Supplying Custer

Supplying Custer

The Powder River Supply Depot, 1876

Gerald R. Clark

THE UNIVERSITY OF UTAH PRESS
Salt Lake City

Copyright © 2014 by The University of Utah Press. All rights reserved.

The Defiance House Man colophon is a registered trademark of the University of Utah Press. It is based on a four-foot-tall Ancient Puebloan pictograph (late PIII) near Glen Canyon, Utah.

18 17 16 15 14   1 2 3 4 5

CIP data is on file with the Library of Congress

Cover photos: Portrait of George Custer (upper left), Library of Congress Prints and Photographs Division, Washington, D.C. *Far West* (upper right) courtesy Overholser Historical Research Center, Fort Benton, MT. Column of cavalry, artillery, and wagons (bottom), U.S. National Archives and Records Administration.

Printed and bound by Sheridan Books, Inc., Ann Arbor, Michigan.

Contents

List of Figures   vii

List of Tables   ix

Acknowledgments   xi

Introduction   1

1. Background   5
2. Exploration and Military Operations in the Lower Yellowstone and Powder River Country, 1805–1875   19
3. The 1876 Sioux War to the Beginning of White Settlement   47
4. Events of the 1876 Sioux War at the Mouth of Powder River   71
5. Archaeology and History at the Powder River Depot   93
6. Conclusions   109

Appendix 1. Excavation Details and Formation of Features D and F   129

Appendix 2. Artifacts Associated with Beverages and Drinking   136

Appendix 3. Artifacts and Organic Materials Related to Food   148

Appendix 4. Artifacts Related to Medicines   160

Appendix 5. Artifacts Related to Tobacco Use   162

Appendix 6. Artifacts and Bones Related to Transportation   165

Appendix 7. Artifacts Associated with Firearms   172

Appendix 8. Artifacts Associated with Clothing   174

Appendix 9. Miscellaneous Artifacts and Minerals   176

Appendix 10. Dog Remains   182

Appendix 11. The Commissary Department Provision Book   183

Notes   191

Bibliography   235

Index   245

Figures

1.1. View of the east bank of the Yellowstone River, with a portion of the Powder River supply depot site. 7
1.2. Map of archaeological Features D and F. 9
1.3. View to the northeast of the Feature D profile. 10
1.4. View southeast of the trash pit after it was excavated. 11
1.5. View south of the rectangular-shaped part of Feature F. 12
2.1. Map of the lower Yellowstone and Powder River country. 21
2.2. Map illustrating the route of W. F. Raynolds's 1859 expedition. 24
2.3. Map illustrating the routes taken during the 1865 Powder River Expedition. 27
3.1. Map of troop movements, supply depots, and battle sites during the 1876 Sioux War. 52
4.1. Map of troop movements near the mouth of Powder River, July 29, 1876. 78
4.2. Map illustrating U.S. Army and Indian positions near the mouth of Powder River, August 2, 1876. 82
5.1. Composite drawing of ale bottle labels. 97
A1.1. Abbreviated Feature D profile. 130
A1.2. Plan map of Feature D. 131
A1.3. Vertical and horizontal dispersion of conjoined fragments from a pipe stem and champagne bottle within Feature D. 132
A1.4. Plan map of Feature F. 134
A2.1. Type 1 ale/stout bottle. 137
A2.2. Type 2 ale/stout bottle. 137
A2.3. Ale bottle shard with partial label. 139

A2.4. Top of a Royal Bottling Company foil wrapper.   140
A2.5. Wine/champagne/ale bottle.   142
A2.6. Soda water/ginger ale/sarsaparilla bottle.   144
A2.7. Tumblers.   145
A2.8. Goblet.   147
A3.1. Can.29.   149
A3.2. Can.536.   150
A3.3. Can.675.   151
A3.4. Can.420.   153
A3.5. Condiment bottle.   154
A3.6. Jar closure.   156
A4.1. Patent medicine bottle.   161
A5.1. Fragments of white clay pipes.   163
A6.1. Horseshoe.   165
A6.2. Fragment of a quillor.   167
A6.3. Remains of a packing or shipping crate at the bottom of the trash pit.   168
A6.4. Metal strapping used to reinforce shipping crates.   171
A7.1. Revolver Ball Cartridge, Caliber .45, and a .44 Smith and Wesson No. 3 cartridge case.   173
A8.1. Buttons.   174
A9.1. Kerosene lamp burner.   177
A9.2. Watch key.   178
A9.3. "Frozen Charlotte" ceramic doll.   179

Tables

4.1. Chronology of Events at the Mouth of Powder River, 1876   72

A3.1. Feature D Bone Frequencies for *Bison* and *Bos*   158

A6.1. Feature D Nail Frequencies   169

A11.1. "Yellowstone Depot—Stanley's Crossing" Provision Book Entries   184

A11.2. "Yellowstone Depot. M.T." Provision Book Entries, August 1876   189

Acknowledgments

Douglas D. Scott and others responsible for the outstanding archaeology conducted at the Little Bighorn Battlefield contributed their time and talent to this project. They assisted with the analysis of artifacts from the Powder River depot and provided information about source materials. Doug offered helpful comments on an early draft of the "Supplying Custer" manuscript. Ephraim Dickson, National Museum of the U.S. Army, Fort Belvoir, Virginia, also provided valuable comments and suggestions on the manuscript; he conducted research in the National Archives that yielded important military subsistence records. Richard E. Fike of Montrose, Colorado, assisted with the analysis of bottles. Bones were analyzed by Danny N. Walker, Office of the Wyoming State Archaeologist, Laramie, and Ken Deaver, Billings, Montana. James T. Rock, Yreka, California, analyzed cans from the depot, and Rick Hill provided drawings of these artifacts. J. Byron Sudbury, Ponca City, Oklahoma, and Michael A. Pfeiffer, Eureka, Montana, contributed their expertise regarding clay smoking pipes. Archaeologist B. J. Earle assisted with fieldwork and illustrated one of the artifacts for publication.

Others who helped with the project include the late James Willert, La Mirada, California, who provided source materials, as did Park Service historians Paul Hedren and Neil Mangum. Leslie A. Perry Peterson, Desoto National Wildlife Refuge, sent data on cultural materials recovered from the steamboat *Bertrand*. Elizabeth Press, librarian for Bass PLC, Burton-on-Trent, England, researched company archives for information about 19th-century Bass bottlers. Stephen W. Taylor, Historical Research Consultants and Genealogists, Staffordshire, England, was contracted to locate data on British ale bottlers. Other individuals and institutions responding to requests for information include Don Rickey, Evergreen, Colorado; Olive Jones, Canadian Park Service; Custer County Library, Miles City, Montana; the Family History Library of the Church of Latter-day Saints, Salt Lake City, Utah; John Slonaker, U.S. Military History Institute, Carlisle Barracks, Pennsylvania; the Greater

London Record Office, London; and the National Archives and Records Administration, Washington, D.C. My wife, Carole Ann, a librarian, provided data on sources of information and edited the volume. She was also a source of encouragement without which the manuscript would never have been finished. Tim Walker of Laurel, Montana, alerted me to an important source of information. Lynn Valtinson, Great Falls, Montana, reviewed the manuscript and provided helpful comments.

Residents of Custer and Prairie counties, coworkers, and members of my family helped recover data from the archaeological features at the Powder River depot, including Prairie County Museum Board members Charlie and Ruth Franks, Wynona Breen, and Mary Haughian. Other Prairie County volunteers were Marcie Lantis, Jackie Dolatta, and Bruce and Merry Kalfell and their sons Kevin and Clint. Lester Jens, who leased state land at the site, shared observations he had made at the depot site. Miles City residents John Halbert, Don Pering, Dale and Diane Hanson, and Don Meier contributed their time and energy. My father, Clairmont Clark of Missoula, Montana, helped excavate, as did my son Scott; Scott also assisted with the photography.

The archaeology was done under a permit granted by the property owner, Glacier Park Company, the land-management arm of Burlington Northern, Inc. Jim Bishop, Glacier Park Company, and Margie Taylor, Meridian Inc., helped with the permit application process. Montana Department of Fish, Wildlife, and Parks employees Dan Vincent, Dave Conklin, Doug Monger, and Beth Riggs helped secure access to state property, as did Mark Ahner, Department of State Lands, Miles City.

Gary Smith and David Wade, Bureau of Land Management (BLM) Montana State Office, supervised the final cataloging of cultural materials from the depot. Thanks to them and BLM summer intern Stephanie Battle, the collections are properly stored at the Billings Curation Center federal repository, where they are available to the public for further study.

Thanks also go to University of Utah Press acquisitions editor Rebecca Rauch. Without her guidance, helpful suggestions, and encouragement at every stage of manuscript review and revision, *Supplying Custer* would never have been published. Other press staff did an outstanding job of preparing the final manuscript.

I am most grateful to all of the individuals and institutions mentioned above; without their generous help the project could not have been completed. Any inadvertent errors, misrepresentations, or faulty conclusions in this volume are attributable to me alone.

Introduction

The Battle of the Little Bighorn is legendary in the history of the American West, and the information available about it is legion. Professional and avocational historians have written thousands of books and articles on Lt. Col. George A. Custer's defeat by Sioux and Cheyenne warriors in what is today southeastern Montana. Beginning in 1983, archaeological investigations of the battlefield also contributed to understanding this central event of the nation's centennial year. Here I report the results of a modest archaeological project conducted not at the battlefield but, rather, at a supply depot used to support troop movements during the 1876 Sioux Indian War. Custer and one wing of his regiment rested several days at this depot on the Yellowstone River before riding west to the Little Bighorn.

Having been raised in Montana, I heard the popular stories of Custer's Last Stand as a child and later became interested in the state's history. However, the real passion I discovered as a university student was the archaeology of Native American cultures on the northern plains. Learning to recognize the traces of human activity left on the landscape hundreds or thousands of years ago fascinated me, as did the potential to understand how ancient peoples coped with their environment and how their cultures changed over time. Thanks to providence and veterans' preference in hiring, I became the Bureau of Land Management's first archaeologist in southeastern Montana. My job was to advise federal land managers about the significance of historic properties and recommend how they should be treated if threatened by activities the agency might authorize on the public lands.

I was on loan from the Bureau of Land Management to the Montana Department of Fish, Wildlife, and Parks when I recorded historic artifacts eroding from a cutbank on the Yellowstone River in 1978. Little did I realize at the time that this archaeological site would broaden my interest in the area's history and lead me into the morass of the Custer myth. The site I found was but a single archaeological feature within a much larger area occupied by the U.S. Army in 1876. Located at the mouth of Powder River, this was one of several primary field camps along the Yellowstone that Custer's commander, Gen. Alfred Terry, established to supply his troops during the war.

The archaeological feature appeared to be a trash pit exposed in the riverbank, with its contents being lost to the Yellowstone as the bank eroded. With the help of volunteers, I excavated the trash pit and a second feature nearby and, over a period of years, sought help to analyze the materials recovered. Analysis of the artifacts confirmed that the trash pit was created sometime during the decade beginning in 1875. However, a firm association with the supply depot was possible only if the contents of the feature were consistent with the historic record. Is there documentary evidence to support a hypothesis that these types of artifacts could have been used, discarded, or lost during the 1876 military campaign? Answering this question required another kind of digging—in books and documents—to find the relevant historic information about Gen. Terry's depot and the broader issues of military transportation and supply.

When researching the history, I found volumes of data and a number of published articles on the supply depot. There was also considerable information about transportation and supply in the Sioux War, but no single source described these issues and their impact on the entire campaign. I have attempted to create a historic context for understanding the archaeology that also emphasizes transportation and supply; it is intended to support my conclusions about the effectiveness of the army's supply effort, but it is not the definitive history of these issues. I hope that the history is interesting to general readers and a useful summary for researchers. There is still much more to be learned about supply and transportation during the 1876 campaign and the Indian Wars in general.

In the first chapter, I provide information regarding the discovery and excavation of archaeological features at the mouth of Powder River. I have also included here a summary of army organization as background for the historic context that follows in chapters 2 through 4. These chapters detail regional history and describe the character of the area in which the Sioux War was waged. Documentary sources from earlier military exploration, punitive campaigns, and army-escorted railroad surveys provide information regarding the challenges of supplying and moving a military expedition in the lower Yellowstone and Powder River country.

Where appropriate, I have given special attention to the mouth of Powder River, including a detailed accounting of 1876 events. This focus on the Powder River–Yellowstone confluence helps identify which historic events might have left an archaeological footprint here. Above all, the historic context is intended to support a conclusion regarding whether or not the archaeological features we studied are associated with Gen. Terry's supply system.

Chapter 5 describes the archaeological features and materials recovered from them; it also connects the archaeology with the depot history. There is a surprising amount of information pertaining specifically to the mouth of Powder River, given that it was not the site of a major battle. In addition to appearing in official army documents, these events are captured in military and civilian diaries and letters, newspaper correspondents' reports, and later, memoirs and interviews with those who participated in the campaign. The documents include a business ledger kept by a trader authorized to sell goods at the supply depot and a "provision book" describing the rations supplied by the army. The analysis focuses on how well the artifacts and other cultural material recovered fit the historic record. Again, the historical information is sufficient to support my conclusions, but much more remains to be found and reported.

In the final chapter I summarize what military planners should have known about the area of operations in 1876 and offer some conclusions about whether supply and transportation issues contributed significantly to campaign failure. The effectiveness of the army's Subsistence and Quartermaster's departments is examined, as well as the performance of traders who sold goods to the troops. I have also summarized in this chapter some interesting conclusions from the archaeological work and describe some mysteries that remain unresolved.

Archaeological projects at the Little Bighorn Battlefield were vastly larger than the modest Powder River depot investigation; methods used to find and recover artifacts and other cultural material were also dissimilar. Despite these differences, I compare cultural materials from both areas to highlight items likely to be found at a field camp as well as a battlefield. This comparison also strengthens the conclusion that the depot archaeological materials are indeed associated with 1876 events and provides background information for some observations not made elsewhere.

Details of the depot excavations and technical descriptions of archaeological features and materials recovered are in appendixes at the end of the volume. The appendixes are intended to be a convenient reference for future research. The trash pit was a kind of time capsule in which all of the items recovered can be dated to events that occurred between June and September 1876. This relatively tight dating enhances the value of the collection for comparative research.

CHAPTER 1

Background

Discovery

The Yellowstone River immediately below the mouth of the Powder has for many years been moderately popular among anglers seeking channel catfish, burbot, sauger, walleye, shovelnose sturgeon, and the occasional paddlefish. Boaters also use the area to access the river, and rockhounds search gravel deposits here for semiprecious Yellowstone agates. While the area can be reached only on unimproved trails that cross private and public property, landowners generally allow access to this stretch of the Yellowstone.[1] Responding to the public's interest in better access to the river, the Montana Department of Fish, Wildlife, and Parks (FWP) studied the feasibility of constructing a road here in the late 1970s and asked me to determine if construction and use of the proposed project would damage or destroy significant archaeological resources.

I first examined the scant archaeological data for the area and learned that the U.S. Army had established a supply depot someplace in the vicinity of the Powder River confluence in 1876. However, no archaeologist had been on the ground here, and no specific artifacts or features had been previously recorded.[2] I would have to conduct a field inventory of the area that would be affected by road construction.

Heading northeast on Interstate 94 from Miles City for the 20-minute drive to Powder River, I noted that the Yellowstone was high; it was early June, when snowmelt in mountains to the west and south typically swells the rivers. The highway runs roughly parallel to the Yellowstone, which is visible to travelers along most of this segment of interstate, crossing 15 named intermittent streams and many more ephemeral coulees too small to warrant appellation. The clear sunny day afforded an unrestricted view of the breaks on either side of the river as well as the Pine Hills a few miles to the south. Grasslands dominate this scene, with the exception of deciduous trees that mark the path of the river and the location of ranch headquarters. Small intermittent streams, the ridges that divide them, and hills flanking the river give the country a rough green texture that quickly changes to brown hues with the rising temperatures and scant rain of a normal summer.

Noting the mouth of Custer Creek on the opposite bank of the river, I crossed the divide east of Camp Creek, and the Powder River came into view, including its juncture with the Yellowstone a mile northwest of I-94. The aptly named Powder's milk chocolate color indicated that it was carrying the usual high load of fine sediment that visibly muddied the larger, faster-moving Yellowstone. Small, sparsely scattered groves of cottonwoods were confined to the rivers' margins. A squadron of pelicans soared above the mouth of Powder River; it was the first I had seen of the majestic birds since the last fall.

Three miles north, Sheridan Butte rose 350 feet above the river valley floor, marking the south edge of extremely dissected river breaks that in this area cover some 15 square miles along the northwest side of the Yellowstone. The easternmost segment of this amazing terrain has been designated the Terry Badlands. Echoes of the 1876 Sioux War reverberate across a landscape with natural features named for U.S. Army officers—Sheridan, Terry, and Custer.

Exiting the interstate, I followed a short connecting link to old Highway 10, which now serves as a local frontage road to the Prairie County seat located five miles to the northeast; the town is named "Terry." I crossed the Powder on the old steel-truss bridge and immediately turned left onto a primitive dirt road along the east bank of the river that passed under the Burlington Northern main line bridge. During spring and early summer, this part of the trail was mostly under water. A few hundred feet from the railroad bridge, the trail continued north onto a wide, relatively flat-lying terrace; from here I had an unobstructed view of about 700 acres north of Powder River between the Yellowstone and the railroad. This segment of the Yellowstone courses north–northeast to a point 1.5 miles below the mouth of the Powder and then curves east and again to the northwest about 1.5 miles farther on. Some cottonwoods were visible at the mouth of the Powder, as were a few on the bank of the Yellowstone where it began its meander to the east (Figure 1.1).

FIGURE 1.1. View of the east bank of the Yellowstone River, with a portion of the Powder River depot site in the foreground.

The trail led north toward the trees visible in the distance. I noted native grasses adapted to sandy and silty soils as well as silver sagebrush near the river, but crested wheatgrass, an introduced species, confirmed that large areas to the east had once been cultivated. Although no buildings or other structures were visible between the railroad and the rivers, the old fields suggested that one or more homesteads were once located here.

Near the cottonwoods on the riverbank about 1.25 miles north of the Powder, I stopped at a small fence that enclosed a military-style gravestone. The marker had been placed here three years earlier to commemorate Private William George, who was wounded at the Little Bighorn Battlefield and died before reaching Ft. Abraham Lincoln, the post he called home on the Missouri River.

A map of the proposed FWP road indicated that I was near the north end of the project. Survey stakes marking the road route roughly followed another existing unimproved trail to the south, very close to the east bank of the Yellowstone, before connecting to the Burlington Northern bridge trail on which I had just driven. Leaving my truck near the grave marker, I walked along the proposed road looking for artifacts or other physical indicators that people had used the area sometime in the past. About a mile north of the Powder River confluence, I discovered clay smoking pipe stems, bottle fragments, and bottle tops covered with foil seals manufactured in London that had eroded from the bank of the Yellowstone. These artifacts were not commonly found in the area and appeared to date to the nineteenth century. I recorded this small area as an archaeological site and recommended that it should be further evaluated to determine its historic significance.

Although the FWP did not pursue its fishing-access plans at the mouth of Powder River and the road was never built, my interest in this archaeological feature grew as I learned more about area history. Further analysis of some artifacts indicated that they were manufactured within a 25-year period that included the 1876 campaign against northern plains tribes. However, because none of the materials recovered from the surface were obviously items the army would supply its personnel, an association between them and General Terry's depot was uncertain. Were there other military or civilian activities at the mouth of Powder River between 1860 and 1885 that might account for the archaeological deposit?

As years passed, the riverbank continued to erode, and it became apparent that the archaeological feature would eventually be lost and with it any hope of answering my question about historic associations. I acquired a permit from the landowner, Burlington Northern,[3] and with help from coworkers, the Prairie County Museum board, family members, and other local residents, I excavated the area now designated Feature D at site 24PE271.[4] We also partially excavated and recorded Feature F, a cluster of sandstone rocks located 300 meters southeast of Feature D on the same river terrace (Figure 1.2).[5]

In addition, we completed an unsystematic, low-intensity examination of the surface, recording a number of artifacts that might be associated with the depot. We located several other potential archaeological features in the vicinity, but none have been evaluated to determine their content, function, or possible association with past events, including the 1876 Sioux War. Historical sources confirmed that our surface survey covered only a small fraction of the area occupied by the army in 1876 around the mouth of the Powder.

Excavation and Analysis

When viewing the cutbank of the Yellowstone from the river, Feature D appeared to be an area about 5.3 meters long by 1.5 meters deep that contained artifacts, bones, charcoal, and lignite, mixed with soil and rocks (Figure 1.3; see appendix 1 for feature details). This area contrasted

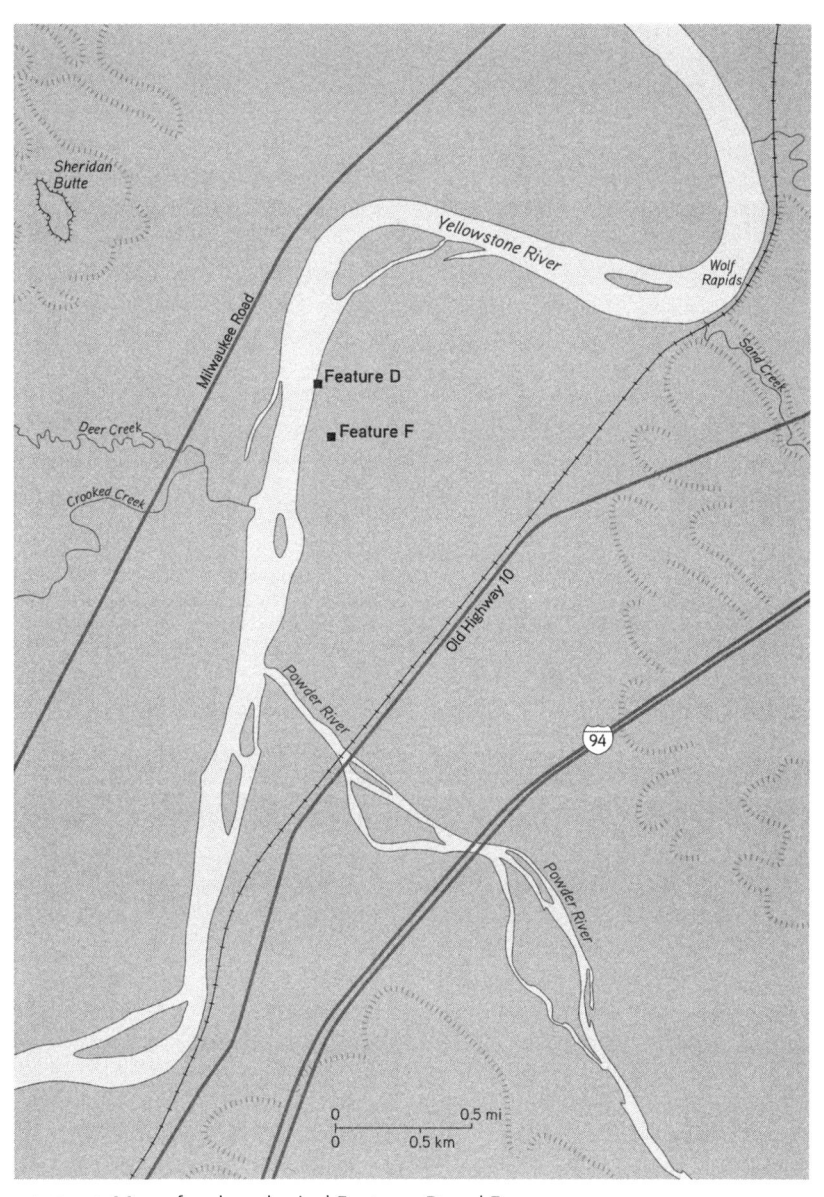

FIGURE 1.2. Map of archaeological Features D and F.

FIGURE 1.3. View to the northeast of the Feature D profile in the Yellowstone River bank. Note the layer of bones and lignite in the central part of the feature.

sharply with the natural strata here, consisting of a soil layer that contained no rocks or cultural material and a lower stratum of solid rock and gravel. On the surface above the cutbank, the feature was defined by a slight depression in the soil nearest the bank. Artifacts identical to some of those in the cutbank were also exposed in the ruts of a trail that passed just east of the depression.

Estimating the maximum extent of Feature D from surface indications, we established an excavation grid six meters long by three meters wide and began digging (see appendix 1 for excavation details). When the excavation was complete, we had removed about 10 cubic meters of soil, rock, and cultural material from the feature (Figure 1.4). Analysis of excavation records revealed that the feature was a pit dug into the river terrace; soil and rock removed from the hole were piled next to it. This excavation was subsequently filled with a mix of soil, rock, and cultural material and abandoned. It was a trash pit, but whether it served any other purpose is unknown.

We recovered hundreds of items from Feature D; most of them were broken, crushed, cut, worn, burned, or intended for a single use and could easily be called "trash" (see appendixes 2—10 for details). I cataloged these materials and determined what they were, when they were manufactured, and their probable use. Other archaeologists with specific

FIGURE 1.4. View southeast of the trash pit after it was excavated. Note the contrast between the silty soil and the river gravels composing the bank of the Yellowstone here.

expertise, such as bone identification, kindly helped analyze the collection. These materials included artifacts associated with beverages and drinking, artifacts and organic materials related to food and transportation, artifacts related to medicines and tobacco use, artifacts associated with firearms and clothing, and miscellaneous artifacts and minerals. The skeleton of a domestic dog was one of the more complete specimens.

Feature F consisted of a cluster of relatively large, flat sandstones, some of them barely visible on the surface (see appendix 1 for details). Partial excavation revealed a carefully laid rectangle of horizontal sandstone slabs 1.7 meters long by 1.1 meters wide, with several vertical slabs along the edge of the rectangle (Figure 1.5). Other stones were scattered about, primarily west of the rectangular area. Many of the 56 stones were stained with charcoal and had turned various shades of red, indicating that they were exposed to high temperatures. Among the rocks, deposits of charcoal were found in the upper 20 centimeters of soil. Lacking associated artifacts to suggest the function and age of this stone feature, I sought explanations in the historic record and, although it was unconfirmed, concluded that it might be the remains of a baking oven.

FIGURE 1.5. View south of the rectangular-shaped part of Feature F.

General Sheridan's Lamentations

Salvaging archaeological data from Feature D before it disappeared into the Yellowstone was a primary goal of the 1985 excavation. I also hoped that analysis of the data would result in a positive identification of the nineteenth-century event or events associated with the features, although by this time the 1876 campaign seemed a most likely candidate. If the features resulted from activities at a military supply depot, could their study confirm some of what is known about the campaign or contribute new insights?

Simply stated, "the intent of historical archaeology is to combine historical documentation with the archaeological record to broaden our picture of the past."[6] Indeed, the process of creating the historic context for understanding events at the Powder River depot allowed me to address broader issues related to army logistics, the branch of military science concerned with "procuring, maintaining, and transporting materiel, personnel and facilities."[7] The depot at Powder River was part of the army's logistics effort, and I have attempted to describe events at the mouth of Powder River in the context of the campaign while emphasizing supply and transportation issues. The depot was an important part of the system that supported troops operating in a large area devoid of settlements, military posts, roads, or railroads in the lower Yellowstone and Powder River country.

In his official report for 1876, Lt. Gen. Philip Sheridan noted that Custer's defeat and subsequent campaign failure were due in part to operating in this vast region about which his field commanders knew little. He also blamed Congress for failing to authorize army posts on the lower Yellowstone; these forts, he argued, would have provided fixed sources of supply from which to pursue the Sioux and Cheyenne tribes in the region. The general's report led me to wonder what military planners should have understood about the area's geography and climate and whether the lack of fixed sources of supply was a significant factor in campaign failure. By drawing the historic context broadly in chapters 2 through 4, I was able to assemble the information needed to address these questions in chapter 6.

The historic context includes early observations regarding the difficulty of travel in the lower Yellowstone and Powder River country. The first military expeditions in this region provide a backdrop for the Sioux War of 1876 and illustrate how well various commanders responded to the supply and transportation challenges they faced. This information helped determine what army planners in 1875–1876 should have understood about the region and allowed me to comment on Gen. Sheridan's lamentations.

Army Organization and Supply, 1876

With the historic context in the following chapters focused broadly on military supply and transportation issues and more specifically on the 1876 Sioux War, it is important to provide some background information regarding army organization in 1876. Sheridan, who led 45,000 Union soldiers to take the Shenandoah Valley during the Civil War, commanded the regular army's Division of the Missouri from 1869 until 1883. With headquarters in Chicago, the geographical division for which he was responsible extended west to include the territories of Montana, Utah, and New Mexico, with the international boundaries of Canada and Mexico defining the north and south limits of the division.[8] He held the single lieutenant general (three stars) position in the army, outranked only by General of the Army (four stars) William T. Sherman and the commander in chief, President Ulysses S. Grant.

While the area for which he was responsible was vast, Lt. Gen. Sheridan's fighting force was but a shadow of his Shenandoah Valley command. Eight years after the War of the Rebellion, Congress authorized the regular army 27,150 officers and enlisted men. Because recruitment lagged behind desertions, deaths, and discharges, actual strength was lower than that authorized. The standing army in June 1876 was 25,331 to man 200 military posts and carry out all duties as assigned, including the Sioux War.[9]

The army was organized into 25 infantry, 10 cavalry, and five artillery regiments, each commanded by a colonel and lieutenant colonel. Because a tactical situation might require splitting the command, cavalry regiments were authorized three majors to lead as many battalions.[10] Each regiment was made up of companies, 10 for infantry and 12 for cavalry, led by a captain and two subalterns, a first lieutenant and a second lieutenant. Company commanders appointed noncommissioned officers, sergeants and corporals, to handle the daily business of the unit. Given mandated limits on personnel, infantry companies typically had no more than 41 men, and cavalry companies, 58. However, when the usual number of men absent for illness, detached service, and other causes was taken into account, many units were missing a quarter of their men.[11]

Gen. Sheridan's Division of the Missouri was divided into three geographic areas, each commanded by a brigadier general (one star). The two areas involved in the 1876 Sioux War were the Department of Dakota under Gen. Alfred Terry and Gen. George Crook's Department of the Platte. These generals each commanded a brigade of several regiments that were spread so thinly over their area of responsibility that the company or battalion was the de facto operational unit in the department. Rarely did all of the companies of a regiment assemble at a single post or other location.[12] Battalions of the same regiment might be serving in different departments.

Officers and enlisted men in regiments of the geographic departments belonging to the army "line" served in the combat branches: infantry, cavalry, and artillery. From the second lieutenant with the least seniority to Lt. Gen. Sheridan, line officers were answerable to General of the Army Sherman. However, more than half of the brigadiers and a substantial number of other "staff" officers served in administrative departments, not to be confused with the Department of Dakota and other geographic departments of the line. Reporting to the civilian secretary of war, army staff was largely outside of the military chain of command.[13]

Army staff provided technical and administrative support to the line regarding issuing orders and keeping records; evaluating the quality of discipline and leadership, arms, and infrastructure; administering military courts and providing legal advice; mapping and construction design; and maintaining communications. The Ordnance Department tested, procured, and distributed arms and ammunition, while the Medical Department supplied surgeons and orderlies. Line soldiers always looked forward to the arrival of Pay Department staff at their post or other duty station. Of the 10 staff bureaus, the Quartermaster's Department and Subsistence Department were the most critical in procuring supplies and distributing them to the line.[14]

While the Quartermaster's Department procured and distributed most supplies, it was also responsible for sheltering and transporting personnel, burying the dead, and maintaining cemeteries. The Subsistence Department determined what foods would be provided to the line and procured the rations. Efficient distribution of food and all other supplies depended on close cooperation between these two departments and the line officers requesting and receiving the stores.

Sixty-four officers under the quartermaster general held ranks from colonel to captain, while the commissary general of subsistence commanded 25 officers, also ranking no lower than captain.[15] These staff officers, like most of the other support bureaus, were located at bureau headquarters or at other locations deemed suitable for carrying out the bureau's mission. Quartermaster officers were often located at a few large army supply depots, and commissary of subsistence officers served at one of nine major purchasing depots.[16] Staff quartermaster and commissary officers were usually assigned only to the headquarters of line divisions and departments, not to individual army posts. Line officers assumed quartermaster and commissary duties at posts and on a campaign. They were often infantry or cavalry company subalterns detailed as "acting assistant quartermaster" or "acting assistant commissary of subsistence" supported by a quartermaster sergeant and commissary sergeant.[17]

The bureaus provided important support to the geographic departments, but there was often friction between the staff and the line, much of it related to who controlled supply and transportation, the staff generals or General Sherman's line commanders. Staff quartermasters and commissaries of subsistence located at division and department headquarters answered to the quartermaster general and commissary general of subsistence in Washington, D.C. Operational commanders often believed that they had little control over their logistics because "the staff decided what was needed where, and how and when to get it there. If the responsible commander had different ideas, he might persuade, but not compel, the staff to modify the decision."[18] Of course, underlying these conflicts was the organizational split in authority between the general of the army and the secretary of war.

Discord between staff and line was not limited to big issues like provisioning a campaign; one feud focused on army regulations governing the flour ration. The Commissary Department provided very basic foods to the enlisted men, primarily salt pork, salt beef, beans or split peas, flour or "hardbread" (hardtack), and coffee supplemented with cornmeal, rice, hominy, sugar, vinegar, salt, and pepper. Fresh beef and desiccated vegetables were sometimes available.[19] Allowed to sell food saved from the ration, companies garnered these funds to buy nonissue foods from commissary stores or local sources and to maintain post gardens. Company funds provided a more diverse and healthy diet as well as facilities that contributed to the well-being of the men. The commissary general of subsistence sought a change in the regulations to prohibit post bakeries from raising funds to support post chapels, libraries, schools, and gymnasiums. The Medical Department weighed in on this issue, stating that the flour ration itself was inadequate to maintain a healthy force.[20]

Sale of "excess" flour from the ration was a big contributor to company funds. The Subsistence Department issued 18 ounces of flour per man per day, which was baked at the post. While each man was given 18 ounces of soft bread, his flour would have yielded about 1 percent more per day.[21] Flour saved from a number of men usually absent from a post was added to the excess and sold to civilian travelers, settlers, or other willing buyers.

Civilians had a much more significant role in the supply system when providing goods and services under army contracts. As Civil War–era stores in primary depots gradually diminished and new posts were needed in the West, the supply departments offered more contracts for goods and transportation. The Quartermaster's Department maintained a policy of purchasing as near as possible to where the supplies and services were needed, taking transportation costs into account. As more settlements were established in the West, commissaries of subsistence also acquired supplies, such as flour and fresh beef, nearer their point of consumption.[22] Understanding the army's need for food, forage, building materials, transportation, and other services, western entrepreneurs were attracted to newly established posts, sometimes forming the nuclei of contiguous towns. Supplying the army was good business. Not surprisingly, control over supply and transportation contracts was another point of contention between army staff and line.

Among the civilians most closely associated with the army supply system were the "sutlers" authorized by the War Department to sell goods to the troops. After the Civil War, these businessmen were officially titled "post traders," but the old appellation continued to be used by many. Soldiers could buy a wide variety of goods from the sutler to supplement basic army-issued rations and clothing.[23] Alcoholic beverages were among the most popular items in the post trader's establishment, which was not unlike a general store and a place to relax and play games, with separate facilities for both officers and enlisted. Sutlers appointed to accompany a military campaign sold goods from the wagon train or from tents at base camps and supply depots.

Soldiers desired access to the sutler's goods but often reviled him for the high cost of his merchandise. Although the sutler had a virtual monopoly after an 1870 law allowed only one trader per post, his transportation costs were often very high, as were the risks he assumed. Sutlers at some isolated posts with small garrisons struggled to make a living, while others diversified and made fortunes in trade, transportation, and even banking. Many with the experience to succeed in the business coveted sutler positions at prime locations, and the one-sutler limit spawned an era of corruption in the appointment of post traders. Citizens with capital could buy a trader's license through a civilian "influence peddler" connected to the War Department.

The 1870 statute mandating a single trader also moved the authority to appoint them from post commanders to the secretary of war. The secretary and his wife soon developed a cabal of friends eager to peddle new post trader licenses and those up for renewal, ensuring yearly profits to middlemen who brokered the deals. Congress was investigating post trader influence peddling, one of several patronage scandals of the Grant administration, while General Sheridan was planning his 1876 campaign against the Sioux and their allies. The investigation identified several influence men, including former army generals and the president's brother. As the head of army staff, the secretary of war was on a collision course with the army line and Congress.[24]

The post trader problem was confined to the secretary's office and did not involve army staff officers; line officers were the first to report the influence peddling, and several testified during the investigation. Indeed, the army had already changed its oversight of the supply system to combat fraud and abuse at western posts. During the Civil War some acting supply officers colluded with their line commanders in fraudulent contracts for personal gain, prompting the quartermaster general to replace all quartermasters serving on the plains and increase supervision by staff officers.[25]

Despite these changes to the army supply system, its organization remained much the same as during the War of the Rebellion, in which many of its senior officers had served. Could these staff and line officers cooperate to do a credible job of supplying the 1876 campaign in the lower Yellowstone and Powder River country? What did they know about the environmental and logistical challenges this region presented to an army pursuing tribes known for their ability to move quickly and subsist on the land?

CHAPTER 2

Exploration and Military Operations in the Lower Yellowstone and Powder River Country, 1805–1875

The 1876 U.S. military campaign against northern plains tribes was undertaken in a vast area devoid of established transportation routes and white settlement; it was the domain of the last large herd of buffalo in America. Within this region, the lower Yellowstone and Powder River country was home to an unknown number of Native American families, bands, and tribes for at least 12 millennia. For much of this time, what is known about these people is captured in the oral traditions of their descendants and the investigations of archaeologists; both lines of evidence confirm that they were nomadic hunters who knew their environment exceedingly well. They understood the behaviors of plains animals and developed communal methods for harvesting many bison or antelope in a single hunt. For thousands of years their sole beast of burden was the dog; their primary weapon was a small spear or dart propelled by a throwing-stick until they adopted the bow and arrow for its superior qualities. A quantum leap in transportation and technology came to the region with the horse and gun some 300 years ago, and tribes with familiar names—Kiowa, Crow, Arapaho, Cheyenne, and Sioux—became the masters of the plains.

The word *plains*, meaning "flat; level; plane," conveys a false impression of the region. Rivers and streams have cut into bedrock formations of sandstone, silt, shale, and lignite to form a steeply dissected terrain across much of the area. From mountain headwaters in the nation's first national park, the Yellowstone flows north into the foothills of the Rockies and then east through the Montana plains to the Missouri River. Named "la Roche Jaune" by an unknown Frenchman, the Yellowstone was Elk River to the Crow, Sioux, and Cheyenne. Primary tributaries of the river run north from the Absaroka and Bighorn Mountains, joining it from west to east as the Stillwater River, Clark's Fork, the Bighorn, Rosebud Creek, Tongue River, and Powder River (Figure 2.1).[1] Rough breaks and badlands stretch from floodplains flanking these streams until they meet the ridges, hills, buttes, and rolling uplands that divide the drainages one from the other. Much of the land is anything but flat.

First White Visitors

The Jesuit priest Father Pierre Jean DeSmet encountered this dissected region in 1851 when leading a party of Indians to treaty negations with U.S. representatives. His route was north of the Yellowstone until the party forded the river 20 miles west of the mouth of Rosebud Creek. From here they journeyed south, crossing the Rosebud, Tongue River, and the upper tributaries of the Powder River to Fort Laramie on the Oregon Trail in what is now Wyoming. Encountering rough country between the Yellowstone and upper Powder River, the party was forced to abandon a broken cart and repair other wagons with rawhide. Fr. DeSmet's summary description of the broken lands south of the Yellowstone would be echoed by later travelers:

> The whole region over which we passed south of the Yellowstone, offers only feeble hopes to civilization. The soil is light, wood scarce, and water wanting during a large portion of the year. It is a country favorable solely to hunters and wandering tribes. All the animals common in the wilderness abound, and during long years to come they will rest undisturbed in their possessions. When all the fertile tracts, yet vacant in the immense Indian territory, will be occupied, then only will the lands below the Yellowstone attract attention; then alone will necessitous and persevering industry succeed in drawing any considerable portion of this region from its present barrenness.[2]

The priest's observation that this region would be the last refuge of the northern plains tribes was prophetic. The Crows struggled to retain their homeland and respond to Sioux incursions. The Sioux with their Cheyenne allies pursued their traditional ways of life here until forced from the area soon after they defeated U.S. troops at the Little Bighorn in 1876.

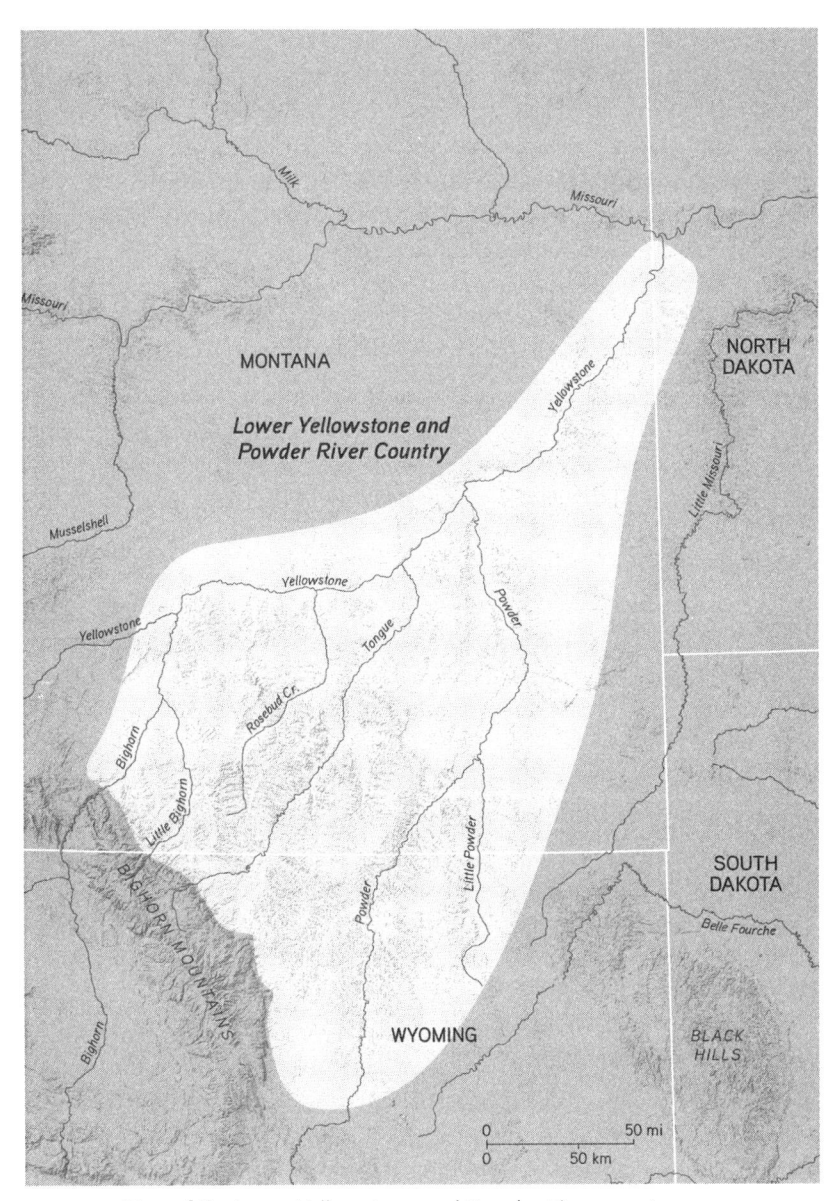

FIGURE 2.1. Map of the lower Yellowstone and Powder River country.

Father DeSmet was not the first to record a trip through the lower Yellowstone and Powder River country. Francois-Antoine Larocque and two companions traveled with Crow Indians from Big Hidatsa Village on the Missouri River to the Bighorn Mountains and back in 1805.[3] The party crossed Powder River about 70 miles above its mouth and proceeded upriver to the Bighorns and then northwest to the Yellowstone River. Larocque attributed a severe shortage of grass in much of the Powder River valley to recent grazing by large herds of bison. Returning down the Yellowstone, he passed the mouth of Powder River on September 23, noting that it had no wood on its banks and was as muddy as when he crossed it in July. The Indians named the river for the fine sand and silt constantly churned by its flow. Captain William Clark of the Corps of Discovery passed the mouth of the Powder a year later, naming the stream Redstone River, but the Indian name prevailed.[4]

Five years after Fr. DeSmet's trek, Lt. Gouverneur K. Warren led the first official exploration of the upper Missouri River since Lewis and Clark's visit in 1805–1806.[5] Mapping the lower Yellowstone River at this time appears to have been unplanned and completed on the lieutenant's initiative when his progress up the Missouri was delayed at Ft. Union near the mouth of the Yellowstone.[6] While waiting here for a boat to be built, Warren bought wagons and teams for a detour up the Yellowstone and proceeded to a point opposite the mouth of Powder River. He was forced to leave his wagons at the east end of what would later be named the Terry Badlands, as this area was impassible with wagons. His party mapped the Yellowstone from Powder River to the Missouri.

Lt. Warren bought wagons for his Yellowstone trip at Ft. Union from Sir George Gore, an Irish nobleman who was completing an extravagant hunting trip. Gore began his excursion through the American West in 1854, traveling from St. Louis to Ft. Laramie on the North Platte River and then hunting west to the Continental Divide and beyond. After wintering on the North Platte, the baronet and his retinue moved north to the Indian hunting grounds of the Yellowstone and Powder River country. Following the Powder to its mouth, the Hibernian hunter turned west and spent the winter on Tongue River. Gore's peregrinations through this region controlled by tribesmen was facilitated by a corps of competent guides led by Jim Bridger, whose many years in the fur trade equipped him with an extraordinary understanding of the West.[7]

Trading companies moved into the upper Missouri and Yellowstone country soon after Lewis and Clark returned to St. Louis, where they reported that the region contained fortunes in beaver pelts. A few trading posts were built on the Yellowstone between the Bighorn and Tongue; most of them were associated with the American Fur Company's Upper Missouri Outfit headquartered at Ft. Union. Constructed in 1850, Ft. Sarpy was the last Yellowstone post used for the Crow Indian trade in buffalo robes and other furs. The American Fur Company was open for business here when Captain William F. Raynolds of the U.S. Corps of Topographical Engineers led the first official cross-country exploration of the region in 1859–1860.[8]

Raynolds Expedition 1859–1860

With the dean of guides, Bridger, again leading the way, Raynolds passed through much of the country that in less than two decades would become the army's area of operations in the Sioux War. After gaining Powder River, he intended to descend this stream to the Yellowstone, but Bridger advised that teams would have a very tough haul bringing wagons through the lower reaches of the Powder River breaks. Staying well south of the Yellowstone to find a wagon-friendly trail, the party instead crossed the divide to Tongue River and Rosebud Creek and then followed Armells Creek to Fort Sarpy on the Yellowstone (Figure 2.2).[9]

After resupplying and conducting some official business with Crow Indian leaders camped at the fort,[10] Raynolds continued west to the Bighorn River. Skirting the east side of the Bighorn Mountains, the expedition reached the North Platte, where the party spent the winter.[11] First Lt. Henry Maynadier led part of the expedition down the Yellowstone on its return journey and noted in July 1860 that Fort Sarpy had been abandoned. As he continued east and passed the mouth of Powder River along the left bank of the Yellowstone, he hugged the north edge of the Terry Badlands, describing them as having clay hills "very regular in form, and the effect of a murage [sic] on the pinnacles made them loom up like tall turrets and castles."[12]

Raynolds and Maynadier not only described the terrain and collected data to map the Yellowstone country but also recorded observations of the region's wildlife, flora, geography, and climate. On August 14, 1859, the captain noted that he was cold when he awoke under the cover of two blankets and by that afternoon the thermometer indicated a blazing 108 degrees Fahrenheit. Less than three weeks later, when they were near the

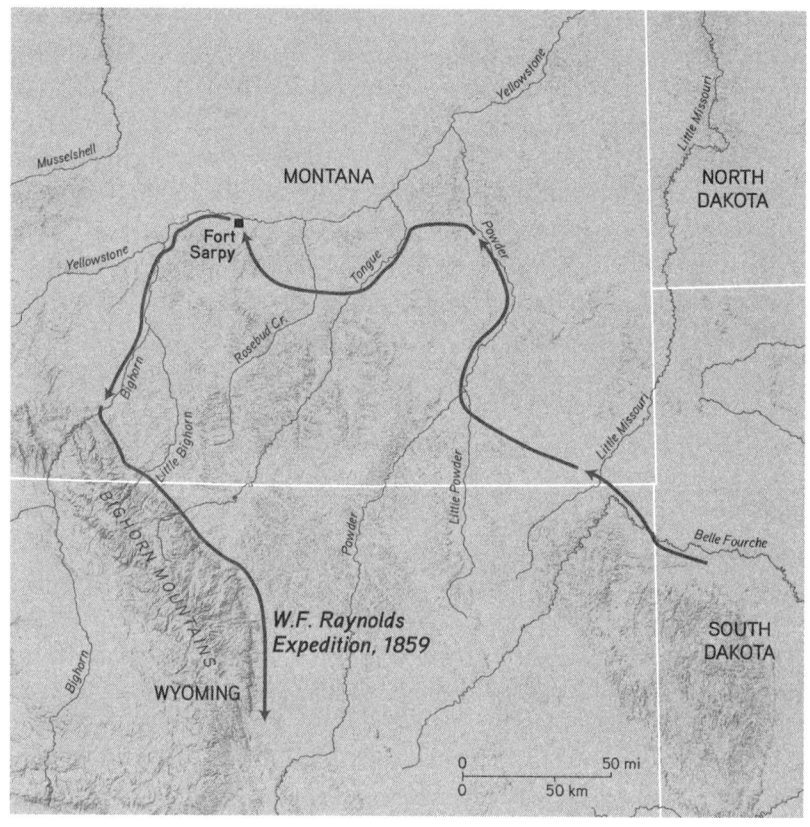

FIGURE 2.2. Map illustrating the route of W. F. Raynolds's 1859 expedition in the lower Yellowstone and Powder River country.

mouth of the Bighorn River, a storm and cold north wind that "caused serious personal discomfort" pelted his party and left the ground impassable for wagons for two days.

From the time he entered the middle reaches of Powder River in late July 1859 until he gained the foothills of the Bighorns in early September, Raynolds worried constantly about "the three great requisites of camping—wood, water, and grass."[13] At several camps the grass was so sparse that the party fed their livestock bark from cottonwood trees. Like Larocque, the captain attributed the scarcity of forage to the recent presence of large herds of bison. Only scattered groups of these herbivores were observed until the engineers sighted the Yellowstone for the first time on August 14, where they marveled at hundreds of thousands of buffalo covering an estimated 50 square miles. The challenges Raynolds experienced in the lower Yellowstone and Powder River country—unpredictable weather, rough terrain, scarce water and forage—also plagued the first large-scale military campaigns against northern plains tribes.

Sully Campaign 1864

The U.S. response to the Minnesota Uprising of 1862 included a campaign two years later that extended west from the Missouri River to the Yellowstone.[14] Rejecting an effort by Fr. DeSmet to broker a peaceful settlement,[15] General Alfred Sully led a formidable force of 4,000 cavalry, 800 mounted infantry, and 12 pieces of artillery across Dakota Territory, battling western Sioux bands and refugees from the Minnesota conflict at Killdeer Mountain and again in the Little Missouri badlands.[16] Sully reported several hundred tribesmen killed and a very large village with most of the Indian's property destroyed. Army losses totaled five killed and 10 wounded.[17]

Operating a long distance from military posts or sources of supply, the general used 15 steamboats and a wagon train of 300 teams trailing a herd of 300 steers for logistical support.[18] He was also obligated to escort a 123-wagon immigrant train on its way to gold fields in Montana Territory. When the expedition met two steamboats on the Yellowstone below Glendive Creek on August 12, it had been on one-third rations for three days and had found very little water for over a week. With grain supplies also gone and but little grass anywhere, livestock died, and many wagons were abandoned. Lack of forage discouraged the general from continuing the campaign, and low water in the Yellowstone precluded steamboats from hauling supplies west for a new fort at the mouth of Powder River. Indeed, Sully was to have built a military post here and another near the mouth of Heart River on the Missouri as supply bases for future military operations in the region.[19]

In an unofficial letter to his commander, Sully lamented his failure to build the posts and echoed Raynolds's comments when describing the difficulty of campaigning in the northern plains:

> Although I may not have been successful in carrying out all the expectations of the government in building posts and entirely finishing the war—that is bringing the Indians to their knees to beg for peace—yet we have done everything that was in the power of man to do with the obstacles before us—want of water, want of grass and want of everything to eat.[20]

As part of yet another large campaign against plains tribes, army planners hoped to have Sully in the field again in the spring of 1865 to build the post at the mouth of the Powder. His command was one of several columns organized to punish Indian bands that raided along major immigrant routes and to forcibly secure the Bozeman Trail, a shortcut through tribal lands to the Montana mines; they were also to clear the way for other potential overland routes on tribal lands. Sully's mission changed before the campaign began, and a Yellowstone post at the Powder River confluence was not built. However, other U.S. forces experienced difficulties associated with campaigning in the lower Yellowstone and Powder River country that summer and fall.[21]

Powder River Expedition 1865

Three columns of the Powder River Expedition were to attack an unknown number of Teton Lakota, Cheyenne, and Arapaho villages, totaling about 3,000 lodges, in the vast region bordered by the Yellowstone River (north), the Black Hills (east), the North Platte River (south), and the Bighorn Mountains (west; Figure 2.3).[22] The lower Yellowstone and Powder River country constituted roughly the north half of this territory.[23] Expedition commander General Patrick Connor personally led the western (left) column of 675 men, including a substantial number of Pawnee and Omaha scouts, supported by 184 wagons. He also inherited Sully's uncompleted task of building a post on Powder River. The middle column under Lt. Col. Samuel Walker included 600 cavalry, with a battery of two mountain howitzers and only 13 wagons; most of the supplies were aboard a pack train of mules. Leading the eastern (right) column, Col. Nelson Cole had the largest force, with 1,400 cavalry and mounted artillery men and three rifled guns. This latter column was supported by a mere 140 wagons.[24]

Connor's expedition was much smaller than planned, although it was a very large cavalry force by post–Civil War standards. The War of the Rebellion ended in April, and many volunteer units were looking to be released from service rather than fight tribesmen on the western frontier. Morale was so poor in some units that Connor threatened to use mountain howitzers to get Lt. Col. Walker's column moving from Ft. Laramie on August 5. This middle column was to march northeast, traveling along the west edge of the Black Hills to the Little Missouri River, then northwesterly to Powder River, down this stream, and then west to meet Conner and Cole on Tongue River.

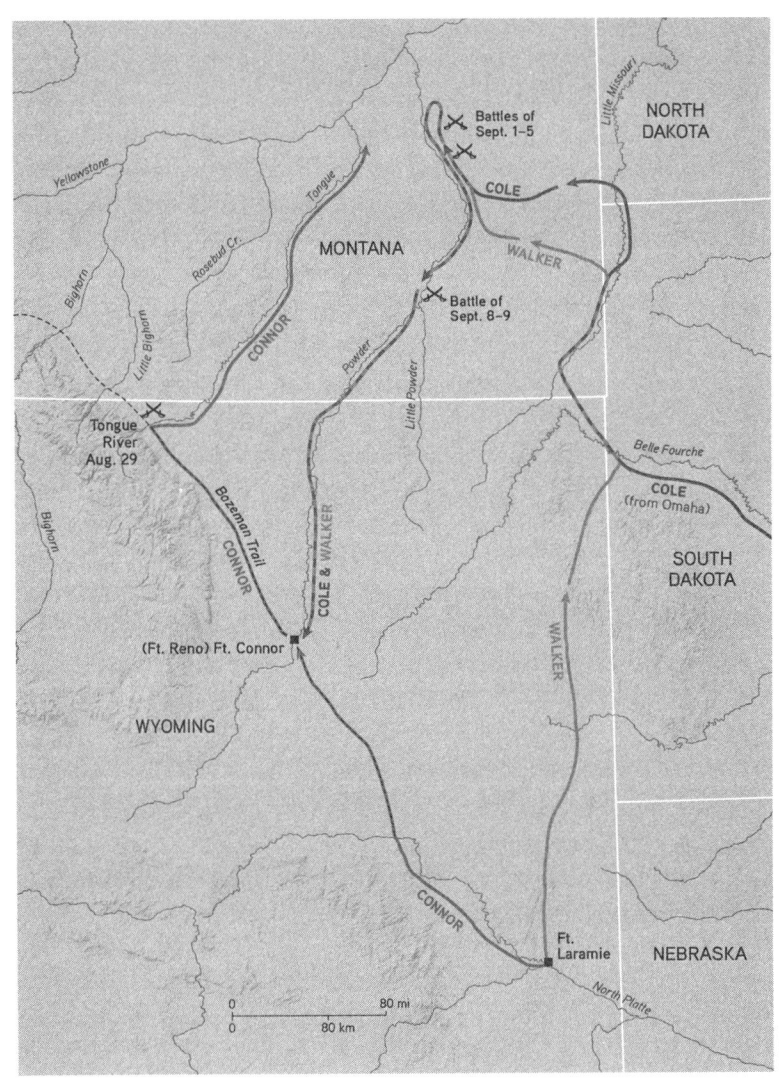

Operations in the Lower Yellowstone and Powder River Country 27

FIGURE 2.3. Map illustrating the routes taken by Connor, Cole, and Walker during the 1865 Powder River Expedition. Battle sites are noted.

When Walker was some 40 miles north of Devil's Tower on August 19, he met Cole's eastern column, which had been on the trail from Omaha since July 1. Cole had not found the large villages thought to be north of the Black Hills and turned west to rendezvous with the other columns on the Tongue, where Conner was to have established a critically important supply depot. From the headwaters of the Little Missouri,

Cole and Walker traveled a short distance from one another to Powder River along routes roughly parallel but north of Capt. Raynolds's trail of 1859.[25]

With the left column, Connor proceeded north from Ft. Laramie on July 30 to the Powder River crossing of the Bozeman Trail. While waiting here for a wagon train of supplies, the general began construction of the new post and sent scouts to search for unsuspecting villages. Three scouting parties engaged enemy warriors in the vicinity; Connor's Pawnee scouts killed 27 Cheyennes in one engagement. Leaving 200 men under Col. James H. Kidd to complete construction of the fort, Connor continued northwest on August 22 to the Tongue River. Scouts located an Arapaho village of 200 to 300 lodges at the head of this stream, where Conner attacked with part of his force on August 29, inflicting casualties, capturing horses, and destroying much of the village property. Though the column was threatened by an effective counterattack, Conner's artillery prevented serious loss among his detachment. The column proceeded down Tongue River toward the rendezvous with Cole and Walker.

From their Little Missouri junction, the middle and eastern columns moved toward the expedition rendezvous on routes determined largely by the availability of scant water and grass. Cole noted that fresh Indian trails continued down the Little Missouri, but he was compelled to turn west to Powder River. Scurvy began to plague many of Cole's men at this time but was ameliorated somewhat by foraging for abundant and pungent wild onions. The condition of horses and mules in both columns was also deteriorating, with some showing stress from lack of forage as early as August 8. By the end of the month, Walker's column shot 10 horses that played out in the descent through the breaks of Powder River. Twenty head of horses and an equal number of mules died during Cole's slow trek through the Powder River breaks as well. High daytime temperatures added to the discomfort of all.[26]

Cole reached the Powder River about 50 miles south of the Yellowstone and, like Raynolds six years earlier, found grass only among cottonwood groves along the river. On August 29, with rations now almost depleted and many men barefoot and in rags, he sent a scouting party west to find Connor and the much-needed supplies. Three days later the scouts returned, having failed to find any sign of the left column or the supply depot because, unknown to them, Connor was still on the upper Tongue and making his way down the valley. The scouts also reported that the route they took would be impossible for wagons and was nearly devoid of grass.[27]

At this time, the columns were located a few miles north of where Capt. Raynolds struck Powder River. From here Jim Bridger found a route west to Tongue River for the captain's wagons in 1859. Bridger was also with the Powder River Expedition, but unfortunately for Cole and Walker, Conner had retained the venerable guide for his own column.

On September 1, warriors stole 20 horses from Cole's command and killed five soldiers who were hunting in small parties. Walker, also nearly out of rations, decided to go north to the Yellowstone, and Cole followed when he saw smoke believed to be emanating from near the mouth of the Powder. Within 25 miles of the Yellowstone, the grass disappeared, as did the Powder River. The valley flanking the muddy riverbed narrowed to become an even greater challenge for the wagon train. With their men on half rations and livestock close to starving on cottonwood bark, Cole and Walker reversed course and headed back up Powder River as the weather changed for the worse. Having suffered in the heat for weeks, both men and animals were now exposed to rain and cold wind, which had a devastating effect on the already weakened livestock. As horses and mules began dying by the hundreds, the command burned wagons and property, littering the Powder River valley for miles.[28]

Indians appeared on the surrounding hills and skirmished with the troops for several days. An estimated 1,000 to 3,000 warriors gathered around the columns on September 5 and again the next day. Small parties of cavalry and tribesmen engaged along the flanks of the columns, but army artillery and Spencer repeating carbines discouraged warriors from a direct assault on the trains. Although most tribesmen were armed only with bow and arrows, the cavalry horses were in no condition to pursue the attackers for any distance.[29]

The western Sioux, or Teton Lakota, who attacked Cole and Walker included many of those Gen. Sully had fought the year before. In the spring of 1865, these tribes harassed Ft. Rice, the new post Sully built, and then turned west to encounter the Powder River columns quite by chance. Other Lakota tribes and Cheyenne bands also joined the attack. Sitting Bull, a Lakota warrior of the Hunkpapa tribe, captured a couple of horses in the Powder River valley. He failed to garner significant war honors during these skirmishes but would distinguish himself in later conflicts with soldiers. Many other prominent Lakota warriors were among the combatants, including the Hunkpapa Gall and Oglalas Red Cloud and Crazy Horse. Cheyenne fighters included Roman Nose, Dull Knife, and Little Wolf.[30]

As combat ended for the most part, another storm brought rain, sleet, and snow into the valley. Reduced to less than quarter rations, the men began to subsist on horses and mules as the animals dropped from fatigue. Many of Cole's soldiers and fully one-third of Walker's men were barefoot as they proceeded up the Powder, thinking that their nearest source of supply might be Fort Laramie far to the south. Finally, on September 13, couriers from Gen. Connor reached the desperate columns with news that supplies were available at his Tongue River location or at the newly constructed Ft. Connor on the Powder River crossing of the Bozeman Trail. Pushing as rapidly as possible given the condition of the commands, Cole and Walker straggled into the fort on September 19 and 20. Casualties among the commands included 13 killed, five wounded, and two missing. Cole's estimate of 200–500 warriors killed was grossly overstated. A best-guess estimate from a review of available data suggests Indian casualties in the range of 25–50.[31]

This first punitive army incursion into the Powder River country failed to accomplish any U.S. strategic goals other than establishing a post on the river. Located at the head of the stream, it was positioned to protect traffic on the Bozeman Trail. Congress would be unwilling to fund the army's coveted post at the mouth of Powder River or elsewhere on the lower Yellowstone until the very expensive Powder River Expedition faded from memory and an 1876 Lakota victory changed national priorities.

Cole and Walker's dismal experience clearly illustrated poor logistics planning and a failure to take local conditions into account. To be sure, many of those who planned the expedition were old hands at supporting large commands during the Civil War; some, including Gen. Connor, were very familiar with the challenges of supplying remote areas of the West. However, details of the expedition supply effort suggest that either army planners did not fully understand the nature of the Powder River country or they were simply too optimistic about a plan they knew was marginal at best.

Connor reported serious trouble getting adequate supplies to launch his campaign, initially planned to begin in June.[32] Plagued with contracting problems, he resolved to leave before the end of July with whatever supplies were available, arranging to have the rest of the material forwarded via a second wagon train when it arrived at Ft. Laramie.[33] This decision allowed the command to reach the Powder River crossing in a timely fashion, but the general could not proceed toward the rendezvous with Cole and Walker on Tongue River until the second train arrived. This 10-day delay was a significant factor in Connor's failure to establish the depot on Tongue River.

When the left column finally departed for the Tongue with a full train, it had rations and other supplies aplenty, including stores needed to resupply Cole and Walker. However, it did not have enough forage to sustain even Connor's column during its descent down the Tongue. Indeed, the general reversed course on September 6 to look for grass, indicating that the command had used all available grain. When horses and mules began dying three days later, Connor slowed the column to find grass and rest the animals; this option was available only because his train was well stocked with rations and other supplies. When it returned to Ft. Connor, the column had been separated from the new post only 33 days.

When outfitting at Ft. Laramie, Connor's acting quartermaster and commissary of subsistence, Capt. Henry Palmer, calculated that the column needed 200 wagons to carry equipment, clothing, shelter, ordnance, and rations as well as grain for the livestock. With only 70 wagons available at the fort, Palmer pressed civilian wagons and teams into service to build a train of 185 wagons managed by 195 teamsters and wagon masters.[34] Finn Burnett, a civilian with the expedition, recalled that the teamsters were ordered to load as much grain on their wagons as possible. When all available wagons were loaded, Burnett estimated that 2,000 sacks of grain were left behind.[35]

Burnett worked for expedition sutler Alvin C. Leighton, who also supplied the wagons and teams to Capt. Palmer. Leighton's 11 four-mule wagons of goods in Connor's train were apparently intended for a store he would establish at the new Powder River fort.[36] He might have sold goods during the column's march, including the trek from Ft. Connor to the Tongue River and back, as both Leighton and Burnett were with the train at that time.[37] Other evidence for the sutler's presence includes references to problems with alcohol abuse the day after leaving Ft. Connor and on August 27.[38] Alcoholic beverages sold by sutlers were often a source of trouble in the garrison and on a campaign.[39]

The middle and right columns apparently did not enjoy the luxury of sutler's goods. Walker's command was outfitted at Ft. Laramie, where all supplies, except forage, were loaded on a pack train. Thirteen wagons carried a week's supply of grain. When empty, the wagons were returned to the fort, and Walker's horses and pack mules were expected to survive solely by grazing along the route. His command started the journey with 40 days' supplies, but rations were lost to damage when the pack mules crossed Powder River many times in what was described as quicksand.[40] This loss would certainly have contributed to the command being on half rations for almost a third of its journey from Ft. Laramie to Ft. Connor. Unimpressed with the performance of his pack train, the lieutenant colonel concluded that pack mules "are a poor way of transporting supplies on such a long march" and that light wagons would have been better even in the rough terrain encountered.[41]

Ordered to take as much grain as possible for the right column, Col. Cole also hired "civilian transportation" to augment government wagons and teams. He left Omaha with 140 six-mule wagons, but it is unclear how many were contract teams. Early in the journey, Cole purchased forage and cattle from farms along the Platte River and trailed 50 head of beef. Although the amount of grain he bought is undocumented, the colonel noted on September 9 that his stock had been without grain for about 60 days; this comment suggests that the column began its trek with no more than 10 to 12 days of grain.

Cole's train also carried 60 days' subsistence rations, although an estimated 20 percent were lost in stream crossings and during loading and unloading. Some units in the command hunted extensively, contrary to Cole's orders forbidding this activity, until rations ran critically short on Powder River.[42] The colonel noted with apparent envy that Walker's pack train was much more mobile than his wagons, pulled by unbroken mules "utterly unfit for the service required of them" and managed by teamsters "in the main worthless."[43]

Long supply trains were indeed needed to support a large force if it was separated from a fixed source of supply for any length of time. The size of the train required depended not only on the number of men and the length of time they would be in the field but also on the number of livestock to be fed. While army horses and mules were expected to graze when possible, horses needed 12 pounds of grain and mules needed 10 pounds each day in field service. Of course, this included the wagon mules, and as the train got larger, more forage was needed to support draft animals. Every man in the force required three to five pounds of supplies per day, also carried on the train. Some simple calculations demonstrate that this kind of transportation and supply system rapidly reaches a point of diminishing returns, where adding more wagons and draft animals provides little additional logistic support.[44]

Cole's 1,400 men required between 4,200 and 5,600 pounds of supplies each day they were on the march; 60 days' supplies therefore weighed 252,000 to 336,000 pounds. If the command carried only 10 days' forage for 1,400 horses and 840 wagon mules, it added about 252,000 pounds. The total weight of supplies, including forage bought en route, was between 504,000 and 588,000 pounds. The six-mule army wagon is estimated to have been capable of carrying an average of 2,000–3,000 pounds and over 5,000 pounds with good six-year-old stock.[45] Cole's less capable two- to four-year-old mules working in difficult terrain should have reduced wagon capacity by an unknown amount. However, if the estimated total weight of supplies and forage is correct, Cole began the campaign with wagon payloads more in the range of 3,600 to 4,000 pounds. Of course, total net weight diminished as supplies and forage were used and the remaining materials were redistributed among the wagons. After Cole's forage was consumed, wagon payloads would then have been in the neighborhood of 1,800 to 2,400 pounds.

Despite the attention given the forage issue, Connor and his subordinates underestimated the amount needed for the campaign.[46] The problem was particularly acute for the middle and right columns when they encountered areas with very little grass after the forage they carried was quickly exhausted. The animals needed more time to graze, thus slowing the columns and delaying their scheduled rendezvous with Connor, an appointment they were unable to keep. Guides unfamiliar with the country and poor maps exacerbated the travel time problem.[47] As their travel time increased, the columns inevitably ran out of rations and other needed supplies. Cole and Walker faced the impossible task of squeezing an additional 22 days from their rations before they reached Ft. Connor. Their campaign was reduced to a squalid fight for survival as they watched the masters of the plains run circles around them. Two years later Col. Cole, in a report to General Grant, noted he could not comprehend "why old Indian fighters had not, with their knowledge, planned a more consistent campaign; created depots here and hunted Indians there."[48]

The Powder River Expedition of 1865 was not only a strategic and tactical failure; it was also very expensive. Reorganized, downsized, and focused on reconstruction duties in the South after the Civil War, the army could not sustain a policy built around heavy columns to subdue the plains tribes. Given political and fiscal realities, the United States again turned to a strategy of negotiating treaties with the tribes and using its limited military capability to defend immigrant travel routes.[49]

Continuing Conflict and Treaty of 1868

Connor's expedition also raised public awareness of the Bozeman Trail, resulting in more traffic along this route to the Montana gold fields and more forts being built to protect the travelers.[50] Peace commissioners appointed to negotiate treaties failed to understand the resolve of Red Cloud and other important Lakota leaders to close the Bozeman Trail and prevent army or immigrant occupation of the Powder River country. Following two years of attempted negotiations and conflict, with substantial losses among troops guarding the trail, peace commissioners continued their efforts in 1868. Raids on immigrant trains and frontier settlements would not cease unless Indian leaders could be persuaded to come to the negotiating table.[51]

Ever one to promote peace, as he had done in 1851 and attempted to do in 1864, Father DeSmet agreed to participate in treaty negotiations and helped commissioners take their case to Lakota holdouts on the lower Yellowstone. Escorted by about 80 friendly Sioux, he traveled to a sizable Hunkpapa village located a few miles west of the mouth of Powder River. Here he met with prominent leaders, including Sitting Bull and Gall (who had battled Sully's force in 1864 and Cole and Walker a year later). Gall attended the peace conference and signed the treaty as head delegate of the Hunkpapas.[52] Red Cloud's Oglala band and others also signed the Ft. Laramie Treaty of 1868.

The United States agreed, among other things, to close the Bozeman Trail to immigrant traffic, abandon army posts along it, and designate the Powder River country as "unceded hunting grounds." This territory, where the tribes were allowed to hunt outside of the Great Sioux Reservation, included lands east of the Bighorn Mountains, north of the North Platte River, and west of the reservation boundary. The treaty established no northern boundary for the hunting grounds, and this detail would become an issue in later conflicts, culminating in the Sioux War of 1876. It also stipulated that others were permitted to enter the unceded territory only with tribal consent.[53]

From the tribes' perspective, the treaty's prohibition against intrusions into the hunting grounds was largely honored until the United States provided army escorts for railroad surveys of the Yellowstone valley. The treaty allowed the development of railroads through the Great

Sioux Reservation, and this provision appeared to apply to the unceded territory as well. Treaty technicalities aside, events would demonstrate that the tribes were prepared to resist incursions into the lower Yellowstone country.[54]

Railroad Surveys 1871–1873

In his expedition report, Capt. Raynolds provided observations on navigable streams and potential railroad and wagon road routes, noting that the Yellowstone valley "affords peculiar facilities for a railroad."[55] The United States had earlier sponsored surveys to locate possible transcontinental rail routes, confirming that a line could be built from the headwaters of the Missouri River across the Rocky Mountains to the Pacific via the Columbia River valley. Such a line was authorized in 1864 to link Puget Sound with Lake Superior. Five years later, Philadelphia bankers financed additional surveys between Carlton, Minnesota, and Bismarck, Dakota Territory, on the east and between the Pacific and Bozeman, Montana Territory, on the west. Because Lakota bands occupied the lower Yellowstone and raided as far west as Montana Territory's Gallatin valley, railroad financiers lobbied for military escorts to complete their survey between Bismarck and Bozeman.

Like many Americans, General of the Army William T. Sherman and his top subordinates viewed settlement of the West as the nation's destiny and railroads as a means to that end. They understood that rails would bring citizens who must be protected, as well as the demise of bison herds on which the Plains Indians depended, which would force the tribes onto reservations where they could be controlled. While Sherman knew that the Lakota would be "hostile in an extreme degree," railroad development "would help bring the Indian problem to a final solution."[56] The government willingly cooperated with Northern Pacific Railroad officials to complete the surveys, though it meant committing scarce military resources that had diminished steadily for several years.[57]

Northern Pacific surveyors were again in the field in 1871. With an infantry escort from Ft. Rice on the Missouri River, the eastern party traveled up the Heart River, crossed the Little Missouri, continued west, and descended Glendive Creek to the Yellowstone. The surveyors returned via the same route without experiencing any resistance from the tribes.

With a cavalry escort from Ft. Ellis, the western party surveyed east almost to the point where Park City is located today. From here surveyors and part of the escort attempted to complete a reconnaissance to the mouth of the Bighorn River but turned back short of their goal at Pompey's Pillar. This party too encountered no resistance from the tribes, but the escort was caught in a fierce winter storm on its return trip. Lacking adequate forage to sustain his horses, the commanding officer sent a small detachment ahead to Ft. Ellis, where a rescue party was organized. Of 91 enlisted men and five officers with the escort, 57 suffered serious frostbite to faces and extremities.[58]

The following year, Col. David Stanley, with 600 men of his 22nd Infantry, escorted the eastern survey party from Ft. Rice to the Yellowstone and on to the mouth of Powder River. While this party followed the 1871 route some distance up Heart River, it then coursed farther south toward the headwaters of the Little Missouri and Cabin Creek and then followed O'Fallon Creek to the Yellowstone River.[59] Leaving most of his command in camp on the Yellowstone, Stanley led a detachment of 200 infantry with a 12-pound Napoleon gun to Powder River, where he expected to meet the western survey party.[60] He moved quickly to finish the mission because Lakota warriors had fired into his camp on O'Fallon Creek and scouts sighted a large party of tribesmen the next day.

Stanley's party included the first military detachment to set foot at the Powder River confluence since Lt. Warren's mapping team 16 years earlier. The colonel's infantry and the surveyors stayed but part of a day and left behind little that might signify their presence. While Northern Pacific engineers constructed a survey mound, some officers uncorked bottles of wine to commemorate the event. The celebration was interrupted when a young engineer, who wandered off hunting agates, was seen riding desperately to escape several mounted warriors. Army scouts rushed to save the reckless rockhound, while the detachment crossed to the left (west) bank of the Powder, putting the river between them and their attackers, who positioned themselves among cottonwoods and willows on the right bank.[61]

Gall, the Hunkpapa leader Fr. DeSmet met near here in 1868, indicated that he wanted to parley, and Stanley offered to meet on a sandbar in the middle of the river. Preferring to keep the river between them, Gall warned that he was prepared to drive the soldiers from the country while the colonel attempted to explain his mission. The conference ended abruptly when it became clear to Gall that the government would not pay for the privilege of traveling through the region. With both sides firing simultaneously, a brief skirmish ensued in which two Lakota men were wounded.

As the tribesmen rode south, Stanley fired the Napoleon gun several times to alert the western survey party he supposed to be nearby. Unknown to him, another force of Lakota warriors, led by Sitting Bull and Crazy Horse, had recently attacked the other party and its escort far up the Yellowstone; there would be no rendezvous of surveyors at Powder River.[62] Warriors under Sitting Bull returned to the lower Yellowstone in time to join Gall in harassing Stanley's party on its journey back to Ft. Rice.[63] The year ended with about 175 miles of railroad survey yet to be completed between Powder River and Pompey's Pillar.

Northern Pacific chief engineer William Roberts recommended a large military escort for the third and final Yellowstone survey to protect the party from Lakota bands that clearly understood the purpose and consequences of his work.[64] Commanding the Division of the Missouri, Lt. General Philip Sheridan enthusiastically began mobilizing a survey escort. He also planned to ship supplies to Ft. Buford for construction of a new fort on the lower Yellowstone, the post Sully tried and failed to build in 1864.[65]

The survey escort was again from the Department of Dakota. Brigadier General Alfred Terry had commanded the department since 1866.[66] Although he had recently returned from temporary duty in the South, he was very familiar with the region and issues surrounding Indian occupation in the unceded hunting grounds; he was a member of the peace commission that negotiated the Ft. Laramie Treaty of 1868. Busy with other duties, the general left much of the planning for the final survey expedition to his field commanders, Col. Stanley and Lt. Col. George A. Custer, 7th Cavalry.[67]

Using Gen. Sully's approach of 1864, military planners developed a logistics strategy that with a few embellishments would be used again in the 1876 Sioux War. Army personnel, civilian employees, and Indian scouts traveled overland from a Missouri River post to a supply depot on the Yellowstone provisioned by steamboats. A new generation of light-draft steamers, designed for upper Missouri service, also ferried troops across the Yellowstone when it was too deep and swift to ford.[68]

While 28 men and a few wagons constituted the Northern Pacific survey party, its military escort was larger than Nelson Cole's ill-fated heavy column of 1865.[69] Col. Stanley's force consisted of 20 companies of infantry and 10 companies of Custer's 7th Cavalry, totaling 1,451 men, 79 officers, seven mixed-blood scouts, and 353 other civilians, including teamsters, wagon masters, guides, a veterinarian, a surgeon, and two sutlers. Also among the civilians was a nine-member scientific corps of naturalists, geologists, paleontologists, an artist, and a photographer. Others included Mary Adams, Custer's African American cook; a sutler's African American servant; two young Englishmen touring the West with a friend from St. Louis; and a Catholic priest—not Fr. DeSmet.[70]

This force, not counting hangers-on, required 2,321 horses and mules for cavalry mounts and draft animals pulling 275 wagons of supplies.[71] The cavalry provided a formidable offensive capability not available in 1872, but it also substantially increased forage requirements. Stanley was concerned from the outset about the rate at which the engineers would travel because this information was critical for calculating supply requirements and the size of his wagon train. He concluded that 60 days' rations and forage would be needed, with grain reduced to five pounds per day. When the train was ready to leave, each six-mule wagon carried 4,000 to 5,280 pounds of supplies, depending on the fitness of the teams. With the wagons already loaded to the limit and just 42 days' forage aboard, Stanley knew that he would have to send a train back to the Missouri for supplies before the expedition reached a depot on the Yellowstone.[72]

The Northern Pacific surveyors were already on the trail from Ft. Lincoln when Stanley's command departed Ft. Rice on June 20. Early summer rain and hail storms contributed to everyone's discomfort and slowed the escort's heavy train and trailing herd of 700 beef cattle. After 12 days on the march, Stanley sent a detachment of cavalry east to Ft. Lincoln with 40 empty wagons to return with additional forage. Continuing west, he overtook the survey party on the upper reaches of Heart River and proceeded across the Little Missouri and Beaver Creek to the head of Glendive Creek. With cavalry detachments riding ahead to find a suitable route for the train, the expedition descended into the Yellowstone valley, where supplies were delivered by steamboats.

Leaving behind one company of infantry and two of cavalry to construct a stockade and guard the supply depot, the surveyors and escort were ferried to the left (north) bank of the Yellowstone River and proceeded west.[73] Skirting north of the badlands that Lt. Warren had found impassible with wagons in 1855, Stanley's cavalry detachments continued to locate routes suitable for the rest of the command. When the terrain permitted, the expedition moved again to the river via a small drainage the colonel named Custer Creek for his commander of cavalry.[74] The steamboat *Josephine* was waiting eight miles above the mouth of Powder River with clothing and more forage.[75]

Welcome to Powell's Books!
You are looking for...

SECTION _____ ROOM _____

SUBSECTION _____ AISLE # _____

AUTHOR _____

TITLE _____

MISC _____

503.228.4651   800.878.7323   visit us online at Powells.com

Welcome to Powell's Books!
You are looking for...

SECTION

SUBSECTION Diet/Nutrition

AUTHOR Lustig/Yudkin

TITLE

MISC

ROOM

AISLE # 315

503.228.4651   800.878.7323   visit us online at Powells.com

The survey proceeded uneventfully until encountering Lakota bands, including Hunkpapa warriors under Gall and Sitting Bull, near the mouth of Tongue River.[76] Custer's cavalry skirmished with 300 tribesmen here and later pursued a village of 400 to 500 lodges near the mouth of the Bighorn River. The Indians crossed to the right bank of the Yellowstone with most of their camp equipment, a feat the cavalry could not duplicate against the river's swift current. Attacked again the next morning, Custer quickly deployed skirmishers to keep the warriors at bay until his units were mounted. When the cavalry charged, the Lakota again fled across the Yellowstone, ending the conflict with an estimated loss of 40 warriors. Stanley reported four soldiers killed and four wounded.

Deciding not to pursue the tribesmen with another attempt to cross the Yellowstone, Stanley advanced another 30 miles to Pompey's Pillar. With the Northern Pacific survey now complete, the command turned north to the Musselshell River and then east to the Yellowstone depot located above Glendive Creek. Other than a minor incident at Pompey's Pillar, the expedition had no more encounters with the Lakota.

Army personnel charged with ensuring adequate expedition supplies and transportation did a much better job than those who planned the 1865 Powder River Expedition, although field commanders noted some problems. Custer chafed when two companies of his cavalry were ordered to guard the supply depot, a job normally assigned to infantry. In a letter to his wife, Elizabeth, he attributed the reduction of his force to "gross miscalculation, as to the amount of supplies and forage in our train and boat."[77]

Regarding the journey back to the supply depot, Custer wrote, "The nucleus of the long train began giving out, forage almost exhausted, horses only allowed 3 lbs a day—14 the regular amount."[78] As Raynolds and others experienced, bison had recently stripped the area of grass. To cope with inadequate grass and forage, Stanley permitted all but two companies of cavalry to push on ahead to the supply depot. He authorized Custer to abandon or burn wagons and any other property necessary to survive. In concert with Custer's famous luck, the detachment chanced onto grasslands the bison had overlooked and arrived at the depot with government property intact. Custer sent a squadron of his regiment back to Stanley's train with 14 wagons of forage.[79]

Col. Stanley's report not only described transportation and supply problems but also suggested remedies for future field operations. Most of his criticism fell on the Quartermaster's Department. He attributed the loss of 80 or 90 mules not only to hard service and short forage but also to faulty procurement and contracting practices. Many teamsters hired had little or no prior experience, and many of the mules purchased were too young for the difficult terrain and conditions encountered. According to Stanley, "This led to a great deal of trouble and damage, as these worthless men killed mules by their want of experience and their careless habits."[80] He repeated Col. Cole's recommendation of 1865 to procure no mules younger than six years.

Regarding the army's seemingly chronic forage-deficiency issue, Stanley noted that grain sent to the Yellowstone depot was more than 20 percent short of the contracted weight. As Custer angrily observed, the grain allotted each animal was reduced below the five pounds per day planned for the expedition; only three pounds was available, a quarter of the full allowance for a horse. The obvious remedy for future field operations was to stock more forage at supply depots and make more wagons and teams available to haul grain. Stanley must have assumed that this solution was self-evident, as he simply recommended that grain sacks should be no heavier than 100 pounds.[81]

Stanley labeled the tentage and fatigue hats provided his command as "worst quality" and "most useless." New cable-screwed shoes, so important to infantry, received his praise, as did the quality of wagons recently built in Philadelphia. The colonel reserved his highest praise for the Commissary Department, which supplied food and water, stating that the expedition was "rather embarrassed with overabundance" of food stores. When the *Josephine* departed Stanley's Stockade for the last time in September, she carried infantry companies and 80 tons of surplus flour, hardbread, and bacon east to the Missouri River. Although his command suffered no shortage of bread, Stanley penned a treatise on the inadequacies of the current hardbread ration issued to troops in the field. He also recommended that hardbread boxes and boxes of canned goods should be reinforced with iron bands and that rice and coffee be double-sacked to reduce waste. Finally, large cattle should not be used, because they become footsore on the trail.[82]

Reporting on the topography and natural resources of the Yellowstone valley, Stanley was not impressed with the country between Glendive Creek and Powder River. He heartily recommended the mouth of Tongue River as the best location in the valley for a new post. His expedition and the river surveys of 1873 contributed substantially to the army's understanding of the lower Yellowstone, including the potential for supplying a campaign with steamboats.[83] Citizens in the territory's

Gallatin valley also now understood that the river was probably navigable far above the mouth of Powder River.

The Bozeman business community and would-be entrepreneurs had eagerly followed the progress of the Northern Pacific surveys and fully expected that the railroad would soon bring prosperity to an economy that was sagging by 1873. As rich placer mines in western Montana Territory played out, the demand for the Gallatin valley's services and products diminished substantially. The community's hopes for economic revival were dashed when bad publicity from the 1872 railroad survey and Custer's report of fights with the tribes in 1873 contributed to the Northern Pacific's mounting financial woes. Unable to sell bonds to spooked investors, the company declared bankruptcy, which ended railroad construction and precipitated the first nationwide economic depression. The 1871–1873 railroad surveys also exacerbated ill will among Lakota bands that continued raiding to the west.[84]

Although the financial panic delayed Northern Pacific plans to lay track between Bismarck and Bozeman, other white incursions into the lower Yellowstone and Powder River country fomented trouble. In the fall of 1873, a man named Vernon who claimed to have been with Stanley's expedition reported having discovered gold on the lower Yellowstone. He found citizens in the Gallatin valley particularly good listeners; one Bozeman resident later recalled, "He was a smooth talker and convinced many of the truth of his story, and quite a large number agreed to go with him to the Rosebud in the spring."[85] This party may actually have consisted of only 10 men, who left the smooth talker to join a more ambitious undertaking.[86]

Yellowstone Wagon Road and Prospecting Expedition 1874

With railroad development stalled for an unknown period, another group of Gallatin valley entrepreneurs organized a party of citizens to explore the feasibility of constructing a wagon road linking Bozeman to the head of navigation on the Yellowstone. Here, they reasoned, a town could be established capable of competing favorably with Fort Benton, the head of navigation on the upper Missouri.[87] The organizers, supported by Territorial Governor Benjamin Potts, were desperately seeking to rescue their community from economic collapse.[88]

When organized early in 1874, the Yellowstone Wagon Road and Prospecting Expedition consisted of 150 men, including miners, frontiersmen, farmers, and stockmen; most were interested only in chasing rumors of gold in the lower Yellowstone and Powder River country, rather than pioneering a road to prosperity. More than 200 horses and mules, 28 yoke of oxen, and 22 wagons provided transportation for the party as well as supplies they believed adequate to last four months. Oxen were no doubt chosen to pull wagons because they required less supplemental feeding than horses or mules and, as planned, they would be eaten when the wagons were emptied and abandoned. Oxen would also be much less attractive to Indians on a horse-stealing raid. The men expected to augment their supplies by hunting along the route, and several brought dogs, including at least three Newfoundlands.[89]

Many of the men were from the Gallatin valley and mining communities in the western part of the territory: They were acclimated to the winters and knew how to survive here; an unknown number had military experience, and some were expert marksmen. Having elected officers and adopted a military-style organization, the party was roughly the equivalent of two or three companies of U.S. cavalry and a detachment of artillery with enough ordnance to sustain a sizable engagement. They were armed with breech-loading rifles and two field pieces, and their store of ammunition included an impressive 40,000 rounds of metallic cartridges and 150 artillery shells and canisters. All in the party knew that they were heading for a part of the lower Yellowstone and Powder River country controlled by the Lakota east of the Bighorn River and by the Crow west of that stream.

Leaving Bozeman on February 12, the expedition followed the 1872 railroad survey route east along the north side of the Yellowstone to Pompey's Pillar and then picked up the trail of Stanley's 1873 survey. Abandoning a plan to establish a road to Tongue River, the expedition crossed the ice-covered Yellowstone opposite the mouth of Armells Creek and proceeded up that stream. Now unquestionably on the unceded hunting grounds, the group moved east across the rugged divide to Rosebud Creek and then south toward the Wolf Mountains, another area rumored to be capable of yielding the next big gold strike.

Near the end of March, between Armells Creek and the Rosebud, the party entered broken terrain that was difficult for wagons, much as Fr. DeSmet experienced when he traveled a few miles west of here in 1851. Working in mud and snow, the men cut a road around a steep ravine and labored to bridge other obstacles throughout the day. After their first encounter with a dozen or more Lakota warriors in this area, expedition leaders carefully chose defensible campsites, dug rifle pits, and ensured that their stock was closely guarded. These precautions would soon prove critical for the group's survival, as tribesmen gathered to battle the intruders.

Lakota warriors struck the party soon after it entered the Rosebud valley, and three significant fights occurred as it moved up this stream and then east to the Little Bighorn and across Lodge Grass Creek to the abandoned site of Ft. C. F. Smith on the Bozeman Trail. The Lakota were reinforced with the addition of Sitting Bull's Hunkpapas and some 350 Cheyenne warriors who joined the battle at Lodge Grass Creek on April 16. Estimates of the number of warriors here vary between 750 and 1,400, but by all accounts, the Indian force was many times larger than the party they attacked.[90]

Indian attacks ceased after this battle, and the expedition was free to plod through mud and cold temperatures to arrive at the abandoned Bighorn River fort on April 21. The men had a much-needed two-day rest, and the livestock were allowed to graze before the party returned to Bozeman in relative safety; they were now on the part of the Crow reservation, east of the Bighorn River, still controlled by that tribe.[91] With better weather and more plentiful game, the expedition began to disband at Pryor Creek; most of the men returned to Bozeman on May 11, where they received a hero's welcome.[92]

The expedition was in the field three months, and for two weeks in April it was constantly pressured by Lakota and Cheyenne warriors. Remarkably, the party had only one man killed and two wounded during several engagements against superior numbers. So few casualties, and even the survival of the group, is generally attributed to competent leadership, good marksmanship, the outstanding firepower of breech-loading rifles, copious ammunition, and two artillery pieces. The selection of excellent campsites allowed livestock to be protected and afforded a clear view of the surrounding terrain. Rifle pits protected their occupants, and the cannons were ready when needed to stop an attack or drive the tribesmen beyond the effective range of their weapons.[93]

The expedition might have ended differently had the tribes not abandoned their pursuit after the battle on Lodge Grass Creek; the prospectors' artillery shells were exhausted, and only a few rounds of canister remained. Food supplies expected to last four months were critically low after 10 weeks; the men had been subsisting on short rations for several days before the Lodge Grass Creek fight, and they used the last of the canned goods two days later. With Lakota in the area, game near the party was scarce, and hunting at any distance was all but impossible.

In addition to supply issues, the party's transportation challenges increased as well. Lakota herds had recently stripped much of the spring grass on the Rosebud, and constantly harassed by tribesmen here, the expedition was forced to confine its stock with little or no time allowed for grazing. Worsening weather made more work for the teams as they struggled to pull wagons on wet, sticky soil. Considering the poor condition of the livestock and a discouraging report from a reconnaissance party, the expedition abandoned an attempt to prospect in the Wolf Mountains and returned to the Gallatin valley via the Bozeman Trail.[94]

The Bozeman *Avant Courier*, whose editor was one of the expedition planners, issued an extra when the first reports from the Yellowstone Wagon Road and Prospecting Expedition arrived on May 1. Indian attacks were said to have prevented the party from reaching the Tongue River and doing any serious prospecting. Regardless, a participant was quoted as indicating "that rich mines exist in the Big Horn Mountains south of the Big Horn," and another noted that "the country is rich."[95] Citizens of the Gallatin valley would soon learn that the expedition did not venture into the Bighorn Mountains or Wolf Mountains and that no gold in paying quantities was found at all.[96] Some participants eagerly shared their stories of battles, booby traps, expert marksmanship, and heroic deeds, which have become legend surrounding the venture.

The expedition not only failed to accomplish publicized goals but also came perilously close to annihilation. While its captain managed a very effective defensive action against Lakota and Cheyenne warriors, he realized that as supplies and ammunition dwindled, livestock condition deteriorated, and the weather worsened, the party could be overrun by the masters of the plains. As the number of warriors grew with each attack, the captain prevailed over a few men who wanted to turn south, deeper into Lakota territory. With the party moving as efficiently as possible toward the Bozeman Trail and Crow country, expedition supplies, ammunition, and livestock lasted long enough to avoid disaster. If the weather had not improved and the tribes had continued their pursuit, the expedition could easily have deteriorated into a condition similar to that of Nelson Cole's command on Powder River in 1865.[97]

Most Gallatin valley residents derived a much different lesson from the 1874 venture. For them, the expedition reinforced an already prevalent view that a few well-armed citizens could defeat and eliminate the

Lakota tribes from the lower Yellowstone and Powder River country.[98] One participant boldly concluded that "the prowess of the Sioux has been vastly overestimated and that a small force of frontiersmen can whip the whole tribe at small cost."[99]

Evidence suggests that those who planned and promoted the expedition hoped that it would punish the Lakota for raids into the Gallatin valley and start a war. Organizers were indeed interested in settlement of the Yellowstone country and improved transportation routes to Bozeman's markets. However, they realized that settlement, steamboat traffic, and railroad development through the Yellowstone valley were impossible until the Lakota were forced from the area. Peter Koch, an advocate for the Bozeman business community, recalled that the valley's economic well-being rested on opening eastern Montana Territory to whites. In his words, the Gallatin men "bravely did their part," referring to the 1874 expedition and the Fort Pease incident a year later.[100] He took pride in suggesting that Bozeman pioneers were a leading cause of the Sioux War of 1876.

While the secretary of the interior officially discouraged civilian miners from entering the Crow reservation in the Yellowstone country, the army was busy prospecting on a much grander scale within the Great Sioux Reservation in 1874. Ordered to escort a reconnaissance of the Black Hills, Custer was charged with finding a location for a new post that would strengthen military control of the region.[101] With many Lakota busy harassing the Crows and chasing prospectors far to the west in Montana Territory, the Black Hills reconnaissance encountered no resistance. Unfortunately for the Sioux, the expedition included a lethal combination of experienced prospectors and journalists. Reports of gold in the hills preceded Custer's return to his headquarters at Ft. Abraham Lincoln.

Much like the tales of fabled gold deposits in the Yellowstone country coveted by Montana miners, rumors of mineral wealth in the Black Hills had circulated among white settlements in Dakota Territory for years; unlike along the Yellowstone, there were indeed rich gold deposits within the Great Sioux Reservation. Despite the government's official policy to keep whites off reservation lands, 1,200 miners were scouring the Black Hills by July 1875. Given pressure from the settlements to allow mining and lacking the military resources or will to keep miners at bay, President Grant tried to persuade the Lakota to relinquish part of their reservation. The Allison Commission failed miserably in this task, but its negotiations clarified the depth of ill will among the Sioux that was created by white incursions into the Yellowstone valley and Black Hills.[102]

The president found himself caught between western interests supporting Indian cession of the Black Hills, by coercion if necessary, and less vocal easterners who pointed to U.S. obligations under the 1868 Treaty. The former general chose a solution to his dilemma already anticipated by his subordinates—military action.

CHAPTER 3

The 1876 Sioux War to the Beginning of White Settlement

Preparing for War

Four months before the Black Hills negotiations, General Sheridan ordered another steamboat reconnaissance of the Yellowstone River, this one to extend above the mouth of Powder River.[1] He wanted more information about the river channel, the character of the surrounding land, and possible sites for the long-sought Yellowstone posts. The general clearly stated that the information was needed because "it may be necessary, at some time in the immediate future, to occupy by a military force the country in and about the mouths of the Tongue River and Big Horn."[2] By June 1875, he learned that the head of navigation was indeed the mouth of the Bighorn and, as recommended by Col. Stanley in 1873, the Tongue River confluence was a superior location for a post. Sheridan adopted this recommendation and sought authorization for new posts even as he advocated immediate action against the tribes in the unceded territory. Plans for a fort at the mouth of the Powder were abandoned in favor of the Tongue River location.

Although there were few Indian attacks on the mining camps sprouting in the Black Hills in 1875, Lakota warriors pushed west of the Bighorn River to harass the Crows and sparse white settlements on the upper Yellowstone. Lakota raiding parties made several attacks at the new Crow agency near the Stillwater River in July. Bozeman citizens raised the alarm in Washington, D.C., when raiding parties spilled into the Gallatin valley. Continuing his crusade to rid the Yellowstone valley of native inhabitants, Territorial Governor Benjamin Potts fumed to the secretary of the interior, "We can have no peace until the Sioux Indians on the Yellowstone are whipped; no other policy will answer the purpose."[3]

As the governor sought military intervention, Bozeman entrepreneurs quickly responded to news of Sheridan's latest Yellowstone River exploration. With the prospect of two new army posts on the river and accompanying steamboat traffic, one of the goals of the Yellowstone Wagon Road and Prospecting Expedition seemed within their grasp; they would establish a trading center at the head of navigation with a connecting road to the Gallatin valley.[4] Not surprisingly, some who organized and participated in the new enterprise were veterans of the 1874 wagon road and prospecting expedition.[5] Named for one of the venture's organizers, Ft. Pease was built about three miles below the mouth of the Bighorn on the left bank of the Yellowstone. Ostensibly established for Crow trade, the fort was guaranteed to attract the attention of Lakota tribes committed to keeping railroads and white settlements out of the Yellowstone valley. It was not long before the trading post was under siege and its organizers were petitioning the army for help.

Sheridan and his top subordinates agreed with Governor Potts's policy statement regarding removal of the Lakota from the Yellowstone country. Many officers responsible for the region had long ago concluded that attacks on white settlements would cease only if the Lakota were confined to their reservation. They were aware that the political landscape was changing in ways that would support a military solution to the "Sioux problem." The president was inclined toward their view in order to extricate himself from the Black Hills dilemma, and he seized the opportunity to appoint a new secretary of the interior who was not an ardent supporter of Indian rights. In these matters, the War Department could act only if requested to do so by Interior. Finally, having failed to acquire the Black Hills through its negotiations with the Lakota, the Allison Commission recommended that the Sioux be compelled to sell; in the commission's opinion, military force would be needed.[6]

President Grant met with military personnel and cabinet members in November 1875 to plan a campaign designed to force the tribes in the unceded territory onto the reservations. Sheridan attended, as did Brigadier General George Crook, recently assigned to command of the Department of the Platte. Although the Black Hills were in General Terry's jurisdiction, Sheridan gave primary responsibility here to Crook, a close friend and West Point classmate. While the president decided to leave in place an order barring whites in the Black Hills, those attending the meeting understood that the army would not enforce this prohibition. They also knew that such a policy would inevitably result in relinquishment of Indian rights to the hills as mining communities were established there. Although he did not attend the meeting, Terry later expressed concern about violating Indian treaty rights but was quickly silenced by Sheridan.[7]

Lacking evidence of recent Lakota raids anywhere in the region of a scope that would justify a major campaign, the president and his planners used a report by an Indian inspector to vindicate their actions.[8] Submitted six days after the planning meeting, Inspector Watkins's report concluded, "The true policy, in my judgment, is to send troops against them [Indians in the unceded territory] in the winter, the sooner the better, and whip them into subjection."[9] Sheridan began preparing his military campaign before the ink was dry on the hastily written report.

Information available to campaign planners about the general character and climate of the lower Yellowstone and Powder River country was considerable. Capt. Raynolds's report of his 1859–1860 expedition provided an extensive narrative description about much of the area as well as a map of major streams.[10] Reports from Conner's 1865 Powder River Expedition as well as the 1872 and 1873 Northern Pacific surveys were also available, including Col. Stanley's specific recommendations for operating in this rugged country. Other officers, including Custer, who participated in the railroad surveys certainly had useful insights into the challenges of campaigning here. However, participants lacked personal knowledge of specific areas where battles would be fought south of the Yellowstone in the Rosebud and Little Bighorn River drainages. Civilian guides and Crow scouts would provide this critical information as the campaign progressed.

Planners should also have taken into account the northern plains climate. Temperature extremes and periods of rain and drought from late spring through early fall contributed to the discomfort of Raynolds's party; these conditions almost resulted in disaster for Cole and Walker on Powder River in 1865. After suffering delays from spring rains and bad soil conditions in 1873, Col. Stanley recommended that overland travel before July was unwise. Certainly officers with experience at posts in the Montana and Dakota territories understood the vagaries of the weather in all seasons and the difficulties associated with overland travel. They also understood the limitations of river transportation when streams were icebound or too low to support steamboat traffic.

Despite considerable knowledge of the northern plains environment among officers in Sheridan's command, his first plan for the Sioux campaign was doomed from the start. Concerned that "unless the Sioux are caught before spring, they cannot be caught at all,"[11] he sought to repeat earlier successes on the southern plains with attacks on winter villages when Indian ponies were in poor condition and the bands were less mobile than in summer. As soon as possible, General Terry was to move a force west from the Department of Dakota, while Crook was to march north from his department to locate and strike any bands encountered in the unceded territory. Sheridan would soon regret his failure to fully take into account the environment in which his forces would be operating.[12]

Information available to Terry suggested that Sitting Bull's band was near the mouth of the Little Missouri, about 150 miles northwest of Ft. Abraham Lincoln. He proposed a quick strike with cavalry from this post, emphasizing the need for stealth because his force would not be able to pursue fleeing Lakotas. He noted, "It would be impracticable to carry supplies of food and forage for more than a few days."[13] The plan changed in mid-January 1876 when Terry became aware that Sitting Bull was actually wintering on the lower Yellowstone between Powder River and Glendive Creek, far from Ft. Lincoln. He was compelled to assemble a larger force and additional supplies from diverse locations, and these tasks could not be accomplished until ice was off the rivers and trains were again moving on once snowbound rails.

Although Sheridan correctly understood the seasonal mobility of the tribes, he also knew that supply issues constrained army tactics and the mobility of troops as well; assembling and keeping heavy columns in the Powder River country would be a challenge in any season. In a response to Terry, Sheridan stated:

> I am afraid that little can be done by you at the present time. I am not well enough acquainted with the character of the winter and early springs in your latitude to give any instructions, and you will have to use your judgment as to what you may be able to accomplish at the present time to early spring.[14]

The delay prompted the lieutenant general to again seek congressional approval for new forts at the mouths of the Bighorn and Tongue rivers.

Crook Strikes First

Complying with Sheridan's winter campaign plan, General Crook launched a strike into the Powder River country from Ft. Fetterman on March 1 (Figure 3.1). He bested Terry's performance largely because troops and supplies were more easily assembled at this post on the North Platte River than at Ft. Lincoln on the Missouri. Cheyenne Depot, located near Ft. D. A. Russell and the town of Cheyenne, Wyoming Territory, at the Crow Creek crossing of the Union Pacific Railroad, was a major military supply facility serving the western plains. Troops with wagon trains of supplies moved north along established roads to Ft. Fetterman via Ft. Laramie, where a recently completed iron bridge spanned the North Platte.[15] Supply trains made this journey in four to six days, or they could save time by using a cutoff, bypassing Ft. Laramie and fording the river.[16]

Crook accompanied the expedition of 10 cavalry troops and two infantry companies that left Ft. Fetterman but assigned the aging Col. Joseph J. Reynolds as commander. Supplies were carried on a modest train of 86 six-mule wagons and 400 mules organized into an impressive five-unit pack train.[17] Managed by experienced civilians, the pack train was able to keep pace with the full command. From a bivouac near the abandoned Ft. Reno on the Bozeman Trail, the colonel pushed on with cavalry (supported only by the mule train) to attack a village of 60 lodges discovered on the Powder River. Each trooper carried a buffalo robe or two blankets, one piece of shelter, and 100 rounds of extra ammunition. Fifteen days' rations on the pack train included only a half ration of bacon; one-sixth of the usual forage allotment was carried for the livestock. There was no room for a sutler and his goods on this streamlined expedition.[18]

Leaving Crook behind with four cavalry companies and the pack train, Col. Reynolds's battalion made a night ride from Otter Creek to Powder River with a single day's ration. Scouts successfully located the village of Cheyennes and a few Oglala and Miniconjou Sioux undetected, but inadequate information about the terrain led to faulty tactical orders and more than a little confusion among the officers.[19] The battalion inflicted a few casualties, destroyed much of the camp, and captured half of the Indian pony herd; warriors later recovered most of their horses.[20]

Having ridden 65–75 miles and fought for five hours in subzero temperatures, many soldiers suffered greatly from exposure and frostbite before Crook and the pack train rendezvoused with the attack battalion the next day. The reunited command moved up Powder River, meeting the wagon train on March 21; two days later the command continued the march south. Forage carried in the wagons and pack train was depleted, and the livestock found little nourishment on the frozen, snow-covered

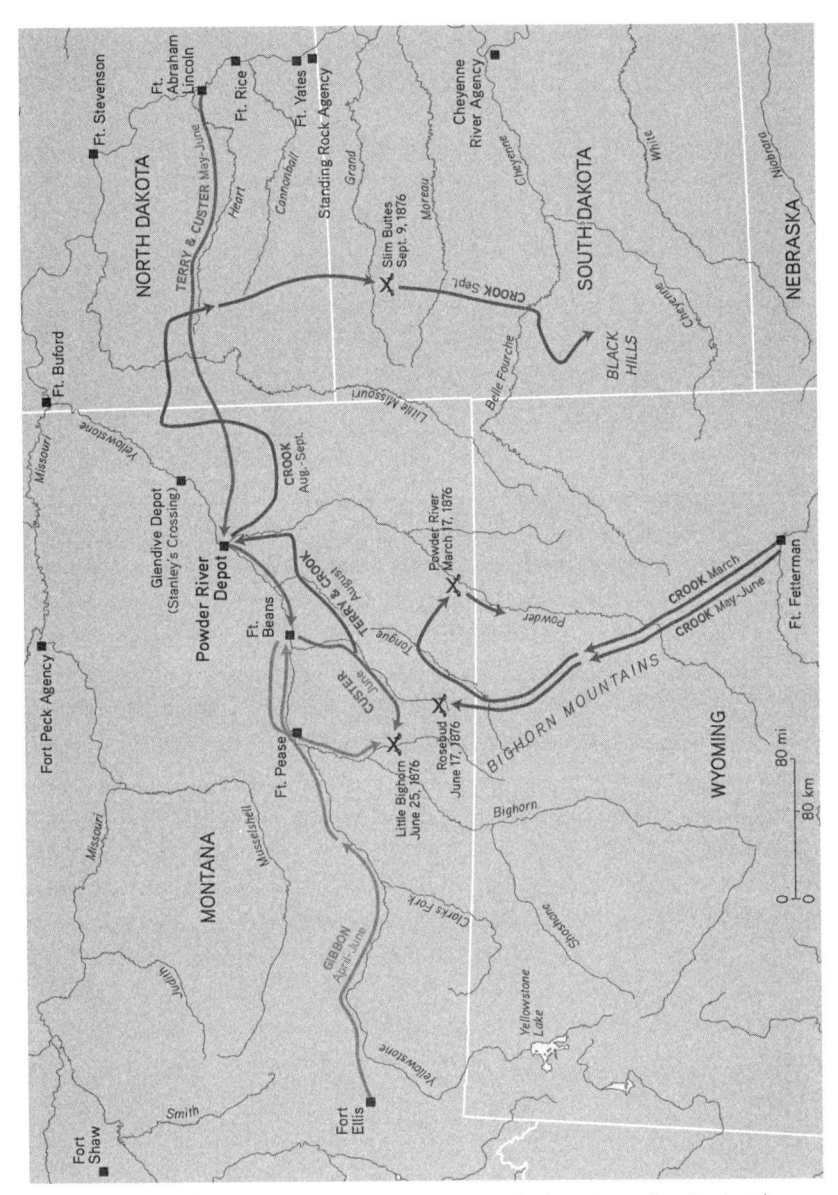

FIGURE 3.1. Map of primary troop movements, supply depots, and major battle sites during the 1876 Sioux War.

grasslands. Ninety exhausted horses and mules were abandoned or killed before the column reached Ft. Fetterman on March 26.[21]

With no access to sutler's goods for nearly a month, many enlisted men went on a drinking spree, while officers fought an internecine war over ambiguous battlefield orders, poor unit performance, soldiers killed in action abandoned on the field, failure to capture all of the village inhabitants, loss of the captured horse herd, and other issues, large and small. General Crook eventually foisted these charges on Reynolds, resulting in the colonel's retirement in disgrace. Field leadership issues aside, Sheridan understood that weather contributed significantly to the limited success of his opening engagement.[22]

The action did not effectively punish the tribes or cause any of them to abandon the unceded hunting grounds for the reservation.[23] On the contrary, as the freezing, hungry refugees of the village made their way north, first to a small Oglala camp under Crazy Horse and then to a Hunkpapa camp east of Powder River, the tribes resolved to stay together to defend themselves. As other Lakota and Northern Cheyenne winter villages in the hunting grounds arrived, the combined camps moved as one to find buffalo and grass. Sitting Bull assumed a prominent leadership roll among all the tribes.[24]

Crook's flaccid St. Patrick's Day attack on Powder River left no doubt that the army would pursue a summer campaign. Maintaining his plan to have several columns converge on the lower Yellowstone and Powder River country, Sheridan left tactics and organization to his departmental commanders. While Crook rested his livestock, resupplied, and awaited reinforcement in Wyoming Territory, General Terry struggled to put his forces in the field as soon as possible. He planned to move the 7th Cavalry overland from Ft. Lincoln (the Dakota column) while a smaller force from posts in Montana Territory would push into the Yellowstone valley from the west (the Montana column). Col. John Gibbon, commander of the Montana Military District, was to assemble six companies of his 7th Infantry and four troops of 2nd Cavalry at Ft. Ellis and proceed down the Yellowstone River.

Montana Column Marches

Terry defined the mission of the Montana column in his orders of March 21. Gibbon's force of 409 enlisted men and 27 officers was to stay on the left bank of the Yellowstone and prevent the Indians from moving north toward the Missouri River. The colonel was free to strike any bands his scouts might find, if the action did not interfere with the primary objective.

Gibbon's cavalry under Maj. Brisbin had only recently returned from a tour of duty "rescuing" the party of Bozeman citizens from Ft. Pease a short distance below the mouth of the Bighorn River. By exaggerating the Lakota threat to their trading venture, organizers convinced the military to send troops. The army not only provided the traders an escort back to Bozeman but also hauled their equipment and goods on army supply wagons emptied on the trek to Ft. Pease.[25]

The Montana column departed Ft. Ellis in early April with 24 government and 12 contract wagons carrying 60 days' supplies.[26] This was not enough transportation to also carry the stores previously freighted to a depot at a new Crow Agency located south of the mouth of Stillwater River. On Terry's orders, Col. Gibbon established a base camp and temporary depot on the Yellowstone east of the Stillwater where supplies could be consolidated as wagons became available. The column continued its march down the left bank of the Yellowstone, arriving at the abandoned Ft. Pease on April 21. Supply trains from Ft. Ellis and Bozeman now had a 100-mile trip to reach the Montana column; each required a military escort of one company.[27]

Beef cattle from a herd trailed with the column and, tended by the troops, supplemented field rations. Officers and enlisted men also had considerable success hunting buffalo and elk in the Yellowstone valley and fishing in the river; the men caught 300 pounds of fish on April 7 and another 80 pounds on April 22. Fresh meat and fish were so often a part of the diet that men complained when circumstances forced them to subsist on ordinary field rations for a few days.[28]

Although no sutler accompanied the wagon train, Bozeman traders floated goods down in mackinaw boats from Benson's Landing, about three miles from where the town of Livingston is now located. Chief among these businessmen was Paul McCormick, one of the partners in the Ft. Pease enterprise.[29] He and another freelance Bozeman trader, James Chestnut, sold butter, vegetables, eggs, tobacco, beer, and other goods to the men.[30]

Apparently, the beer was limited to a single cask shared among officers. There is little mention of alcohol until June, when the column met a steamboat carrying the sutler with the Dakota column. However, Gibbon's medical officer, Holmes O. Paulding, discovered seven bottles of medicinal whiskey stolen at Ft. Pease and on May 29 reported that some officers were drinking rum.[31]

The Montana column relied on Gibbon's scouts to find a route for the supply trains. During his first month in the field, the colonel succeeded in hiring a number of Crows and civilian scouts and guides who were intimately familiar with his area of operations. Scouts included some veterans of the Yellowstone Wagon Road and Prospecting Expedition and the Ft. Pease venture as well as Mitch Boyer, a mixed-blood Sioux who had lived with the Crows. As a youth, Boyer was among the guides under Jim Bridger's leadership who shepherded Sir George Gore through the lower Yellowstone country in 1855–1856.[32] At age 72, Bridger was no longer guiding for the military, but his disciple would render important service to Gibbon and Terry in 1876.[33]

The Montana column remained unaware of Lakota warriors in its vicinity until the Crow scouts discovered their horses missing on May 3. With increasing signs of raiding parties near his position and intelligence suggesting that they were coming from the southeast, Gibbon marched his column down the Yellowstone from Ft. Pease on May 10. Six days later, Lt. James Bradley, Co. A, 7th Infantry, and his scouts found a large Sioux and Cheyenne camp on Tongue River. The following morning, Gibbon organized an attack force, but, as Custer experienced during the 1873 railroad survey, cavalry could not cross the rising Yellowstone. The colonel's failure to quickly inform Terry of this event, as well as the additional intelligence from his scouts regarding the location of the Lakota, is one of the outstanding command issues of the campaign.[34]

Dakota Column Departs

As Gibbon's cavalry struggled to cross the river on May 17, Terry marched his long-delayed Dakota column from Ft. Lincoln with only a general notion of where he might encounter the Sioux. Modeling his movement after the final Northern Pacific survey expedition, he planned to move his command overland with a supply train to the Yellowstone, where he would establish depots provisioned by steamboats. The plan allowed flexibility to position supplies on the river where they would most effectively support troop movements. Pack trains of mules taken from wagons could carry supplies for cavalry deployed from the wagon train or river depots, as either reconnaissance detachments or combat forces.

Unlike the blocking mission given Gibbon's smaller command, the Dakota column's assignment was clearly offensive. It included Custer's

12-company regiment of 7th Cavalry for strike-force capability. The column also included two companies of 17th Infantry, a company of 6th Infantry, and a battery of three Gatling guns served by a 20th Infantry detachment. Accompanying the 52 officers and 897 enlisted men were 43 Arikara and Dakota scouts, several quartermaster scouts, two interpreters, and some 200 civilians in charge of the wagon train and a beef herd. Considerably smaller than the 1873 railroad survey escort, the command's supply train consisted of 114 six-mule government wagons and 36 smaller contract wagons to support the march from Ft. Lincoln to the Yellowstone.[35]

Terry's commissary of subsistence officer purchased rations for the column in Sioux City, Iowa, and in Chicago, Illinois; those bought in Chicago were transported via rail to Sioux City or Bismarck, where they were shipped on steamboats to Ft. Lincoln and Ft. Buford. Because it was the Missouri River post closest to the lower Yellowstone country, Ft. Buford would serve as a primary supply depot as the campaign progressed. The wagon train from Ft. Lincoln carried only enough subsistence stores and other supplies to support the column until it reached a depot to be established on the Yellowstone near Col. Stanley's abandoned 1873 stockade above Glendive Creek.[36]

Two contract steamboats of the Coulson Packet Co., the *Josephine* and the *Far West*, transported supplies to what would be the first of several field depots. Leaving Bismarck on May 9, the *Josephine* carried a load of freight to Ft. Buford, where a 6th Infantry battalion under Maj. Orlando Moore boarded, and continued up the Yellowstone to a location some distance above Stanley's 1873 depot.[37] On May 18 Moore established the depot here, referring to it as "Stanley's Crossing."[38] His three-company battalion remained here as the depot guard. The steamers continued to shuttle commissary and other supplies from Ft. Buford, including 10 tons of goods belonging to field sutler John Smith. Terry's column would have access to a variety of commissary goods and a cornucopia of sutler products when at the Yellowstone supply depots. The sutler's prices were typically very high.

Smith had been an Indian trader and also participated in the notoriously corrupt military sutler business for many years.[39] His résumé included ventures on the Platte River, at posts along the Bozeman Trail, and finally at Ft. Abraham Lincoln. Having been field sutler for Custer's Black Hills Expedition in 1874, he won the lucrative job with the Dakota column and proceeded to establish a business network to support this enterprise. He called on an old partner, Alvin Leighton, to help assemble the goods and capital needed to complete his task. Leighton was a partner in the post trader position at Ft. Buford and had extensive business interests in the region. He was the field sutler with Patrick Conner's column in 1865.[40]

Ft. Lincoln's post trader was also given the opportunity to sell his wares to the departing Dakota column. At Heart River, his clientele included hundreds of soldiers who had just been paid in the field. After crossing the river, the column marched west on rolling prairie, following Stanley's old trail to the Glendive supply depot. Weather and terrain slowed Terry's progress in the Little Missouri badlands, where he learned that Sitting Bull's band had vacated the region months ago. When conditions permitted, the column worked its way north of Sentinel Butte and into the Beaver Creek drainage. Before it moved northeast toward fresh supplies accumulated at Stanley's Crossing, couriers delivered dispatches from Col. Gibbon and Maj. Moore indicating that the tribes would be found west of Powder River. One of the couriers bearing a message from Col. Gibbon's camp near the Rosebud confluence was John Williamson, a Gallatin valley veteran of the Ft. Pease venture, now scouting for the Montana column.[41]

Given this long-overdue intelligence, Terry changed his itinerary and sent messengers directing Moore to deliver supplies to the mouth of Powder River, where a new depot would be established. On June 6, with Company C, 6th Infantry, under Capt. James Powell as boat guard, the *Far West* arrived at the Powder River confluence carrying 15 days' rations, medical supplies, 75 tons of forage, and ammunition for the general's command. The next day several of Terry's Arikara scouts reported to Powell that the Dakota column was bivouacked on Powder River about 20 miles south of the Yellowstone.[42]

Between the Dakota column bivouac and the mouth of the Powder lay the rugged river breaks that foiled Col. Nelson Cole's attempt to reach the Yellowstone with his wagon train in 1865. Terry, with two companies of 7th Cavalry, rode north from the bivouac on June 8 through this same terrain, arriving at the mouth of the Powder that evening. Although he found no suitable wagon route, Terry was greeted by a detachment of 7th Infantry with news that the Montana column was now near the mouth of Tongue River. He sent a message back to Col. Gibbon with one of the Montana civilian scouts, George Herendeen, who had participated in both the 1874 wagon road and prospecting expedition and the Ft. Pease fiasco a year later. The next morning, Terry proceeded up the Yellowstone on the *Far West* to meet Col. Gibbon and plan the next phase of the campaign.

After conferring with subordinates, Terry decided to send Maj. Reno with six companies of 7th Cavalry (right wing) and a Gatling gun to scout the Powder and Tongue river valleys. Reno was to determine if Indian bands observed on the Rosebud had gone east toward Powder River. Custer's left wing of cavalry and the rest of the Dakota column were to move to the mouth of Powder River with the wagon train while Gibbon's command marched back to the mouth of Rosebud Creek. The two wings of the 7th Cavalry were to rendezvous at the mouth of Tongue River, where further movements would take into account what Reno learned from his reconnaissance. Major Moore was to complete the transfer of supplies from Stanley's Crossing and establish a new depot at the Powder River confluence.[43]

Terry's detachment again failed to identify a suitable wagon route through the breaks during its return to the Dakota column bivouac. On his arrival here, the general used the remaining supplies in his wagon train to outfit Reno's cavalry wing for its mission. An estimated 90 to 97 pack mules managed by five civilian packers carried 12 days' rations, one-sixth the normal forage allotment, and additional ammunition for the scouting party. The column's few professional packers had a scant two days to work with the poorly trained mules and to teach soldiers the art of throwing a diamond hitch, balancing a load, and caring for a pack mule; the results were mediocre at best.[44]

Reno Scouts South and West

On June 10, Reno's right wing rode up the Powder River valley. Terry sent a cavalry detachment to find a wagon route to the Yellowstone, which had eluded him earlier. When the detachment failed to return in a timely fashion, Custer led the column though the breaks to uplands east of Powder River and then north to the new supply depot at the mouth of the river.

Giving the right wing time to complete its reconnaissance, Custer and six troops of the 7th Cavalry remained at the new depot for five days. Officers and enlisted alike engaged in some rest and recuperation and bought a variety of goods from sutler Smith's clerks. Cavalrymen continued to work with the mules that would make up their pack train.

When Custer led his wing west from the Powder River depot on June 15, he left behind 124 enlisted men of his regiment and the band;

these soldiers were to guard company property, but many simply did not have suitable mounts. The Dakota column's wagons, infantry, many civilian employees, and a few Indian scouts also remained at the depot with Moore's three-company guard from Ft. Buford.[45]

Lakota and Cheyenne Strike Crook

Riding west along the right bank of the Yellowstone, Custer reached the mouth of Tongue River on June 17, but Reno's wing had not yet arrived. Unknown to anyone in Terry's command, Gen. Crook's column was fighting its second battle of the campaign, this time at the head of Rosebud Creek. On May 29, Crook left Ft. Fetterman with 15 companies of cavalry and five of infantry, a total force of 74 officers and 1,000 enlisted men. Supplies were carried aboard 120 wagons and a very large pack train of 1,000 mules. He established a base camp and supply depot on Goose Creek, a tributary of Tongue River, from which he again sent a strike force supported by his seasoned packers and well-trained pack mules. Although they had never been ridden, some of the mules were pressed into service as infantry mounts.[46]

At Crook's urging, 261 Crow and Shoshone allies joined the column two days before Lakota and Cheyenne warriors attacked the command near the head of Rosebud Creek. The ensuing battle lasted several hours, and thanks to quick action by his Indian allies and some officers, Crook's casualties were light. The Sioux and Cheyenne suffered 21 killed and many wounded, but they stopped the army from approaching closer to their camp, now located on a tributary of the Little Bighorn River. Before withdrawing to their village, the attacking warriors did enough damage to send the general back to his base camp to await reinforcements and more supplies.[47] Crook declared this tactical defeat by a smaller force a victory because he held the field at the end of the day.

Sitting Bull, Crazy Horse, and other prominent Lakota leaders were among the 500 to 700 attacking tribesmen. Their camp included bands that had consolidated after Reynolds destroyed the village on Powder River in March. Moving west to Tongue River and then Rosebud Creek, the village grew to 450–500 lodges as other bands arrived. This was the camp Lt. Bradley and Gibbon's Crow scouts located in May. It was also the nucleus of the village Custer would encounter on the Little Bighorn, when its population had more than doubled in just eight days. Sheridan and Crook learned that warriors had left the reservation in significant numbers. Terry remained unaware of this critical intelligence as he and Custer waited at the mouth of Tongue River for the tardy Maj. Reno.[48]

While the Wyoming column battled the tribes on the upper Rosebud, Terry's right wing of 7th Cavalry was a mere 40 miles farther down the steam completing its reconnaissance. Reno arrived at Tongue River on June 15 but did not descend to the Yellowstone as ordered. He turned west, found the recently abandoned Lakota campsites, and followed the Indian trails west for some distance before returning down the Rosebud valley to the Yellowstone River.

Terry's Force Consolidates and Plans

On June 20, Terry's cavalry wings finally came together on the Yellowstone a few miles west of Tongue River. In meetings among officers aboard the *Far West*, Terry decided that Custer would pursue the Indian trail up the Rosebud with his united regiment while the Montana column marched west along the Yellowstone to Bighorn River and then south to the Little Bighorn valley. Gibbon planned to be at the mouth of the Little Bighorn on June 26; based on information now available, Terry assumed that the Sioux were likely camped someplace on this stream. In keeping with his original plan, he attempted to position Gibbon's force where it could prevent the Lakota from escaping to the north. All of the officers involved continued to worry that the tribes could not be caught if they learned of the army's approach.

Because the Dakota column scouts were west of the country with which they were most familiar, Terry transferred Mitch Boyer and several Crow scouts from Gibbon's command to the strike force. Terry also hired George Herendeen to accompany Custer. Boyer and the Crows were intimately familiar with all of the country between the Rosebud and Bighorn River; Herendeen had traveled much of the route Custer would follow when with the Yellowstone Wagon Road and Prospecting Expedition in 1874.[49]

As the Montana column proceeded west toward the Bighorn, Custer's 12 companies drew supplies from the *Far West*, moored at the 7th Cavalry bivouac about two miles below the Rosebud confluence.[50] The strike force was issued 15 days' ration of hardbread, coffee, and sugar and 12 days' ration of bacon to be transported by a pack train of 175 mules. The pack train also carried an extra 50 rounds of ammunition for each man, totaling 24,000 rounds. No ammunition for the Gatling batteries was taken because these guns were sent with Gibbon; Custer believed that the guns would slow his progress. Individual troopers carried in saddlebags 100 rounds of carbine ammunition, 24 pistol cartridges, 12 pounds of oats, and two horseshoes. A debate among Custer and his officers ensued regarding the total amount of forage required for the command.[51]

The lieutenant colonel understood that many animals in the pack train that had supported Reno's scouting mission were not in good condition. Several officers argued that the forage should be decreased to lighten the load on the mules, but Custer, who liked using pack mules, suggested that more grain would improve mule fitness.[52] Leaving the final decision on forage to company commanders, Custer told them to take extra salt and to be prepared to live on horsemeat.[53] He intended to pursue the tribes until he found them, even if it required more than the 15 days for which his command was provisioned. The companies appear to have taken about one-sixth the usual forage allotment, but they also carried extra salt.

While the cavalry regiment prepared for its departure, sutler John Smith was doing business from the steamer, and another trader from Bozeman landed a mackinaw boatload of goods near the bivouac. Popular items in the traders' inventory at this time included straw hats and liquor. Some officers filled flasks and canteens for their journey.[54]

On the morning of June 22, Custer led his troops a few miles west to Rosebud Creek, where he was forced to attend to poorly packed mules in the supply train. After repacking and adjusting loads, the command marched up the creek to the Indian trail Reno's scouting party encountered on June 16 and followed this stream as it coursed south and west. Instead of continuing to the head of the Rosebud before crossing to the Little Bighorn as planned, Custer used the discretion afforded by his orders to pursue the trail as it turned west before he reached the upper Rosebud valley. Learning the general location of the Indian camp along the Little Bighorn, he intended to rest his command in a secluded area until Gibbon was in place at the mouth of the stream. However, fearing that his position had been discovered, Custer ordered an attack on June 25 with only a general idea about the location and size of the village.

Battle at Little Bighorn

Splitting his force into battalions, Custer sent Capt. Benteen south with three companies (117 men) to scout the upper valley and, if he found no Lakota, to join the rest of the command. He ordered Reno's three companies (170 men) to follow Reno Creek to the Little Bighorn and attack wherever they encountered the village. Custer rode north along bluffs east of the Little Bighorn with five companies (225 men) to attack from another direction. The number of men in each company was reduced by one noncommissioned officer and six or more troopers detailed, with six civilian packers and two Indian scouts, to move the badly lagging pack train forward; Capt. McDougall's company was assigned to guard the train, bringing the total personnel committed to the train to 143.[55]

As Custer rode along the east ridge, Reno crossed the Little Bighorn and advanced north toward the village but stopped short of the objective as warriors gathered in his front. The major dismounted his command, formed a skirmish line, and, when flanked, moved into timber near the river.

Advancing north on the high ground, Custer saw for the first time one of the larger Indian villages ever assembled on the plains.[56] He quickly sent a courier to summon Benteen, but what he did next continues to be debated among professional and avocational historians. It appears that he further split his command into battalions, with one proceeding down a coulee toward the middle of the village while a second took a position on a ridge still farther north.[57] Sioux and Cheyenne warriors massed around both these units, killing everyone in Custer's two battalions.

Believing that his tenuous defensive position in a grove of trees had been infiltrated, Reno ordered a retreat to bluffs east of the river. The withdrawal turned into a disorganized route. With half of the command killed or missing, Reno's battered troops consolidated about 3.5 miles south of Custer's final position. Benteen soon joined the remnants of Reno's battalion, although the captain was slow to respond to two urgent requests from Custer to hurry forward with ammunition packs.[58]

All reserve ammunition was still with the pack train, nearly an hour behind the two battalions now forming a defensive position on the bluffs. Sent to expedite the train, Lt. Hare had civilian packers cut out two mules with ammunition packs and hurry them forward. Capt. McDougall arrived soon after with the head of the train, but small groups of exhausted mules continued to straggle in for some time.[59]

When Benteen's battalion arrived at the defensive site, it helped organize Reno's shattered command and attempted to move toward the sound of heavy gunfire to the north. The firing was from Custer's fight; after destroying him, the warriors moved swiftly toward the battalions approaching from the south. Averting heavy casualties with an organized retreat back to Reno's poorly fortified position, Benteen led a defensive action that lasted until nightfall and much of the next day. On the evening of June 26, the weary, thirsty command watched as the tribes paraded up the west side of the valley toward the Bighorn Mountains with all of their horses and most of their possessions.

Although the tribes lost 30 to 40 dead and many wounded, they had won a stunning victory.[60] Sitting Bull, Crazy Horse, Gall, and other leaders contributed to the victory, but it was the resolve of individual warriors to protect their families that won the day.[61] Indian combatants had perhaps a three-to-one advantage, and they faced a fragmented force with overconfident leaders. Sheridan, Custer, and other officers were convinced from the outset that the tribes would not stand and fight under any circumstances.[62]

Gibbon's force arrived on June 27 to discover that the tribes had indeed fought. The Montana column and survivors of the 7th Cavalry attended to 60 wounded and buried 263 dead combatants. Terry's reunited but significantly reduced force carried the wounded to the mouth of the Little Bighorn, where they were placed aboard the *Far West* and taken to the mouth of the Bighorn. The steamer ferried the command to the left bank of the Yellowstone, where Terry established a new base camp. He then sent the *Far West* toward Ft. Lincoln with the wounded and an initial report of the action on June 25 and 26. After stopping at the Powder River depot on the Fourth of July long enough to bury a soldier who died en route, boat captain Grant Marsh set a speed record to Ft. Lincoln, traveling 710 miles in 54 hours.[63] General Sheridan heard of Custer's fate on the eve of the nation's centennial celebration in Philadelphia.

Shocked by the defeat at Little Bighorn, Sheridan sent reinforcements and ordered Crook and Terry to continue their pursuit of the tribes. He suggested that they coordinate their efforts but left much to the discretion of his department commanders. Crook left his Goose Creek base camp on August 5 with about 2,000 men, including 25 troops of cavalry, 20 companies of infantry, and 200 to 300 Shoshone allies. He carried rations for 15 days on the pack train but lacking additional mules, was unable to take forage. To lighten the load on his now inadequate pack train, he stripped the command to a bare minimum of equipment and traveled north to the head of the Rosebud and down that stream toward the Yellowstone.[64]

On July 17, Terry ordered his men at the Powder River depot to join the rest of his command at the mouth of the Bighorn. The *Josephine* and *Far West* ferried Moore's personnel, goods, wagons, and equipment across the Yellowstone, and he proceeded up the valley to a point 12 miles west of Little Porcupine Creek. Receiving orders to establish the new depot at the mouth of the Rosebud, Moore backtracked to a point opposite that steam. When the Montana and Dakota columns arrived here on July 30, the soldiers named this new base camp "Fort Beans."[65] The paymaster disbursed $68,000 to the men, and John Smith's clerks were again enjoying brisk sales of sutler's goods.[66]

Reinforcements on the way, Terry prepared to move his force up the Rosebud in pursuit of the tribes that had mauled his 7th Cavalry. He ordered Moore to return to the abandoned Powder River depot site on the *Far West* and retrieve a large store of forage left there. The major departed on July 31, taking three companies of infantry and a detachment to serve a Gatling gun and 12-pound Napoleon gun. Along the way, Moore met the *Carroll* coming up the river with some of the promised reinforcements and learned about their encounter with an estimated 200 warriors at the mouth of the Powder. There was abundant evidence of recent Indian activity at the depot site when he arrived on August 2, and the major wisely set up a defensive position on a low ridge surrounding his grain-loading operation on the Yellowstone. His artillery kept a number of mounted warriors at bay, but an army scout was killed when he and two other men engaged in an unauthorized reconnaissance.[67]

With the arrival of additional troops and forage at Ft. Beans, Terry led his reorganized force up Rosebud Creek on August 8. He now had 1,700 men, including 12 companies of cavalry, four infantry battalions, and 75 Indian scouts. Supplies for this heavy column included shelter tents and 35 days' rations carried in 240 wagons.[68] The command also trailed a herd of beef cattle.[69] Two days later, Terry's well-supplied but cumbersome force met Crook's streamlined expedition in the Rosebud valley. The meeting was not planned. Each simply believed that the tribes would be found in the other's field of operation, with Terry marching toward the Bighorn Mountains and Crook following weeks-old Indian camps toward the Yellowstone River.

Crook and Terry Meet

The generals agreed to combine their forces and follow the large Indian trail Crook had been following, which now turned east toward the Tongue River.[70] Terry restored the Wyoming column's rations to 15 days' supply and, following Crook's example, reduced his command's rations and stripped it of most supplies, all to be carried on a pack train.[71] He sent wagons and equipment with six companies of 5th Infantry under

Col. Nelson Miles back to Ft. Beans. Miles was to patrol on the steamboat, guard fords along the Yellowstone east of Rosebud Creek, and see that supplies were moved back to the Powder River depot site. With the largest force on the northern plains since Sully's 1864 expedition, Terry knew that his supplies would be stretched thin. He also understood that the supply system would collapse when the steamboats could no longer negotiate the low water levels that are normal for the Yellowstone in late summer and fall.

The rivers swelled temporarily on August 11 when a cold front and rainstorm chilled and drenched the commands' bivouac on Tongue River. From here the large Indian trail diverged in several directions; Terry and Crook followed the largest of these down the Tongue and then east to Powder River.[72] Unable to escape cold temperatures and rain for several days, the commands suffered, as the sick list grew longer. Many men displayed symptoms of scurvy and dysentery. All were fatigued, and most needed to replace worn clothing and shoes.

The tribesmen had set fire to much of the country over which the commands passed, and soldiers were forced to destroy mounts and pack mules weakened by the lack of grass and grain.[73] The generals led their weary, demoralized armies north to the Powder River depot site for much-needed rest and supplies. The Indian trail they followed turned east from Powder River in the vicinity of the Dakota column's bivouac in June, about 20 miles south of the mouth of the Yellowstone. The trail was at least two weeks old.[74]

Terry and Crook arrived at the mouth of Powder River on August 17, finding a guard of 5th Infantry that Col. Miles had posted there, but few supplies had been transferred from the Rosebud base camp. Lacking adequate vessels to ferry wagons across the Yellowstone, Miles's command was unable to start its overland trip from Ft. Beans to the Powder until the day Terry and Crook arrived at the old depot site. Terry was more concerned about patrolling the Yellowstone to determine if any Lakota had crossed to the north than hurrying supplies to Powder River. He used the *Far West* to send Miles and scout Buffalo Bill Cody on a quick reconnaissance to Glendive Creek. When they returned two days later to report having found no Indian crossings, Terry ordered the steamer to the Rosebud for supplies and closed the depot at Ft. Beans.

Army supplies were scarce when the columns arrived at the mouth of Powder River, but traders were again ready to do business. Field sutler Smith plus Bozeman traders with an armada of mackinaw boats were overrun with eager customers. The steamer *Carroll,* unable to ascend above Wolf Rapids on August 21, brought supplies from Bismarck and a new sutler temporarily authorized to conduct business at a post to be established at the mouth of Tongue River. The wagon train from Ft. Beans finally arrived at the 5th Infantry camp on the left bank of the Yellowstone on August 22.[75] The following day, the *Far West* returned with supplies and equipment from the Rosebud camp, having been delayed by low water at Buffalo Rapids.

Crook and Terry Part

The legion camped at the mouth of Powder River responded favorably to a brief rest and a little variety in diet, but heavy rains returned on August 22. Two days later, General Crook led his command up Powder River in the mud without a full 15 days' rations or his Shoshone allies; disgusted by the way the army conducted a war, they left. Crook also failed to inform Terry of his departure, although the two brigadiers had earlier agreed to pursue the Indian trail they passed 20 miles above the Powder River confluence. Crook was eager to take the Wyoming column south toward his department. The next day Terry's command followed after the generals agreed to a new plan of operations. Crook was to pursue the Indian trail east while Terry patrolled the Yellowstone and sent supplies to Glendive Creek for the Wyoming column. But a message from Sheridan caused Terry to revise the plan before it was implemented.

Understanding that his ponderous force had little chance of overtaking the tribes, Sheridan changed his strategy. Again mimicking an earlier conflict on the southern plains, his troops would relentlessly harass the Indians in their hunting territory until forced onto reservations. Only with Custer's defeat on the Little Bighorn did Congress appropriate funds for additional posts and personnel and give the army control of the Sioux reservation. Sheridan could now disarm, dismount, and discipline the tribes into compliance with military rule.[76] Finally able to build the posts he wanted in 1873, Sheridan ordered Terry to construct temporary quarters at the mouth of Tongue River to accommodate 500 men of the 5th and 22nd Infantry under the energetic and ambitious Nelson Miles.[77] Stores and materials were already on their way up the Yellowstone on a flotilla of additional contract steamers.

Terry realized that all of his steamboat capacity and a lot of luck would be needed to transfer supplies for a new cantonment at Tongue

River before the Yellowstone would no longer support river traffic. Water levels were already perilously low, and no boats could pass above Wolf Rapids without first unloading cargo. Freight from boats that could not ascend the rapids was piled on the left bank of the Yellowstone for transshipment. The *Far West* continued to operate above these rapids and would not descend below them until the last possible moment. Taking these factors into account, Terry sent most of his force to the mouth of O'Fallon Creek to be ferried to the left bank of the Yellowstone. He then proceeded back to the Powder River confluence followed by Maj. Moore's infantry and the wagons. Steamers ferried men and equipment at Powder River to the left bank of the Yellowstone, where the infantry used wagons and teams to move stockpiled cargo above Wolf Rapids and loaded it onto the *Far West* for transport to the mouth of Tongue River.[78]

With the shipment of goods to Tongue River under way, Terry took his main force north from O'Fallon Creek on August 27. Still concerned that Sitting Bull had moved north toward the upper Missouri, Terry's column, supplied by a pack train, marched to the head of Bad Route Creek and back to the guard post Col. Miles had established at Glendive. This brief scout to the north failed to yield results when a cavalry detachment narrowly missed a Hunkpapa camp under Long Dog.[79]

Terry received a message that the Wyoming column would not resupply at Glendive; Crook would instead continue to follow Indian trails to the south. On September 5, Terry ended his campaign, ordering the Montana column back to Forts Ellis and Shaw. Maj. Moore's command marched back to Ft. Buford with Reno, who, after another unsuccessful scout for Long Dog's village, led the 7th Cavalry to its Ft. Lincoln headquarters. Terry, Buffalo Bill, and several officers who were granted leave took the *Josephine* to Ft. Buford, where the officers directed the supply operation for the cantonment at Tongue River before returning to St. Paul and other destinations.[80]

As Sheridan predicted after the 7th Cavalry was defeated at the Little Bighorn, his two large armies did little damage to the tribes before the campaign came to its inglorious end. Crook's command was subsisting on horse meat en route to the Black Hills when it stumbled on a camp of 37 Sioux lodges. The Wyoming column inflicted a few casualties and destroyed the camp, but, like Reynolds's fight on Powder River, the battle at Slim Buttes accomplished little.

After the Campaign

On his own in the lower Yellowstone country, Col. Miles relied on a new supply system to continue work on the Tongue River post and sustain winter operations against Indian bands that had scattered to the north and south. Wagon trains now moved material overland from the Missouri River to the Glendive Cantonment, a depot and forwarding station constructed opposite the mouth of Glendive Creek garrisoned by six companies of infantry. This supply line ran parallel to the left bank of the Yellowstone but was often several miles north of the river to avoid rough terrain such as the Terry Badlands. Road camps were established at key crossings, including Spring, Clear, Bad Route, Cherry, and Custer creeks. While guarding supply trains, troops from the Glendive and Tongue River cantonments had a number of skirmishes with Lakota warriors.[81]

Terry and Crook's officers applied Sheridan's new strategy with great success. Beginning in October, Miles harassed Sitting Bull's bands between the Yellowstone and Missouri rivers until they departed for Canada. In January 1877, Miles attacked Crazy Horse on Tongue River, and Crook's forces under Col. Ranald Mackenzie destroyed a large Cheyenne village on the east edge of the Bighorn Mountains. Beset by superior forces and unable to sustain their way of life, the tribes were forced to move to the reservation; Crazy Horse surrendered in May, and many others followed. Sitting Bull found refuge north of the U.S.–Canada border, the Medicine Line, until the buffalo on which his people depended had nearly vanished. He surrendered at Ft. Buford in 1881.

Colonel Miles supervised construction of a permanent post at the mouth of Tongue River in 1877. It was named for one of the officers killed at the Little Bighorn, Capt. Myles Keogh. Even before all the Lakota bands vacated the area, white settlement and commerce came to the lower Yellowstone country. Entrepreneurs quickly established Milestown (later Miles City) near the new post. The community rapidly developed into a regional trading center, with roads and stage service to Bozeman, Bismarck, and Deadwood. Farmers settled in the fertile river valleys, while hide hunters set about extirpating the last great herd of buffalo on the American plains.

During a particularly frigid winter in 1880, bison gathered near the mouth of Powder River, where thousands were killed by hunting parties from the Miles City area.[82] The northern herd migrated south from the Canadian plains, and fewer returned each year. Tribes north of the Medicine Line, including Sitting Bull's expatriated Sioux bands, could no longer find enough bison to feed themselves. White hunters had all but slaughtered the entire herd by 1883.[83] The hunters' success provided a new opportunity for the open-range livestock industry, and Miles City became the terminus of the Texas or Northern Trail over which cattle were driven from various places to the south.

As the Bozeman entrepreneurs had desired for a decade, steamboat traffic flourished on the lower Yellowstone beginning with the construction of the cantonment at Tongue River. When water levels permitted, steamers transported materials to Ft. Keogh and a second post built on the Bighorn River. From 1877 to 1882, steamboats also facilitated civilian commerce related to the hide trade, ranching, and settlement.

Although a steamboat port never developed in the Yellowstone valley to compete successfully with Ft. Benton, the Bozeman business community was delighted when railroad construction crews pushed west from Bismarck. Northern Pacific tracklayers reached Miles City in 1881, and two years later, the last spike was driven to connect the line with the West Coast. As freight trains carried the last buffalo hides from the northern herd to eastern markets, the steamboat business on the Yellowstone began to collapse.[84]

The Northern Pacific encouraged settlement in the Yellowstone valley to generate revenue from selling land it received from the government and then hauling the goods imported to and exported from area settlements. Farming continued to grow in the valleys through the 19th century and rapidly spread to upland areas as railroad advertising stimulated a homesteading boom between 1900 and 1918. The Chicago, Milwaukee, St. Paul and Pacific built into Montana after 1906 with an advertising campaign extolling the blessings of cheap land and no-risk dryland farming methods. In response to the Milwaukee's enormously successful campaign, settlers filed for homesteads on public land, purchased railroad property, and bought from private speculators.[85]

Although located at the confluence of two major streams, the old Powder River depot site looks much the same as it did in 1876. Homesteads were built here between 1889 and 1922, but they have been either consolidated into larger ranches with headquarters elsewhere or acquired by the federal government and torn down. A few building foundations with associated trash and fields planted with crested wheatgrass are the only visible evidence of the homestead era. The first wagon road between Ft. Keogh and Ft. Buford was north of the Yellowstone and several miles from the Powder River confluence. A road connecting Ft. Keogh with

Ft. Lincoln and Bismarck in 1878 crossed the Powder River a mile south of the confluence. The town of Terry was established five miles northeast of the depot site in 1882 along the Northern Pacific route. Built on the south side of the Yellowstone, the Northern Pacific line crosses the Powder River about a quarter mile southeast of its mouth. Old Highway 10, now a local frontage road, lies close to the railroad, and Interstate Highway 94 is roughly parallel another half mile to the south near the original Keogh-to-Bismarck Trail. The Milwaukee line, now abandoned, bridged the Yellowstone a mile below Wolf Rapids and then followed along the north side of the river. Calypso, one of the Milwaukee stations, was built about a half mile west of the Yellowstone crossing; like the homesteads, it now consists of foundations and trash.[86]

Fr. DeSmet's 1851 characterization of the lower Yellowstone and Powder River country was essentially correct. Other than along perennial streams, the land was not suitable for small-scale agriculture, although abundant grasslands supported grazing herbivores. As the Jesuit noted, plains tribes found the area a cornucopia of natural resources, where "all the animals common in the wilderness abound." It was also one of the last areas of the plains claimed by thousands of homesteaders seeking their fortune on small dryland farms. These settlers soon discovered that the Northern Pacific and Milwaukee advertisements were simply propaganda; the land was not an agricultural Eden on which a farmer with 320 to 640 upland acres could make a living. Most of them left the country after a few years, and those who persevered built larger, viable ranches that cover the landscape today.

CHAPTER 4

Events of the 1876 Sioux War at the Mouth of Powder River

From the Dakota column's bivouac on Powder River, General Terry sent Reno's 7th Cavalry wing scouting to the south on June 10 with the command's remaining supplies aboard a hastily organized pack train. The following day, Custer led companies making up the left wing of his regiment and the rest of the column through very difficult terrain to the Powder River depot (Table 4.1). With the wagon train nearly empty, the cavalry companies used this 20-mile trek to the Yellowstone River as an opportunity to continue training men and mules in the art of packing; the cavalry regiment would continue to depend on pack mules for its supply needs when away from depots on the Yellowstone.

R and R at Powder River Depot

Reaching the Powder River confluence the evening of June 11, Terry discovered that the *Far West* had arrived that morning from Stanley's Crossing with the second company of Maj. Moore's infantry guard and sutler John Smith's goods. Quickly erecting tents for a makeshift store, Smith's crew was ready and waiting to do business. Having marched 317 miles in 24 days, officers, enlisted men, and civilian employees stormed the trader's tents to buy goods not available while on the march. As Arikara scout Red Star noted, alcoholic beverages, including whiskey, brandy, wine, and ale, were among the most popular items available at the sutler's store:

> Here was a large tent owned by a white man who was trading. This white trader was selling liquor to the soldiers. The tent was black with soldiers buying liquor, it looked like a swarm of flies.

TABLE 4.1. Chronology of Events at the Mouth of Powder River, 1876

Jun 6	Capt. James Powell and Company C, 6th Infantry, arrive at Powder River with supplies from Stanley's Crossing.
Jun 8	From the Dakota column bivouac 20 miles south on Powder River, Gen. Terry arrives with two companies of 7th Cavalry and meets a detachment from the Montana column.
Jun 11	A second company of the 6th Infantry depot guard arrives with sutler Smith and his goods. Terry returns to the Powder River depot with the Dakota column minus Reno's wing of cavalry sent to scout south along Powder River and then west to the Tongue.
Jun 13	The last of Major Moore's 6th Infantry depot guard companies arrive with the remaining supplies from Stanley's Crossing.
Jun 15	Custer's wing of 7th Cavalry departs. The depot guard and several hundred other men remain at the Powder River depot.
Jun 16	Major Moore reorganizes his depot guard battalion.
Jun 28	Gen. Terry's Arikara scouts arrive with news of the battle at Little Bighorn.
Jul 4	The steamer *Far West* stops on its way to Ft. Lincoln with the Little Bighorn wounded. Depot personnel bury battlefield casualty Private William George, Co. H, 7th Cavalry, and celebrate the centennial of Independence Day.
Jul 20	Major Moore's battalion and all other personnel at the depot take the supplies on the wagon train to Rosebud Creek. The Powder River depot is abandoned, but some forage is left there.
Jul 29	Three companies of 22nd Infantry are deployed to cover the passage of the steamer *Carroll* past the abandoned depot after tribesmen are seen here. Rifle fire is exchanged at long distance.
Jul 30	Two steamers carrying 5th Infantry reinforcements for Terry's command sight warriors in the vicinity of the abandoned depot.
Aug 2	A detachment under Maj. Moore returns to the abandoned depot to recover forage and skirmishes with warriors. Scout Brockmeyer is mortally wounded, and a warrior is killed.
Aug 11	Company H, 5th Infantry, is posted at the mouth of Powder River opposite the abandoned depot site.
Aug 15	Recruits for the 2nd Cavalry and 7th Infantry from Ft. Ellis are posted at the abandoned depot site.
Aug 16	The combined commands of Gen. Terry and Gen. Crook arrive at the mouth of Powder River.
Aug 17	Sutler Smith arrives with goods from the Rosebud depot (Ft. Beans).
Aug 21	The supply train arrives from the Rosebud depot.
Aug 23	Court-martial of Sgt. DeLacy, 7th Cavalry.
Aug 24	Gen. Crook's command departs.
Aug 25	Gen. Terry's command departs; an infantry guard is left at Powder River.
Aug 26	Terry returns with infantry companies. Several steamers arrive with supplies for the new Tongue River Cantonment.
Sep 6	Gen. Terry closes the campaign, and the mouth of Powder River is abandoned.

There was no guardhouse at this camp and when the soldiers were arrested for being drunk they were taken out on the prairie and guarded there.[1]

Custer did not use alcohol but noted in a letter to his wife that the steamer delivered new supplies for the mess including onions, potatoes, and dried apples.[2] Items bought on account from the sutler provide examples of other food and nonfood items available at the depot.[3] Among the goods were peaches, succotash, corned beef, turkey, lobster, corn, beans, salmon, oysters, pickles, ketchup, and cheese. Fresh eggs, butter, and lemons were available too. Other items included boots, boot blacking, gloves, hats, goggles, underwear, shirts, pants, overalls, socks, and handkerchiefs. Smith also offered mirrors, knives, tin pans, plates, cups, washbasins, pails, brooms, coffeepots, kettles, pins, envelopes, water kegs, fishhooks, head nets, and toothbrushes. He sold a few products commonly used to treat upset stomach such as ginger ale and magnesia. Second only to alcohol, the item most sought at the store was tobacco, sold in plug and as cigarettes and cigars. Pipes and cigarette papers were also available, as were matches.

Soldiers could purchase a variety of foods and condiments from commissary stores at much lower prices than similar items carried by the sutler.[4] Canned goods included asparagus, clams, green corn, raspberry jam, cranberry sauce, currant jelly, lobster, milk, onions, oysters, peaches, pears, pineapples, plums, two kinds of green peas, salmon, sardines, soup (two flavors), and tomatoes. Also available were butter, cheese (two types), Java coffee, crackers, sugar-cured ham, macaroni, mackerel, jars and bottles of pickles, and lemon extract. Foods could be enhanced with cinnamon, cloves, ginger, molasses, mustard, red pepper, Worcestershire sauce, and syrup. The Commissary Department also sold tobacco at cost.

Although enlisted men could purchase these kinds of foods from the Commissary Department or sutler, few could afford to buy them in quantity.[5] Many subsisted on the basic ration issued to them by the commissary, consisting of flour or hardbread, salt pork, salt beef, beans or split peas, and coffee supplemented with cornmeal, rice, hominy, sugar, vinegar, salt, and pepper. Companies were permitted to sell excess flour and other surplus rations to civilians and use the cash to purchase nonissue foods for the rank and file. The nonissue commissary items were available to all soldiers at cost, but most were purchased by officers, who were required to buy all of their rations.[6]

While men recuperated and enjoyed access to commissary stores and sutler's goods on June 13, the steamer brought more supplies along with Capt. Murdock's Co. D, 6th Infantry. Pvt. Wilmot Sanford of this company observed drinking and gambling when he arrived at 8:00 PM. The next day he noted that many in his unit were inebriated, including Pvt. McGowan, who was thrown in the mill for being drunk while on duty.[7] Not everyone was at leisure this day; a fatigue party loaded commissary goods, forage, and some sutler's wares for shipment up the Yellowstone.[8]

Infantry soldiers handled boat cargo and organized the depot, while cavalrymen prepared for the march to Tongue River and rendezvous with Reno's scouting wing. Custer's men honed their packing skills and attempted to break in wagon mules for pack train duty. Results of the weeklong seminar in pack train management were disappointing for both men and mules.

On June 15 the steamer ferried two guns of the Gatling battery and 25 reserve mules across Powder River; the left wing of 7th Cavalry and its unruly pack train forded this stream and proceeded west while the band played "Garry Owen," one of Custer's favorite tunes.[9] An estimated 11 mules per company, plus the replacements for any stock found unfit in Reno's train, brought the total to 91 pack animals.[10] Apparently, each company initially managed its own pack mules, but when this organization proved unsatisfactory, a single train was formed at the rear of the command. With Custer on the march, Terry boarded the *Far West* with his staff and Company B, 6th Infantry, as boat guard and steamed up the Yellowstone.

More than 500 men remained at the Powder River depot.[11] Moore's three companies of 6th Infantry from Ft. Buford and Terry's two-company wagon escort of 17th Infantry served as depot guard and other duties as assigned. Relieved as boat escort, Nelson Bronson's infantry detachment remained at the depot until space was available on an eastbound steamer to Ft. Buford. Terry also left 14 members of the 7th Cavalry band at Powder River as well as one officer and 124 enlisted men, ostensibly to care for the regiment's property. Like many of the enlisted cavalrymen, several Arikara scouts remained at the depot simply because they did not have suitable mounts. Two contract surgeons were left to establish a hospital here; their first patients were four 7th Cavalry privates who became sick or suffered injuries when on the march.[12] One hundred forty quartermaster civilian employees who worked with the wagon train and beef herd also remained here, as did the wagons.[13] Animals included more than 500 mules not selected to support the 7th Cavalry in the field and an undetermined number of dogs. Before accompanying Terry on the *Far West*, sutler Smith detailed clerks to maintain a store at Powder River for about 300 men.[14]

The number of men at the depot fluctuated as detachments escorted steamboats and acted as couriers. Infantry served as pickets, handled freight, managed the mule herd, and assumed all other chores associated with a field camp. Pvt. Sanford noted that Moore reorganized his command on June 16, assigning each company a specific bivouac area. Half of the companies erected work tents where three to four men slept, while the rest of the units used two-man dog tents.[15] Soldiers constructed sinks (i.e., latrines) and shades for both officer and enlisted; the shades required constant maintenance to repair wind damage. Camp chores included picket duty, hauling wood and water, cooking, and kitchen police. To improve their menu, the men of D Company constructed an oven, allowing them to have fresh bread for much of their stay at the depot. Although no confirmation was found in documentary sources, other companies probably built ovens as well.[16]

Perhaps typical of soldiers in any age, Pvt. Sanford was always interested in what was served at meals. In addition to fresh bread, his company had butter, baked beans, apples, applesauce, bacon, coffee, and pie. After the *Josephine* arrived on June 24, Company D enjoyed fresh beef for much of its stay at Powder River. The steamer brought lettuce, onions, and radishes on July 1, probably from gardens maintained by the 6th Infantry at Ft. Buford.[17] The men also supplemented their diet by fishing and hunting. Although Pvt. Sanford noted that buffalo were seen by hunting parties, he mentioned only venison and rabbit being served in his company.[18] Of course, the sutler's store continued to offer a variety of goods.

Smith's clerks sold quantities of alcohol in early June while the cavalry was at Powder River, and sales remained strong until the depot was abandoned in July. Sanford noted incidents of drunkenness and related disciplinary problems throughout this period, recording many in his company inebriated on June 14 and 17 and July 4, 5, and 8. Partying officers kept the entire camp awake the night of June 23, and D Company's Lt. Thibaut was drunk on July 5. Several enlisted men of the company served time in the mill for being drunk on guard duty and a variety of other offenses including missing reveille or retreat, fighting, forgery, and threatening an officer; some of the transgressions resulted in courts-martial. Three soldiers who deserted on June 20 were probably not from Company D; several members of the 7th Cavalry deserted on July 7.

While there were disciplinary problems at the depot, many sought recreation in harmless activities such as gambling for tobacco, fishing, agate hunting, or prospecting for gold. Literate soldiers wrote letters and read whatever material was available. All enjoyed frequent concerts by the 7th Cavalry band.[19] According to Cpl. Samuel Meddaugh, another 6th Infantry diarist, many participated in games and sport to break the monotony of camp life.[20] Soldiers here also had a penchant for pets, including "eagles, owls, crows, horned toads, and queer rats like a kangaroo."[21] Pvt. Sanford slept with a dog.[22]

News from Little Bighorn

On June 28, camp routine was interrupted when 21 of Custer's Arikara scouts arrived at Powder River with the first report of combat on the Little Bighorn.[23] Although the scouts wondered if the depot officers believed them, Private Sanford and Cpl. Meddaugh did not question the veracity of the scouts' report. The depot command became fully aware of General Terry's loss on July 4 when the *Far West* stopped briefly on its record-breaking run to Ft. Lincoln with the battlefield wounded. Mary Adams, Custer's African American cook, was the first ashore with news that all members of the lieutenant colonel's family who had accompanied the expedition were dead.[24] The steamer was under way after collecting personal effects of 7th Cavalry officers killed in action, taking aboard Dr. Ashton, who was serving at the depot hospital, and leaving a private's body for burial.[25] Private William George died of wounds received at the Reno–Benteen defensive position.

As the nation commemorated its centennial year at a grand exposition in Philadelphia, soldiers at the depot held a big Fourth of July celebration. Their salute to America was modified to accommodate a funeral for Pvt. George, although the celebration, planned for days, was otherwise unrestrained. Fatigue parties were sent across the Yellowstone River to gather firewood on June 28 and 29 and July 3 for an Independence Day bonfire atop Sheridan Butte, a mile northwest of the depot. Preparations included constructing a platform from which speeches could be delivered and brewing a couple of barrels of beer.[26] A brew made by the soldiers from hops, oats, and yeast was a fraction of the cost of the sutler's whiskey and ale.

On July 4, Major Moore cautiously posted vedettes up to a mile from the depot, well beyond earlier pickets established on the perimeter.[27] Fires were lighted on the hills, the band played, and there was plenty of drinking. Private Meddaugh described the mother of all bonfires on Sheridan Butte, which "made a fine sight against the sky, and no doubt could be seen for many miles, much to wonder of the Indians who may have seen it."[28] Tribes may indeed have noticed the bonfire; three days later Indians were reported to be "all around" the depot.[29]

General Terry received a message on July 15 indicating that reinforcements were on the way. He arrived at Powder River aboard the *Josephine* on July 17 to begin ferrying depot personnel and all matériel to the left bank of the Yellowstone. The depot was to be moved west to facilitate the new offensive that in four weeks would lead Terry and General Crook back to Powder River. When ferrying operations were completed on July 20, Terry returned up the Yellowstone via steamboat. Maj. Moore's command proceeded overland with the wagon train the next day, leaving a significant amount of sacked forage that could not be carried on the wagon train.[30]

Tribesmen at Abandoned Depot

As Terry's force currently in the field gathered at the mouth of Rosebud Creek, reinforcements were steaming up the Yellowstone from Bismarck. When the *Carroll* with six companies of 22nd Infantry under Col. Elwell Otis approached Powder River on July 29, all aboard saw fires burning in the direction of the abandoned depot. Two newspaper correspondents among the passengers left a detailed, if confusing, record of the day's events, which produced the first casualties since the action at the Little Bighorn.[31]

The steamboat was making little headway against the current as she entered Wolf Rapids about 2.25 miles northeast of the mouth of Powder River. From here, James Howard of the *Chicago Daily Tribune* observed some 200 warriors gathering on the right bank of the Yellowstone a short distance below Powder River. Perched atop the boat's pilot house with field glasses, he also spied 40 to 50 tribesmen on the left bank of the Yellowstone. To cover the movement of the boat through this area, Col. Otis ordered a landing on the right bank at the first opportunity and deployed Companies I and F under Capt. Francis Clarke (Figure 4.1). *New York Herald* correspondent James O'Kelly accompanied this detachment.

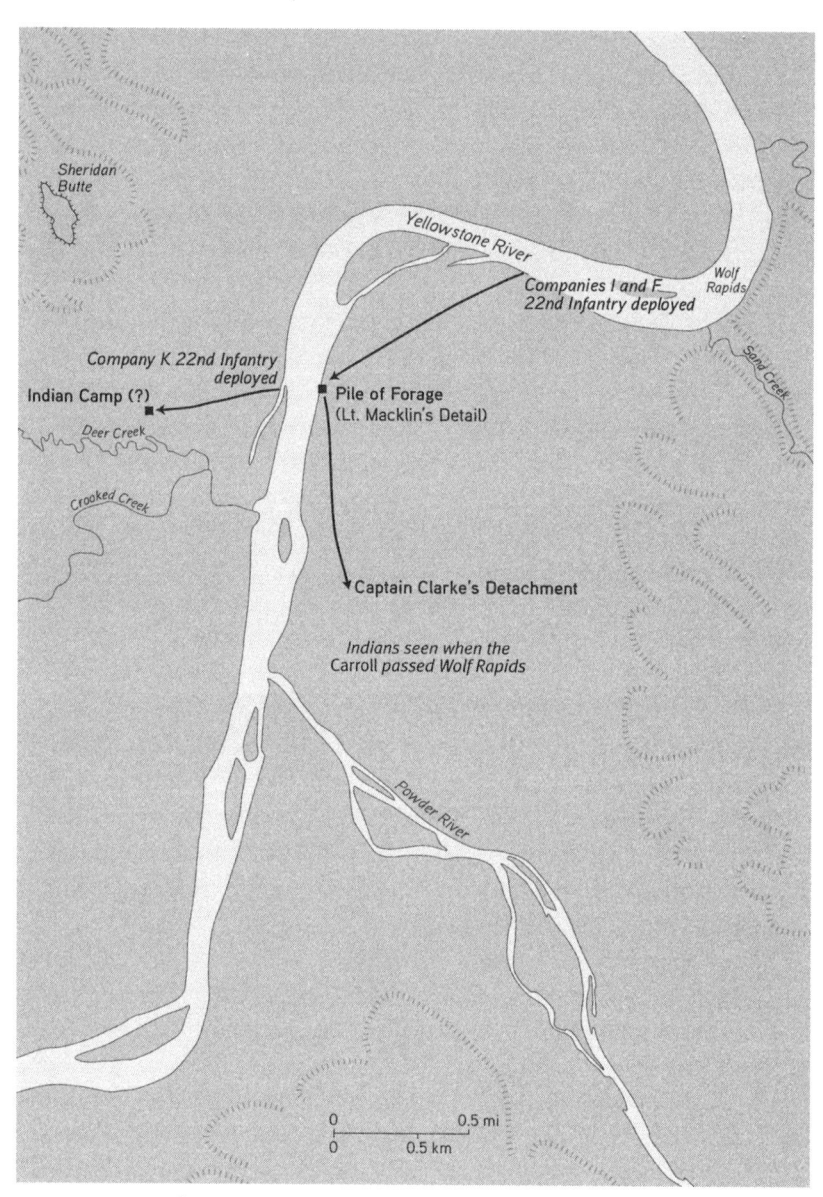

FIGURE 4.1. Map of troop movements near the mouth of Powder River, July 29, 1876, indicating where three companies of 22nd Infantry were probably deployed to cover the passage of the steamer *Carroll* past the mouth of the Powder. Troop movements and Indian positions are approximate based on newspaper accounts.

In skirmish order, Clarke's force advanced south, roughly parallel to the slow-moving steamer, and soon arrived at the abandoned depot site. Here O'Kelly observed, "There were scattered about the broken boxes of horseshoes, boxes of horse nails, debris of potato barrels, and some civilian clothing." He also mentioned seeing a wagon that had apparently been thrown into the river. Farther south he encountered a substantial pile of corn and oats that he surmised the Indians had been dragging to the riverbank to transport it to the left bank of the Yellowstone. The location of the forage was described as "a hollow in the bluff." Having found no warriors, Clarke left a detail under Lt. Macklin to destroy the forage as the rest of the detachment continued south along the right bank of the Yellowstone.[32]

After Clarke's detachment disembarked, Col. Otis ordered the *Carroll* to proceed upriver, where it soon came under fire from tribesmen on the left bank of the Yellowstone. Infantry companies aboard returned volleys of rifle fire into an Indian camp on the left bank; Clarke's force also appears to have fired on this camp from across the river. Correspondent Howard, who remained on the steamer, described the firing as well over a half mile to targets consisting of horses and warriors trying to gather them. The fusillade from the steamer had the desired effect of scattering the warriors beyond the effective range of their weapons and resulted in a number of dead and wounded ponies.

When the steamboat reached a position closest to the Indian camp, Otis ordered a landing on the left bank of the Yellowstone. Here he deployed Capt. Mott Hooten's Company K to reconnoiter and kill the wounded horses. Howard accompanied this party and reported that the detachment pillaged weapons and equipment found in the abandoned camp. Otis decided not to destroy the village, opting instead for a quick withdrawal from the left bank when he became concerned about a possible threat to Clarke's force on the other side of the river.

Lt. Macklin was north of the rest of Clarke's detachment attempting to destroy the pile of forage at the abandoned depot site when his detail came under fire from across the Yellowstone. While Hooton's company occupied their camp, warriors gathered to the north where they were not immediately threatened by Company K and could shoot across the river at Macklin's exposed detail, albeit at long range. Otis recalled Company K and steamed across the river to pick up Macklin and the rest of Clarke's detachment. The colonel concluded that little could be accomplished at Powder River so late in the day and ordered the *Carroll* to proceed toward the rendezvous with Terry's command at the mouth of the Rosebud. The incident was listed as one of the official actions with Indians during the 1876 campaign, and the army reported one warrior killed and a single casualty on the steamer, a slight wound to Pvt. John Donahoe, Co. G, 22nd Infantry.[33]

Soon after the action of July 29, Col. Nelson Miles and his 5th Infantry regiment passed the mouth of Powder River on the *Josephine* and *E. H. Durfee*. These additional reinforcements for Terry also reported seeing tribesmen in the vicinity of the abandoned depot site, but the steamers were not fired upon.[34] George Miles, the colonel's civilian nephew aboard the *Durfee*, recorded the following in his diary entry of July 30: "Passed Custer's old depot near the Powder River, a few dead mules and old tent poles, etc., one old wagon. This place was smoking for it had lately been set on fire by the Indians." The next day, Mr. Miles noted meeting the *Far West* on its way to Powder River to recover a large amount of forage left there and to "look after some Indians who had fired on the *Carroll*."[35]

Fight for Forage

Terry ordered Maj. Moore to salvage the grain Macklin's detail failed to destroy at Powder River on July 29 and return it to Fort Beans, the burgeoning camp at the mouth of the Rosebud.[36] Moore was to take a force sufficient to protect the grain-loading operation and "attack any hostile Indians that might be encountered."[37] However, lacking a functional cavalry detachment, the major was ill prepared to assault even a small band of mounted warriors. With him on the *Far West* were two companies of 6th Infantry, a company of 17th Infantry, and a 7th Infantry detail to serve a Gatling gun and 12-pound Napoleon gun. Another detail of 17 dismounted 7th Cavalry troopers served as boat guard. Medical officer Dr. Henry Porter was aboard, as were three quartermaster scouts: George Morgan, Vic Smith, and Wesley Brockmeyer.[38] Grant Marsh was captain of the *Far West*, and Dave Campbell was pilot.

In a report of his operation to retrieve the grain, Moore noted that smoke was rising from distant coulees and hills east of the abandoned depot site as his command approached Powder River on August 2. Suspecting that Indians were still in the vicinity, the major steamed past the depot site to Wolf Rapids and then returned to the landing where the grain was piled. While Moore deployed his force along a low ridge near the landing, Indians appeared southeast of his position, toward Powder

River. An attempt to bring the warriors into rifle range by concealing most of his men below the ridge failed. The major then opened fire with the Napoleon gun, first toward Powder River and then in an arc toward Wolf Rapids. As tribesmen dispersed to the hills and ravines east of the landing, he concluded, "The whole ground in the bend between Powder River and Wolf Rapids on our left was commanded by artillery."[39] Soldiers began loading the 75 tons of grain with a brief interruption about 11:00 AM when Indians were seen to the southeast near Wolf Rapids; the artillery crew resumed firing, and the tribesmen scattered once more.

Two hours later, the relative calm of the hot summer day was disturbed when pilot Campbell and scouts Morgan and Brockmeyer mounted their horses to reconnoiter toward Wolf Rapids. Soldiers on the skirmish line then reported about 20 warriors riding to cut off the foolhardy threesome, who were yet unaware of the immediate danger (Figure 4.2). A shot from the Napoleon gun sounded the alarm and discouraged all but a few tribesmen who were closest to their quarry. The three men had reversed course and were riding hard for the command's position when Brockmeyer's horse fell. The scout was shot by a single warrior who dared to come close. This warrior was subsequently killed by a man identified by Maj. Moore only as "the other scout." The major stated that a detachment under Lt. Frank Garretty, Co. C, 17th Infantry, was "promptly hastening to the aid of the scout."[40] Tribesmen were again seen on the bluffs in the direction of Powder River, but no further action ensued before the *Far West*'s departure at 4:00 AM on August 3. Attended by Dr. Porter, Brockmeyer died after suffering for several hours; Moore's command buried him during one of several short stops on the way back to the Rosebud.[41]

Other accounts differ significantly from Moore's official report regarding the events of August 2. The 6th Infantry's Cpl. Meddaugh and Pvt. Sanford were present at this action. The corporal stated that Morgan killed the tribesman and that soldiers who went forward to aid Brockmeyer slashed the Indian's body with their knives.[42] Sanford claimed that the warrior had two bullet wounds and was killed and scalped by Vic Smith.[43] Maj. Moore identified Smith as the third scout with his command on August 2 but did not mention him being in the action, unless Smith was the warrior's killer identified in Moore's report only as "the other scout."[44]

Smith's memoire affirms his presence at this event and provides details not found elsewhere.[45] He arrived at the mouth of Powder River

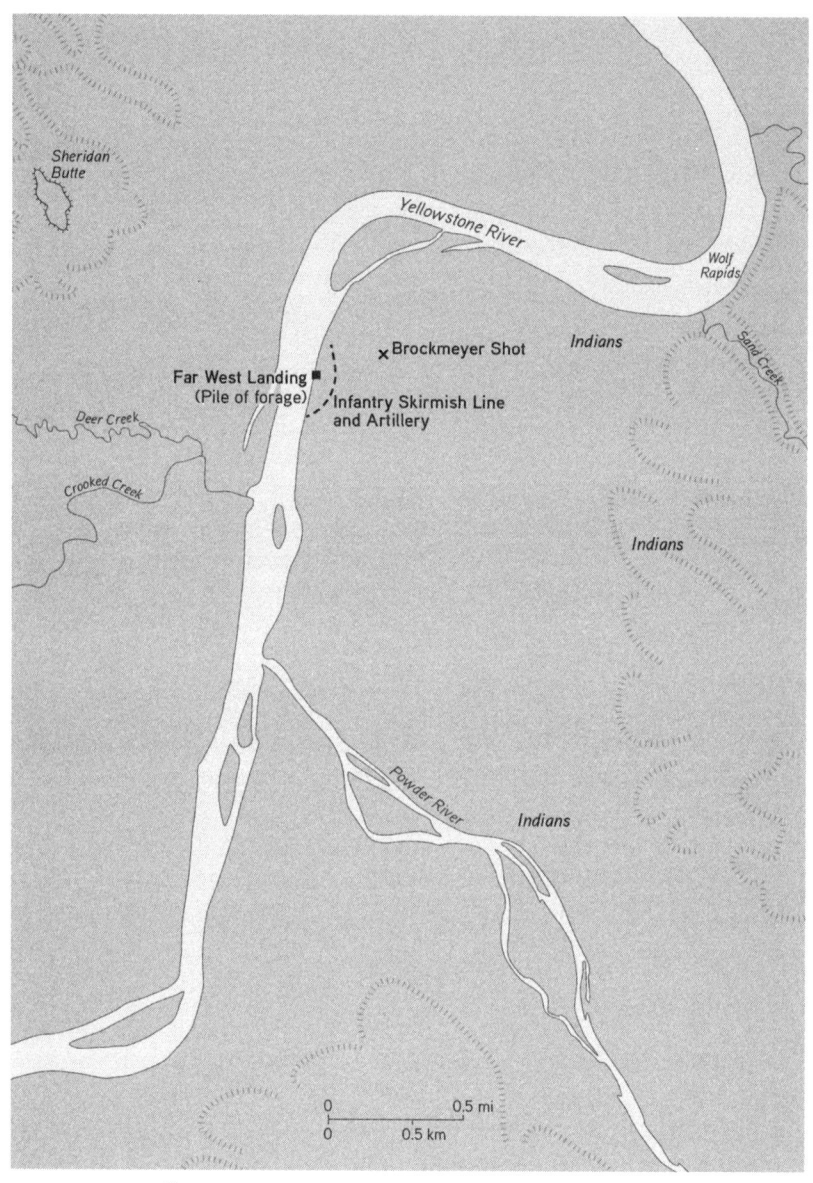

FIGURE 4.2. Map illustrating U.S. Army and Indian positions near the mouth of Powder River, August 2, 1876. Indian positions and the location of scout Brockmeyer's fall are approximate, based on official reports and eyewitness accounts.

Events of the 1876 Sioux War at the Mouth of Powder River 83

with Moore's command, landing where Indians had taken corn and all the sacks, leaving only oats on the ground. While soldiers and deckhands loaded grain onto the steamboat, Brockmeyer and Smith rode three miles to a high bluff from which they could see, using field glasses, a sizable Indian camp about 12 miles up the Powder River valley.[46] When returning to the steamboat landing, Smith saw six Indians on a knoll about 300 yards distant; one of them followed the scouts at a safe distance to within 300 yards of the landing.

When Smith arrived at the landing, Moore refused his request to kill the brave, who remained a few hundred yards from the troops. The warrior made rude gestures toward the troops, whereupon Moore opened fire with artillery and the tribesman fled uninjured. Smith requested permission to return to the bluffs south of the landing from which he had seen the village, but Moore again refused.

Smith then retired to his steamboat cabin and slept until he was awakened by pilot Dave Campbell with a request to borrow Smith's horse to ride into the hills with Brockmeyer and a person Smith identified only as "the herder." As Smith continued his nap, the three men were attacked by a half dozen mounted tribesmen about two miles from the landing. Campbell, Brockmeyer, and the herder made a hasty retreat toward the *Far West* with the warriors pursuing them. Moore again ordered the Napoleon gun into action, with such accuracy that "two Indians were seen to fall, and one horse went down to rise no more."[47] Two of the tribesmen turned back toward the hills, and a single warrior continued his pursuit of the three men.

Meanwhile back in his cabin, Smith awoke at the sound of artillery. Quickly assessing the situation, he commandeered Major Moore's fine steed from the steamer and rode bareback toward the retreating party, rifle in hand.[48] As he and the men rapidly converged, the pursuing warrior fired, hitting Brockmeyer's horse under its backbone. Unable to retrieve his rifle from beneath the fallen horse, and deserted by his companions, Brockmeyer ran but was soon overtaken and shot by the warrior. Smith began firing when about 200 yards from the warrior, who now rode toward Smith. When the two were some 50 yards apart, Smith delivered a fatal shot from his Winchester, killing the tribesman.[49]

While Moore fired the Napoleon gun a few more times, Marsh and the boat crew went looking for Brockmeyer, a task that took about 15 minutes because the prostrate scout was difficult to locate in the tall sagebrush. Smith noted that someone scalped the warrior without indicating who did the grisly deed. He retrieved Brockmeyer's horse, which had regained its feet, and removed the saddle blanket so that it could be used to carry the wounded scout back to the steamer, presumably by Marsh's crew. After Brockmeyer's death the horse recovered and was sold at auction.[50]

These accounts create more questions than they provide answers for the events of August 2 at the abandoned Powder River depot. A few consistent themes confirm that Brockmeyer, Campbell, and Morgan rode away from the landing. When attacked, the men retreated, and Brockmeyer was wounded by a single pursuing warrior. One or more of the scouts then shot the Indian. Brockmeyer was taken back to the *Far West*, where he died; he was buried along the Yellowstone as the command returned to the mouth of the Rosebud.

Most other details of the action vary among the accounts in ways that cannot be easily reconciled. Maj. Moore reported that 1st Lt. Garretty promptly hastened his company to help the scouts, with no mention of Marsh's rescue party. Marsh recalled that he and his crew rushed to help the scouts because Moore refused to order troops forward. The *New York Herald* reported that Moore threatened to court-martial eight soldiers who volunteered to accompany Marsh's rescue party and that the boat crew called the major a coward for failing to order troops to the scene.[51] This newspaper article and an account by Capt. Walter Clifford, Co. E, 7th Infantry, who probably got the information from others, identified pilot Campbell as turning back to assist Brockmeyer and having a hand in killing and scalping the warrior.[52] The person who killed the warrior who shot Brockmeyer is elsewhere identified as Morgan or Smith. Brockmeyer is described as being shot point-blank while pinned under his horse and as being shot while running away from his downed horse. His companions are said to have heroically made a stand to help him and kill his attacker or to have abandoned him to his fate.

Smith recalled that Brockmeyer was buried on August 3 on the steamboat's return to Ft. Beans; he says that the burial was on an island in the Yellowstone "so Indians might not find and mutilate the body."[53] There is, however, no mention in the record that the body of Pvt. William George was reinterred by Moore's command. Cpl. Meddaugh, who witnessed George's burial on July 4, noted in his diary entry for August 2 that Indians had removed the body from its grave at the old depot site. Meddaugh also noted that the body of the warrior who shot Brockmeyer was slashed and decapitated by soldiers; the head was "used for a football in camp for several days."[54] If that is the case, the man's head would have had to have been transported back to the Rosebud base camp. Dr. Porter reportedly sent this man's scalp to Bismarck to be displayed in public.[55]

Two Indian accounts document contact with soldiers at the mouth of Powder River between the depot's abandonment on July 20 and the fight of August 2.[56] Cheyenne warrior Wooden Leg recalled that after the battle at Little Bighorn, several tribes returned east and camped on Powder River, not far from the Yellowstone. They stayed here for several days before splitting up to find game and better grass for their horses. The Cheyennes first went from this camp to the mouth of the Powder River, where they found a large pile of sacked corn by the Yellowstone. The Indians ate some of the grain, fed some to their captured cavalry horses, and left most on the ground after taking the sacks. Wooden Leg noted that some of the warriors shot at a passing steamboat but those aboard did not return fire or stop.

Oglala warrior Black Elk also recalled camping on Powder River before the tribes dispersed, when Lakota scouts reported finding corn on the Yellowstone. Some young warriors went to investigate and "had a fight there with the soldiers of the steamboat."[57] A warrior named Yellow Shirt was killed in this fight. If Black Elk's account refers to Moore's action on August 2, Yellow Shirt might have been the warrior who shot Brockmeyer and was then killed by the army scout.[58] However, the army also reported a warrior killed here when Col. Otis's command engaged tribesmen on July 29. There is not enough information to identify which event Black Elk was recalling.

Although details of the fights on July 29 and August 2 are often confused or contradictory, the significance of the events is clear. With the exception of a few scattered bands, the tribes were camped on Powder River not far from the Yellowstone during this period. From this big camp, young warriors gathered at the mouth of Powder River to harass the steamboats and engage Moore's forage-recovery operation. As reinforcements gathered at his Rosebud Creek base camp, most of the Indians Gen. Terry sought were a few miles south of his old depot site. Terry's pursuit of the tribes would lead him and Crook back to Powder River long after the tribes had departed.

There was no further military presence at the mouth of Powder River until troops under Col. Nelson Miles began patrolling the Yellowstone to ensure that Indians did not escape Terry and Crook's combined forces by moving north of the river. With the *Far West* providing transport on

August 11, Miles posted Co. H, 5th Infantry, on the left bank, opposite the old depot site. Capt. Samuel Overshine built fieldworks here and deployed a three-inch rifled gun.[59]

Four days later, 1st Lt. William P. Clark, 2nd Cavalry, landed a small flotilla of mackinaw boats with recruits from Ft. Ellis for the 7th Infantry and his regiment. Having met Col. Miles at Ft. Beans on August 11, he was, perhaps ironically, ordered to transport forage to the mouth of Powder River. Clark not only took grain back to the old depot site from which it recently came but also had with him James O'Kelly, the *New York Herald* correspondent who had accompanied Otis's troops when they tried to burn the forage at Powder River on July 29. Free-lance Bozeman trader Cy Mounts and his goods were with this party as well.[60] In his August 15 diary entry, Clark states the following:

> Left landing at 5 o'ck reached mouth of Powder river at 11 AM dropped below about a mile received orders from Gen Miles to go into camp. Soon after he came on the Str. Far West and landed a Gatling Gun which was placed in rear of Camp—This is the place from which the corn was taken by the Indians in July and where they were in considerable force in the early part of the present month.[61]

Clark established this outpost on the right bank of the Yellowstone at the old depot location, where on August 16 he continued to secure "a large quantity of grain which had been scattered by the Indians in order to procure sacks for the corn taken away by them for food."[62] The warriors could not have known that taking grain sacks from the abandoned depot would create a minor logistics problem that would hound the soldiers for weeks.[63]

Terry and Crook at Powder River

Terry and Crook arrived at the mouth of Powder River the following day to resupply their commands and rest both men and animals. Col. Miles's infantry continued to occupy guard posts at fords along the Yellowstone and patrol the river. Everyone else eagerly awaited supplies traveling overland on the wagon train and those transported via steamer from Ft. Beans to Powder River. The commanders wanted to pursue Indian trails as soon as possible, but officers and enlisted alike looked forward to supplementing their field ration as well as replacing worn shoes and unserviceable equipment. Having subsisted only on grass during the march, many horses and mules were incapable of further service without rest and grain.[64] A number of cavalry mounts were reported abandoned during the last three days of the march.[65]

Collectively the largest force sent against the northern plains tribes since Sully's 1864 campaign, the two commands made up a five-mile-long column while on the march from Rosebud Creek to the mouth of Powder River. Occupying hundreds of acres at the Powder River confluence, both commands wanted to ensure adequate grazing for their livestock. Sixth Infantry Pvt. Sanford noted that the companies of his regiment camped at their old depot location along the right bank of the Yellowstone with the 7th and 22nd Infantry.[66] The 5th Infantry detachment Miles posted earlier was camped on the left bank of the Yellowstone, opposite the main infantry camp.

A day after arriving, Terry moved his headquarters and the main infantry camp a mile down the Yellowstone. Terry's cavalry was located on the Powder about 1.5 miles from the Yellowstone and some two–three miles south of the infantry.[67] All of Gen. Crook's command bivouacked west of the Powder along the Yellowstone.[68] After extinguishing a prairie fire that began in the 5th Cavalry camp, Crook moved his force one–two miles up the Yellowstone for better pasture and water.[69]

Having endured field rations, storms, and camps without shelter for some time, soldiers and civilians were disappointed that few supplies and only limited commissary goods had reached the mouth of Powder River by August 17.[70] However, most were overjoyed to see eager entrepreneurs from the Gallatin valley land two mackinaw boats full of goods.[71] Much like the scene at sutler Smith's tent when the Dakota column arrived in June, soldiers stormed the boats for vegetables, canned fruit, eggs, and other goods. Mackinaws with more goods from Bozeman continued to arrive during the next few days.[72]

John Smith soon arrived at Powder River to sell his wares between August 17 and August 25. The Smith and Leighton ledger documents charges to 25 officers during this period, all but two of whom were from Terry's command. Nonfood purchases were dominated in descending order by socks, gloves, matches, coffeepots, pans, pails, tin cups, boots, and shirts. A single item each of overalls, drawers, a toothbrush, and a hatchet were charged. The most popular food items bought on account were cans of corn and lobster, followed by crackers, cheese, and butter sold by the pound. Other canned goods included beans and succotash.[73]

Officers in Terry's command charged far more tobacco and alcohol to their accounts than all other items combined. A 6th Infantry sergeant bought 22 pounds of tobacco, and a 2nd Cavalry captain bought 20 pounds, while four other officers charged a pound each. The large quantities were no doubt intended for companies or other groups of soldiers. Ten officers charged cigars in quantities appropriate for an individual or small party of comrades.

During the last half of August demand for tobacco greatly exceeded both Smith's supply and that of Terry's subsistence stores.[74] The day after the columns arrived at the Powder River confluence, 1st Lt. Edward Godfrey, Co. A, 7th Cavalry, stated, "The P.T. [post trader] sold nearly everything out — tobacco and such things at outrageous prices."[75] Crook's adjutant, 1st Lt. John Gregory Bourke, cited the scarcity of tobacco as proof that officers in charge of supply at Powder River were incompetent:

> I will note that all the tobacco obtainable was eleven pounds. I know this because that number of orderlies at our Hdqrs. used tobacco and I, accordingly, put in a requisition for the allowance of one pound each. Shortly after it was handed to me the Commissary Sergeant, Bubb came up greatly excited and said that there was no tobacco at all, that he wanted to keep the eleven pounds for emergencies, etc, but it was then too late; it had been distributed among the men of the detachment.[76]

While it is hard to imagine what emergency would require the last shred of cut-leaf or plug, tobacco was clearly "the weed that a soldier likes even better than he does whiskey."[77] The Wyoming column's Lt. Col. Eugene Carr noted that lack of tobacco was a "great privation" to his men and responded to their desperation by allowing some of them to charge on his account.[78]

In contrast to trade at the depot in June and July, there was little mention of alcohol sales and only a single incident of drunkenness reported in August. One account states that beer was available from the Bozeman traders, and another notes that Montana column transportation manager Matt Carroll set out a barrel of bottled ale for some officer friends.[79] The reason for this relative sobriety is likely revealed in Pvt. Sanford's comment of August 21: "No whiskey sold to inlisted men."[80] This prohibition, however, was not extended to officers.

Most entries in Smith's ledger at this time were for whiskey and brandy. Eleven officers charged 23.5 gallons, two demijohns, one quart, and one canteen of whiskey, and seven officers bought 94 individual drinks on account. One officer paid $6.00 for two bottles of brandy; whiskey prices were $6.00 per gallon or 12.5 cents per drink.[81]

The total amount of liquor Smith sold at Powder River in August cannot be determined because he might have kept other ledgers and there is no record of cash sales. If the Bozeman traders sold liquor, no record has been found. Many men were probably buying in quantity to share with officers in their unit or others, and the liquor appears to have been consumed over several days. Regardless, Lt. Ernest Garlington, Co. H, 7th Cavalry, would recall, "Unfortunately, when we got to the Powder River camp we found a trader located there who had plenty of whiskey." He went on to recount an incident involving an officer in his regiment.[82]

On August 23, Garlington was detailed to serve in a regimental court-martial, the first in which he acted as judge advocate. After an extended search, he found an infantry officer in Crook's command who could write out from memory the oath to be administered to members of the court. His next challenge was coaxing the reluctant president of the court, Capt. Thomas Weir, Co. D, 7th Cavalry, to convene the proceedings. The tenacious lieutenant succeeded after several foiled attempts, and the court-martial began under a cottonwood tree with members seated on "roots and stumps." Presiding with a demijohn of whiskey held between his knees, Capt. Weir would occasionally adjourn the court, "have Sergeant DeLacey and the witness step a few paces to one side, when he would tilt the demijohn, take a drink, and ask the other members of the court to join him, which none did." DeLacey, the accused, was charged with being absent without leave and conduct to the prejudice of military orders and discipline. His $10.00 fine was suspended by the regimental commander. Lt. Garlington hounded the president for several days to sign the proceedings and commented on Weir's promising early service and gallant Civil War record.[83]

Capt. Weir was with Benteen's battalion at the Little Bighorn and on joining Reno's shattered command at its hilltop defensive position, requested permission to lead a reconnaissance to determine Custer's whereabouts. He led Company D to an elevated area now called Weir Point, a mile north of the defensive position. Benteen followed later with

Cos. H, K, and M, and still others were headed north when all units retreated back to Reno Hill as a large force of warriors from Custer's part of the battlefield rode in their direction. Weir had a heated exchange with Reno because the major failed to organize an advance in the direction of Custer's apparent position.[84]

The captain and many others no doubt needed rest and recuperation at Powder River, and in the frontier army that often included alcohol. Drinking was a prominent pastime for soldiers in garrison and in the field when alcohol was available, to deal with stress, boredom, loneliness, and other conditions of military life. While the incidence of severe alcoholism was high, it does not appear to have been any more prevalent on the frontier than elsewhere.[85] General cultural norms of the day contributed to this problem because alcohol was commonly used as medicine and was thought to be particularly good for the heart and lungs. Combat-related issues, such as post-traumatic stress disorder, were not understood and probably contributed to alcohol consumption after any battle.[86]

As recorded in Smith's ledger, Capt. Weir charged nine drinks, several ales, two quarts of whiskey, and a bottle of brandy to his account at Ft. Beans between August 1 and August 7. Two days before DeLacey's court-martial at Powder River, the captain bought two gallons of whiskey.[87] Tragically, he died less than four months later, probably from complications of alcoholism.[88]

Although the traders' goods contributed to the comfort of the men, lack of adequate shelter made rest or recuperation impossible for many. Emulating Crook, General Terry stripped his force to bare essentials when the commands marched together from Rosebud Creek; each soldier carried only a blanket and four days' rations. Troops in neither command had tenting when a cold front brought rain on August 11 to the bivouac on Tongue River. Makeshift shelters of brush and driftwood constructed at the mouth of Powder River proved woefully inadequate as rain and cool weather gripped the area again on August 21. The next day, Terry's men got access to their tenting when the 5th Infantry detachment arrived on the left bank of the Yellowstone with the wagon train from Ft. Beans.[89]

Even tents failed to keep the men dry on August 23 and 24. By most accounts, the camps were pelted by a deluge that few would forget. Lt. Godfrey noted that the dog tents did not afford enough protection for men in these extreme conditions.[90] Indeed, Pvt. Sanford reported two feet of water in his tent at the 6th Infantry camp the morning of August

24, and his unit's quartermaster was equally flooded.[91] Some of Terry's officers apparently fared better than most; camped with his uncle's 5th Infantry, George Miles stated in his diary entry for August 23:

> This evening we had one of the hardest wind and rain storms that I ever saw, quite a number of the tents came down and the poor soldiers were just drenched. I slept on the ground but managed to keep nice and dry, as we had a good ditch around our tent and canvas on the tent floor.[92]

Still without tenting, the Wyoming column suffered the most, as revealed in numerous accounts of officers and newspaper correspondents.[93] Despite the inclement weather, Crook bade a final farewell to the mouth of Powder River on the morning of August 24 after acquiring rations and new shoes for his men. In pursuit of now weeks-old Indian trails to the east, he again limited the amount of material carried by individual solders and had only his pack train for supplies.[94]

Intending to follow Crook, Terry modified his supply system to include not only pack animals but also a limited number of wagons. He ordered steamboats to ferry the 40 wagons and four companies of the 5th Infantry to the right bank of the Yellowstone.[95] Leaving Company B, 5th Infantry, and Capt. Sanger's 17th Infantry to guard wagons and supplies transferred from the Rosebud, he started his command up Powder River on August 25. The next day couriers brought news of recent Lakota activity on the lower Yellowstone and new orders from Sheridan to expedite construction of a post at the mouth of Tongue River. Sending most of his command back to the Yellowstone near O'Fallon Creek, Terry returned to the mouth of Powder River with his staff and a company of 2nd Cavalry; Major Moore and the 6th Infantry companies followed with the wagons. Here Terry found several steamers with supplies and additional troops for the new post. After leaving orders for disposition of the supplies for Tongue River, he proceeded down the Yellowstone to join the rest of his command near O'Fallon Creek.[96]

Water levels in the Yellowstone continued to fall, forcing steamboats to off-load cargo below Wolf Rapids. Soldiers were busy using wagons left at Powder River to transport stores from a landing below the rapids to an upper landing where supplies were loaded on the *Far West*, the only steamer still capable of operating between Powder River and the Tongue.[97]

Following Terry back to the old depot site, Maj. Moore's command arrived with additional wagons on August 27, and the steamboat ferried them to the left bank of the Yellowstone. The next day, Moore, with four companies of 6th Infantry, escorted a wagon train to Ft. Buford, traveling up the left bank of the Yellowstone for several miles before turning up Custer Creek and then east around the badlands.[98]

The *Far West* carried supplies to Tongue River with Co. B, 5th Infantry, 50 cavalry recruits, and young George Miles aboard. Capt. Sanger's two companies of 17th Infantry remained at Powder River to move supplies between landings for transshipment to Tongue River. The *Far West* was forced to abandon the river above Wolf Rapids on August 30. Receiving orders to close the depot site on the evening of September 5, Sanger transported everything left at Powder River to Custer Creek, where supplies were forwarded to the Tongue and some wagons were sent to the Glendive Cantonment.[99]

Beginning in the fall of 1876, Col. Miles actively pursued Lakota and Cheyenne bands from his base at the mouth of Tongue River. The cantonment, later Ft. Keogh, was initially supplied via a trail north of the Yellowstone from Ft. Buford to the Glendive Cantonment and then to the Tongue. Located north of the Terry Badlands, this trail was several miles from the Powder River confluence. Steamboats also hauled supplies during the spring rise when passage above Wolf Rapids was no problem and there was no need to stop at the Powder River.

CHAPTER 5

Archaeology and History at the Powder River Depot

Connecting Archaeology and History

Among documented events in the lower Yellowstone and Powder River country, three warranted consideration as potentially associated with archaeological Feature D before it was excavated.[1] Analysis of artifacts recovered from the surface suggested that they were manufactured sometime between 1865 and 1885. Within this period, events occurring at or near the Powder River confluence that might account for similar materials were the 1872 railroad survey, the 1876 Sioux War, and construction of the Northern Pacific Railroad (1881–1883).

A 200-man detachment from the 1872 railroad survey occupied some part of the land east of the Yellowstone River and both north and south of the Powder. This party built a survey mound, offered a libation of wine, and had a brief fight with Lakota warriors. If any physical remains of this event have survived, they might be expected to include a stone pile, wine bottles, rifle bullets and cartridge cases, arrowheads, a cannon fuse, and shell fragments, with the latter spread over a broad area. Staying but a day, the party is unlikely to have discarded the diverse materials found in Feature D.

Analysis of artifacts, bones, and other items recovered from excavation of the feature narrowed the range of dates with which the archaeological deposit is associated and eliminated the 1872 survey from further consideration. Of the two remaining events, an association with the Sioux War is the most plausible, but confirmation rests on a detailed examination of the documentary and archaeological evidence in tandem. Diaries, memoirs, and ledgers of those who participated in the campaign provide information about military activities and where they occurred at the Powder River confluence. Although sometimes inconsistent or contradictory, these and other documentary resources contain many clues about what was built and the kinds of items that were used and possibly discarded, lost, or left behind when the army abandoned the area. Compiling the preponderance of evidence from multiple sources of information should lead to defensible conclusions.

Artifacts, bones, and even fly pupae from Feature D provide evidence regarding when and how the feature was constructed (see appendix 1). Items for which a date of manufacture can be determined provide a time frame before which the artifact could not have been used. Most of the artifacts clearly suggest the kinds of activities they represent, but some also offer clues about what they contained and where they were made. If they are indeed associated with the campaign, some artifacts provide details about the supply system and the scale of trade in early post–Industrial Revolution America. This kind of information can be determined only from the archaeological record when relevant documentary sources no longer exist.

Several documentary sources help define where units of the Dakota column camped at the mouth of Powder River in June and July 1876. Private Wilmot Sanford's diary contains information about where the 6th Infantry depot guard and others set up field quarters. Sanford noted that when he arrived at the mouth of Powder River on June 13, his Company D camped with all of the troops from Ft. Buford on the bank of the Yellowstone, about a mile from the cavalry, which was located on Powder River. The 6th Infantry guard units changed positions three days later, with Company D placed second of four from the river; the wagon train extended from near the company farthest from the river to the riverbank, where the sutler's store was also located. On June 19, Sanford commented that the camp was on "nothing but a sand bed" near the right side (right or east bank) of the Yellowstone.[2]

Other accounts that help identify the location of the June–July camp include Maj. Moore's report of the action on August 2 when he returned with a detachment to retrieve forage left at the Powder River depot. The major ordered the *Far West* to steam past the abandoned depot site to Wolf Rapids and return to the boat landing where the grain had been left. Moore stated, "The ground near the landing, on account of a circular ridge, made a strong military position, which I at once occupied."[3] *Far West* captain Grant Marsh recalled that after advancing to Wolf Rapids, he turned the steamer about and returned back "to the landing where the oats had been stored, some distance below the mouth of the Powder."[4] Finally, when 1st Lt. William P. Clark landed mackinaw boats of recruits on August 15, he established a camp about a mile below the mouth of Powder River and noted, "This is the place from which the corn was taken by the Indians in July and where they were in considerable force in the early part of the present month."[5]

Collectively, these accounts confirm that the depot guard camp in June and July and Lt. Clark's August 15 camp were in the same location, although the guard camp would have been much larger. The location of the forage abandoned in July and retrieved on August 2 is well documented as about a mile below the mouth of Powder River on the right bank of the Yellowstone. Field observations confirm that there is only one "circular ridge" near the riverbank between Powder River and Wolf Rapids on which Maj. Moore could have deployed his troops. At 0.9 miles north of the Powder, a low ridge meeting the cutbank on the Yellowstone continues to the north and east for about a quarter of a mile. Feature D was located about 75 meters north of the point where the circular ridge begins, placing the trash pit in close proximity to the depot guard camp, Moore's forage-recovery effort, and at least one steamboat landing site.

This area is within a half-mile corridor where the Yellowstone is deepest along its right bank. An 1879 map of the river channel indicates that this is the only river segment deep enough to accommodate a steamboat landing between the Powder and a big bend in the Yellowstone 1.5 miles to the north.[6] The pile of forage Moore retrieved would almost certainly have been located where a steamer delivered it to the depot in June or July, marking the location of at least one landing.

Feature F is 300 meters southeast of Feature D. It is a good candidate for the remains of an oven constructed by one of the 6th Infantry companies composing the depot guard.[7] Pvt. Sanford noted that the men of Co. D made an oven to bake bread and that the next day Sgt. Gayle was firing it.[8] The sergeant made the first batch of bread on June 26 and baked on eight days between June 27 and July 9. The oven was repaired on July 10, but there is no documentary confirmation that it was used again before the guard departed the depot on July 20.[9] While the evidence suggests that Feature F might have been the location of a company oven, more work is needed to confirm its function and association with the depot and a specific company (see appendix 1).

When Terry and Crook's combined forces arrived at the Powder River confluence on August 17, Pvt. Sanford stated that his unit "camped in our old camp ground on the Yellowstone at the mouth of the Powder river."[10] He also noted that part of the 5th Infantry as well as the 7th Infantry recruits brought from Ft. Ellis by Lt. Clark were already encamped at the same location. Sanford's comment that the next day his company moved a mile down the Yellowstone agrees with Terry's diary entry of August 18, indicating that the general relocated his headquarters and infantry camp down the Yellowstone.[11] On August 20 Sanford walked to his old campground and visited the sutler, suggesting that the sutler's store was near its previous location in June and July. Much of the terrain between Powder River and Wolf Rapids and land west of the Powder was occupied until August 26. However, which, if any, units camped at the old 6th Infantry guard camp after August 18 is unconfirmed.[12]

The archaeological features are clearly located in the area occupied by Terry's command, but determining if Feature D is associated with 1876 military activities also rests on how well its contents comport with the historic record. Following is a discussion relating items recovered from this feature to the documentary record, with emphasis on establishing when the items were manufactured and, to the degree possible, what they contained. Do the data allow me to conclude that all of the items would have been available by 1875 and 1876 and that they are items that could have been discarded at this location by the forces of Terry or Crook?

Feature D Cultural Material

Foil seals from bottle tops and fragments of bottles that contained ale or stout are among the commonly occurring artifacts from Feature D. These embossed seals and a composite bottle label identify most of the foil wrappers and bottles with the Royal Bottling Company. While no other labels could be discerned, foil wrappers from three additional firms were recovered: E&J Burke, M. B. Foster and Sons, and E&G Hibbert.[13] These British and Irish companies were export bottlers authorized by brewers to sell their products, but they were not owned by the brewers. By the mid–19th century several of these firms dominated a worldwide trade in export beers.[14]

The Royal Bottling Company (RBC) was apparently authorized to export Bass products, but no further information about this firm was located.[15] The brewer, however, is a familiar British company that continues to market its beers in the United States. Begun by William Bass

FIGURE 5.1. Composite drawing of ale bottle labels from fragments of Bass and Royal Bottling Company labels on several bottle shards. Illustration by B. J. Earle.

in 1787, the firm proudly announced in 1870 that its product "could be found in every country in the globe."[16] Three years later Bass controlled almost 25 percent of all beer exports. E&J Burke was also an authorized Bass exporter, but its primary business was with the Guinness brewery in Dublin. Guinness's origins date to 1759, and by 1833 it was Ireland's largest brewery. Like Bass ale, Guinness stout was distributed globally during the last half of the 19th century.[17]

The three bottling companies, Hibbert, Foster, and Burke, exported both Guinness and Bass products, but they differed in market emphasis. By 1873 E&G Hibbert dominated the U.S. market for Bass, although M. B. Foster and Sons was by far the largest distributor of Bass ale worldwide.[18] From 1849 to 1874, E&J Burke was the sole agent for the U.S. trade in Guinness and continued to be a significant distributor into the next century. On a global scale, Burke was the dominate export bottler of Guinness stout, much as M. B. Foster controlled most of the Bass trade.[19]

A composite label drawn from Feature D bottle shards confirms that the RBC bottles contained Bass pale ale (Figure 5.1). The yellow label with the Royal Bottling Company's trademark, a representation of St. George slaying the dragon, appears to have been applied on top of the lower portion of the Bass label with its trademark, a red triangle. Introduced in 1855, this triangle is still found on Bass products today. Most bottle shards have no labels adhering to them, and all of the surviving label fragments appear from their colors to be associated with the RBC.[20]

From 1868 through 1886 E&J Burke was authorized to use green paper for its Guinness stout labels with the familiar Irish harp.[21] This green label was used only in the U.S. market, where Burke was the sole authorized bottler until 1874. Other than foil-covered bottle tops, no bottle fragments from Feature D could be positively associated with E&J Burke. Lacking Burke labels or green label remnants, there is no physical evidence that any of the bottles contained stout. However, there is insufficient data to conclude that all ale/stout bottles contained only Bass ale.

Bottled ale is a common entry in the Smith and Leighton ledger of items the sutler sold on account.[22] Thirty-three officers and civilians charged from one to several bottles at 50 cents or 75 cents each, suggesting that ale was sold in two sizes or qualities; at least two and possibly three sizes of ale bottles were indeed recovered from Feature D. Diamond R wagon master Matt Carroll charged three barrels, and General Terry's chief ordnance officer bought 1¾ barrels of ale, no doubt to be shared. When Terry met members of the Montana column aboard the *Far West* on June 8, Captain Walter Clifford recorded that he enjoyed a bottle of ale on the steamboat.[23] Lt. Charles Roe, also with the Montana column, noted on August 18 that Carroll shared a barrel of bottled ale with him and other officers when they arrived at the mouth of Powder River.[24] The reference to barrels comports well with the fact that British and Irish export bottlers often shipped their products in flour barrels.[25]

The sutler's ledger records only two beer sales from a cask rather than bottles, a half gallon to 7th Cavalry Quartermaster Sgt. Thomas Causby and a gallon to a civilian employee; both sales occurred on August 3 at Ft. Beans. Other than a cask, probably from Bozeman traders, shared among officers of the Montana column in May,[26] this is the only indication that domestic beer was sold to Terry's command.[27] While lager beer would have been brewed in Montana Territory towns such as Bozeman and Helena, as well as Bismarck, Chicago, St. Paul, and Sioux City, it spoiled quickly in the summer heat.[28] Larger American breweries began pasteurizing in 1873 and exporting in quantity when refrigerated railcars were developed after 1876. Before pasteurization, the U.S. bottled beer trade was dominated by British, Irish, and other European firms such as E&J Burke and M. B. Foster and Sons.[29]

Officers charged a much greater volume of liquor than ale at the sutler's Yellowstone store, although few whiskey and brandy bottles were found in Feature D.[30] When the Dakota column arrived in June Smith's clerks sold stock liquor from 45-gallon casks, while finer brands were in bottles packed in barrels.[31] Pvt. Sanford, Arikara scout Red Star, and others reported many enlisted soldiers and a few officers drunk during this period. Several campaign participants commented on the rush to the sutler when Terry and Crook's combined forces reached the mouth of Powder River in August. Officers again charged copious amounts of liquor, but it was not sold to the enlisted ranks at this time.

Although there is no documentary evidence, small, paneled tumblers recovered from Feature D might also have been used to serve liquor. Any liquid could have been drunk from a stemmed goblet found in the feature, but the vessel does suggest wine or champagne. Bottles of the type usually associated with the fruit of the vine were recovered from Feature D; however, the British and Irish bottlers sometimes sold ale and stout in this type of bottle as well (see appendix 2, note 9). A few foil wrappers embossed with bunches of grapes are evidence that at least some of these bottles contained wine or champagne. The Smith and Leighton ledger provides the only documentary evidence that wine was available to Terry's column. The day before he charged two gallons of whiskey and three barrels of ale to his account, wagon boss Matt Carroll purchased wine for $25.00.[32]

In addition to liquor, wine, champagne, and beers, Smith sold ginger ale. Terry's ordnance officer, who also bought bottled ale by the barrel, charged ginger ale to his account totaling $48.00.[33] The sutler's ledger documents that several other officers, including the general, purchased the spicy beverage at 50 cents a bottle. Consistent with this record, shards of thick-walled, round-bottomed bottles and embossed metal disks indicate that Feature D contained a minimum of 10 bottles designed for highly carbonated beverages such as soda water, ginger ale, or sarsaparilla. The disks and some bottle fragments are embossed with "CANTRELL AND COCHRANE, BELFAST AND DUBLIN." One of these bottles had "MEDICATED AERATED WATERS" in raised lettering, but others might have held ginger ale, another popular beverage made by this Irish firm.[34]

Ginger ale was among many products thought to have medicinal qualities in the late 19th century. Smith's ledger also documents sales of magnesia and Seidlitz powder, patent medicines for stomach and intestinal problems. Often fed badly prepared food and exposed to poor sanitation, frontier soldiers suffered from a variety of deficiency and diarrheal diseases.[35] A 7th Cavalry private left at the Powder River depot in June was diagnosed with typhoid fever and died of pneumonia at the Ft. Buford hospital.[36] By the end of July 1876, 35 to 40 men of the Montana column were reporting to sick call every night with symptoms of "camp fever" and scurvy.[37] Twenty sick men were transported via steamboat from Ft. Beans at the mouth of the Rosebud on August 2.[38] Later that month, 34 sick and disabled men in General Crook's command, including 14 cases of acute dysentery and diarrhea, were evacuated from the mouth of Powder River on the *Far West*.[39] Others such as 2nd Lt. Frances Roe, 2nd Cavalry, suffered temporary bouts of dysentery and "fearful pains" in the stomach but remained on duty.[40] Treatment of diarrheal diseases often involved purging the digestive tract with laxatives, leaving the patient ever more dehydrated.

One bottle recovered from Feature D is embossed "TARRANT & CO DRUGGISTS NEW YORK." Tarrant and Company marketed a variety of medicinal products from 1859 to 1905.[41] One of their products advertised to "physicians and medical staffs of the Army and Navy" was Tarrant's Seltzer Aperient. The ad stated, "As a means of alleviating all maladies in tropical climates it has been found particularly valuable."[42] Like other purgatives, it probably worked as well on the banks of the Yellowstone as it did along the Amazon or Orinoco.

The sutler's ledger indicates that he carried fresh and canned goods that would combat deficiency diseases such as scurvy, including lemons, canned peaches, succotash, corn, and beans. Smith's clerk recalled selling goods at the Powder River depot for several days when the Dakota column arrived in June, and sales were brisk to those who had been on field rations for a month.

Army records indicate that the Commissary Department provided foods for soldiers to purchase when at the depot that offered variety to their diet and prevented deficiency diseases. Ten varieties of canned fruits and vegetables were available as well as potatoes, dried apples, and peas. As an alternative to bacon, salt pork, or salt beef, protein was available from canned clams, lobster, milk, oysters, salmon, and sardines; bulk cheeses, cured hams, and mackerel could also be purchased.[43]

Unlike the Dakota column, which marched from Ft. Lincoln to the Powder River depot, the 6th Infantry depot guard traveled via steamboat from Ft. Buford to the Stanley's Crossing and Powder River depots, where it had access to commissary and sutler's goods. Pvt. Sanford's diary indicates that the enlisted men from these units were interested primarily in the sutler's alcohol and had little need for his high-priced canned goods. They were eating very well in June and July, with frequent issues of fresh beef, baked beans, and apples supplemented with venison and rabbit supplied by hunting parties. Individual soldiers contributed fish to the company mess. When possible, 6th Infantry companies assigned to escort the steamboats also brought back fresh vegetables, probably from their gardens at Ft. Buford.[44] This fare differed markedly from the usual bacon, hardtack, coffee, and sugar provided when on the march.

When Terry's and Crook's forces arrived at the mouth of Powder River in August, demand was high for fresh foods and canned fruits and vegetables, particularly among Crook's men. They had been on field rations the longest, without access to commissary stores or sutler's goods. Terry's supplies had not yet arrived from the Ft. Beans depot on the Yellowstone, but many participants noted that they had access to fresh eggs, potatoes, onions, and canned fruits and vegetables brought by Gallatin valley traders on mackinaw boats.[45] Egg sales by these traders would account for the presence of the many eggshells in Feature D; there is no evidence that eggs were available from sutler Smith or commissary stores.

Most of the cans recovered from Feature D probably contained fruit, vegetables, or preserves, and a few are definitely sardine cans; others were designed for dry materials such as yeast or lemonade powder. In addition to canned fruits and vegetables sold by the sutler and commissary, the latter stocked cans of sardines and yeast powder. All of the can specimens are consistent with the canned goods available for purchase and with activities that occurred at the depot such as baking bread. Private Sanford noted that his sergeant baked bread in an oven constructed at Powder River, an observation supported by records indicating that 85 barrels of flour were among the commissary stores at the end of June. These records also indicate that most of the bread ration in the coming weeks would likely consist of hardbread, with 61,530 pounds on hand.[46]

A stopper from a "Lea and Perrins" sauce bottle and a condiment bottle, probably ketchup, recovered from Feature D comport with the documentary record as well. Commissary stores included bottles of Worcestershire sauce, and sutler Smith sold ketchup.

Beef and fish bones in the archaeological assemblage are certainly consistent with Pvt. Sanford's frequent references to fresh beef and fishing at the depot guard camp. Bison bones recovered from Feature D suggest that buffalo meat was also available, but no documentary evidence for its consumption at the Powder River depot was found. Sanford notes that bison were observed from the guard camp in June and July, and it is possible that other companies or the civilian hunter assigned to the camp provided buffalo meat.[47]

Among the bones from Feature D are the remains of a dog. Although there is no evidence to suggest that it was ever intended to be a menu item, this canine nonetheless met a violent end as a result of three chops to its neck with a sharp steel implement.[48] It was a mature dog, slightly smaller and more muscular than a coyote but not built for speed like its wily native cousin.[49]

Numerous accounts from the 1860s and 1870s document the presence of dogs in garrison and on the campaign trail. Like Gen. George Crook, many officers enjoyed hunting for sport, and some, including Col. Carr, 5th Cavalry, and Lt. Col. Custer, kept hunting dogs for this purpose. Officers in Col. David Stanley's 22nd Infantry maintained a regimental pack of dogs.[50] Carr had greyhounds with him when campaigning against southern plains tribes in 1867, and Custer was rarely without his dogs, which, at various times, included foxhounds, staghounds, and greyhounds.[51]

Staghounds accompanied Custer from Ft. Lincoln in May 1876 and were reported to have pursued antelope across the plains of Dakota Territory with great abandon. When the Montana column was near Ft. Pease in April, Lt. James Bradley noted a greyhound at the abandoned trading post and surmised that it had belonged to the post's former civilian inhabitants.[52] As Crook's force departed the mouth of Powder River in August, 1st Lt. John Bourke observed that the Wyoming column had recently acquired a fine Newfoundland and that solders will sometimes steal dogs.[53]

Enlisted men did not have time to hunt or the resources to afford hunting dogs; most did not own a personal firearm.[54] The documentary record indicates, however, that the rank and file had dogs and other pets. Five days after his company arrived at the Powder River depot, Pvt. Sanford recorded in his diary that he had a dog sleeping with him and penned, "Plenty of others here."[55] The breed of dog killed and thrown into Feature D could not be identified, but it was smaller than any of the hunting breeds known to have been used by officers.[56] Perhaps it was simply a pet, a "non-descript canine of no particular race, breed or utility."[57]

Feature D also contained many clay smoking pipe fragments. Sutler Smith and the Bozeman traders sold tobacco in various forms, and it was available from the commissary at cost. When the latter source dried up late in the campaign, there was near panic among the troops. While most of the men used chewing (plug) tobacco, documentary and archaeological evidence confirms that some smoked.[58] Lt. Thaddeus Capron with Crook's command noted that he lost his pipe a few miles from Powder River, and Smith's ledger indicates that three officers of different regiments charged pipes at $1.00 each.[59] These were probably not made of clay like the estimated 58 pipes in Feature D. Even at sutlers' prices, clay pipes would have sold for a few cents in 1876.[60]

One type of clay pipe recovered from Feature D has "MCELROY" impressed into the stem and an embossed design on the bowl. As with the Royal Bottling Co., no record of a McElroy pipe-manufacturing company was found.[61] However, a pipe with this bowl design was sold by D. McDougall and Co. beginning about 1850 and was on the company's price lists published in the mid-1870s.[62] The McDougall firm of Glasgow, Scotland, manufactured clay pipes from 1846 until the 1960s.

A number of campaign participants mentioned seeing coal or lignite as they traveled through the lower Yellowstone and Powder River country. Pvt. Sanford noticed this sedimentary material along the bank of the Yellowstone as he bathed in the river on a hot June day. Two months later a reporter for the *New York Times* observed, "The banks of the river are traversed everywhere by coal seams, but the coal is loose, friable stuff and useless for fuel."[63] A dense layer of friable lignite was found in the middle levels of Feature D in a context confirming that someone deposited it there. A naturally occurring seam of lignite about 100 feet south of Feature D is clearly visible in the riverbank today.

Several pieces of agate were also recovered from the feature, broken in a manner that indicates someone had purposefully fractured cobbles of this mineral. Gem-quality river cobbles of Yellowstone agate are widely sought by rockhounds and lapidaries today, as they were in the late 19th century. When Col. Stanley faced off with Lakota chief Gall at the mouth of Powder River in 1872, a young Northern Pacific engineer hunting agates too far from the military escort narrowly escaped mounted Sioux warriors. In August 1876, Crook's adjutant general, 1st Lt. Bourke, made this comment about the Yellowstone River: "The bottom of the river is thickly strewn with agates: they are to be picked up at every step of our promenades. Everybody has taken one or two, intending to have them cut as souvenirs of the Expedition."[64] Novice rockhounds sometimes break an agate cobble to determine the quality of its interior, creating fragments like those in Feature D. If the rock does not exhibit the colors or patterns sought, it is discarded.

When deployed at the abandoned Powder River depot with two companies of 22nd Infantry on July 29, correspondent James O'Kelly observed, "There were scattered about the broken boxes of horseshoes, boxes of horse nails, debris of potato barrels, and some civilian clothing."[65] Like the pile of forage retrieved by Maj. Moore's command in August, these items were left behind when Terry ordered his depot moved west after the battle at Little Bighorn. They are commonly used items that would be expected at a military supply depot, as are many such artifacts recovered from Feature D. While these items would not ordinarily be mentioned by campaign participants or in records, they are not out of place in the context of an army supply depot.

Several types of artifacts from Feature D are associated with packaging supplies and transporting goods or personnel, including a horseshoe, horse nails, harness parts, a packing crate, nails, and metal strapping (see appendix 6). A harness specimen is part of a wheel-mule quillor that fastens to the hind quarters of mules closest to the wagon. A badly deteriorated wooden box, fragments of burned boards, nails, and metal strapping are the remains of shipping crates. Measuring 24 inches by 14 inches by 8 inches, this type of box could have carried one of many commodities shipped to the depot. All that remains of an unknown number of burned crates are the nails used in their construction and metal strapping that reinforced them for shipping.

The single artifact from Feature D that could be classified as camp equipment is a burner for a kerosene lamp. The thumbwheel, which is turned to adjust the height of the wick, is embossed "M.L.COLLINS PAT. FEB. 4. 1866." Supplies of kerosene were very limited before the U.S. petroleum industry began to develop after 1859. Lamp patents for this new fuel proliferated in the early 1860s, and a decade later, kerosene dominated the lighting market in this country.[66] Fearing the potential for fires in garrison, the army prohibited the use of kerosene lamps in enlisted men's barracks until 1879; this prohibition did not extend to officers' quarters. The specimen in Feature D suggests that kerosene lamps might have been permitted in field camps.[67] However, candles were probably the most illuminating commodity at the depot, where commissary stores included 1,771 pounds of them at the end of June.[68]

No uniquely military insignia, button, or other item of clothing or equipment was recovered from Feature D, and a revolver cartridge is the only confirmed army-issue artifact; it was designed for the Model 1873 Colt and the Smith and Wesson Schofield.[69] These guns were the same caliber but used slightly different-sized cartridges.[70] By the end of 1874, 7th Cavalry companies had been issued the Model 1873 Colt.[71] Both revolvers were in service with cavalry regiments in 1876, although the Colt was the dominate sidearm. The army's Frankford Arsenal stopped making the .45 Colt cartridge in 1874 and manufactured only the shorter "Revolver Ball Cartridge, Caliber .45."[72]

A .44-caliber cartridge case was also recovered from the feature. It was manufactured for the .44 Smith and Wesson No. 3 (aka American) revolver, a popular handgun in the early 1870s commercial market.[73] The army purchased this model as well, and by 1873 four cavalry regiments had a substantial number of them. After distribution of the Colt and Schofield .45s to cavalry units, fewer than 100 Smith and Wesson Americans were in military service in the summer of 1876.[74]

Company I was the only 7th Cavalry troop issued the Smith and Wesson .44, with 78 on hand in December 1871.[75] Three years later, Company I received 83 Colt .45s but also reported 29 Smith and Wesson .44s as well as 4,119 rounds of .44-caliber ammunition. In June 1875 only the Colts were reported for Company I. However, this troop still had 2,700 rounds of .44 ammunition, suggesting that some of the men might have acquired their Smith and Wessons.[76]

Personal items from Feature D include those that would not be out of place at a supply depot and others that are out of the ordinary. Certainly, it is not surprising to find buttons and a watch key here. Buttons include those commonly used for military shirts and trousers and one manufactured for civilian work clothes. The watch key is a type used for winding a kind of pocket watch manufactured in America from about 1850. Two other artifacts would probably not be expected at a military field camp: a stone marble and a doll, most often associated with children.[77] If it were complete, the solid porcelain doll would be about 2¼ inches tall. It is a "Frozen Charlotte," popular between about 1850 and 1914.[78]

With the exception of the two artifacts that seem so strangely out of place, materials from Feature D either are like those mentioned in the historic record or are the kinds of things that would be expected at Terry's Yellowstone supply depots or at Crook and Terry's August camp. The availability and use of a variety of canned and fresh foods, alcoholic beverages, and tobacco at the Powder River confluence are solidly confirmed. Likewise, bones from the feature confirm that fresh beef was available here and that bison may also have been served. The personal items, packing crates, harness parts, and horseshoe and even the dog remains are consistent with the record. The following analysis demonstrates that the artifacts could have been manufactured and transported to the mouth of Powder River by the summer of 1876.

Dating Feature D

The identified manufacturers and distributors of products represented in the archaeological assemblage were doing business well before the army's centennial campaign, and many are still doing business today. All were viable companies in 1875 and 1876. The best clues for dating the materials include technologies used in the manufacture of the bottles and cans, patent dates on other items, and dates derived from similar materials in other dated archaeological sites. Taking all of these considerations into account, the latest secure date for the manufacture of any artifact is 1875, when the Frankford Arsenal began production of the Revolver Ball Cartridge, Caliber .45. Feature D would not have existed before this date. Determining a date beyond which the feature could not have existed using only data from the artifacts is complicated by the fact that an item made in 1875 might have been used or lost some months or years later. Less ambiguous is a terminal date suggested by the presence of bison bones in the feature.

After the tribes reluctantly moved back to the reservations or sought refuge in Canada, hide hunters entered eastern Montana Territory, where much of the last American bison herd was located. Some 5,000 hunters and skinners were working the northern herd in 1882, and by fall of the following year, few buffalo were found.[79] The only herd surviving in 1883 was well east of the lower Yellowstone in Dakota Territory, and it was quickly extirpated. From the analysis of its contents, then, Feature D was constructed between 1875 and 1883. Of the events known to have occurred at or near the Powder River confluence, only the 1876 Sioux War and the 1880–1883 construction of the Northern Pacific (NP) Railroad fall within this time frame.

Thousands of bison hides were shipped from Miles City, the town that grew near Ft. Keogh at the mouth of Tongue River. Completion of the railroad to this point in 1881 provided transport for the hide business

Connecting Archaeology and History at the Powder River Depot 107

and facilitated the development of new settlements in the Yellowstone valley. Fifteen hundred men were reported working on grading crews between Glendive and Miles City in 1880, and the following year 2,000 men and 1,600 mules were laying track between Glendive and Billings.[80]

Although none have been located near Powder River, railroad construction camps along the Northern Pacific's Yellowstone Division would date within the period 1880 to 1882. The company's grading, bridging, and tracklaying operations were well coordinated and supplied by moving men and materials on newly completed track in close proximity to the work.[81] Feature D is located a long mile north of the NP's Powder River crossing, and, based on proximity alone, it is unlikely to have been associated with railroad activities.

None of the items recovered from Feature D were manufactured specifically for railroad use, although many would not be out of place in a construction camp; an exception is the presence of British-export ale bottles. After adopting pasteurization and developing a new bottle style suited for highly carbonated lager beers, large American breweries quickly captured the export trade to the west. The 1882 *Year Book* noted that Anheuser-Busch was

> the first...to introduce bottled beer into the United States, and which, unknown a dozen years ago is now kept in every grocery store, hotel, liquor house, and nearly every family in the country. The creation of this trade has practically destroyed the importance of English and German bottled beer and ales, it has certainly reduced it by fully seventy-five percent.[82]

Lager in aqua or amber export-style bottles was distributed to a number of communities west of the Mississippi by the late 1870s. Exports of both bottled and cask lager from the large U.S. firms expanded as quickly as the railroads that provided cost-effective distribution in refrigerated cars. When the NP reached Helena in 1883, a single distributor sold more than 1,600 casks of Milwaukee-brewed Schlitz in less than three months.[83]

By 1880 bottled beer, if allowed in Northern Pacific construction camps, would undoubtedly have been lager in export-style bottles. American preference at this time strongly favored lager rather than ale, and the domestic beer would also have cost much less than British imports. Less expensive unpasteurized cask beers from local breweries would also have been available from Bismarck and other settlements along the NP route that were eager to profit from railroad development.

Connecting Feature D to the army's 1876 campaign does not rest on ale bottles alone. The foregoing analysis demonstrates that no other event at this location would have produced materials so similar to those identified in army records and the diaries, memoirs, and ledgers of those who participated in the campaign. The data support my conclusion that all of the recovered items would have been available in 1875 and that they are items discarded by the forces of Terry or Crook. In the next chapter, comparing Feature D artifacts with items recovered from the Little Bighorn battlefield provides some interesting details and further affirms the feature's association with Sioux War events.

CHAPTER 6

Conclusions

U.S. Army Management of Transportation and Supply

The historic record supports several conclusions about the army's management of transportation and supply in the 1876 campaign and specifically how the Powder River depot functioned as part of the supply system. Lt. Gen. Sheridan's official report of operations in the Division of Missouri provided his assessment of successes and shortcomings from which he concluded that the troops did as well as expected, "for long experience has taught me how difficult it is to catch an Indian in the summer season."[1] Understanding the many challenges Gen. Terry faced getting his column into the field, Sheridan reported the following:

> The impracticability of operations against these Indians from Fort Lincoln, on the Missouri River, during the existence of the wild storms of Dakota in the early spring, became pretty well settled by the result already experienced, and satisfied me that the recommendation for the establishment of the two military posts in what is known as the Yellowstone country, made in my last annual report and in my report of 1874, in anticipation of hostilities with the Sioux, was the only view to take of this subject which promised undoubted success, and I again renewed my solicitations for the establishment of the posts at the mouth of Tongue River and the Big Horn. This advice, if adopted, would have given us abundant supplies at convenient points, to operate in the very heart of the country from whence all our troubles came.[2]

In the next three pages, the lieutenant general twice restated his previous requests for the Yellowstone posts and asserted that, had they been built, "there would have been no war."[3]

Sheridan's repeated assertion that building the Yellowstone posts earlier would have averted war rested on the assumption that the tribes would not have contested construction of these posts or white settlement in the Black Hills. This seems an overweening supposition, given the resolve of some bands to remain in the unceded territory and to retain the Black Hills. A statement that his field commanders had "to operate blindly in an almost totally unknown region, comprising an area of almost ninety thousand square miles" was a partial truth,[4] embellished to support Sheridan's argument regarding the Yellowstone posts. Although his forces operated in a very large region with difficult terrain, Sheridan and his subordinates understood a good deal about the geography and climate of the lower Yellowstone and Powder River country by 1876. Some of the scouts and guides with the campaign knew the area very well.

When the Yellowstone could support steamboat traffic in the spring, Terry's mobile supply system was a reasonably good surrogate for depots at the posts coveted by his commander. Supplies delivered by steamboat were in place when the Dakota column was to have first arrived at the Yellowstone River near Glendive Creek. When Terry decided to bypass this depot at Stanley's Crossing and push on to Powder River, supplies were rushed to the mouth of that stream to meet the Dakota column on June 11. Steamboats continued to move supplies and communications from Ft. Buford at the mouth of the Yellowstone to Terry's depots as needed. After the Little Bighorn disaster, steamers evacuated the wounded and brought reinforcements and more supplies. Steamers also remained available for patrol duty on the river and to relocate supplies as circumstances of the campaign dictated.

There were occasions when commanders wished they had more steamboat support. Col. Gibbon's failed attempt to cross the Yellowstone with an attack force in May might have had a different outcome if the Montana column had had steamboat support at that time. Gen. Crook would have been most grateful for an additional steamer to deliver supplies more quickly from Ft. Beans to the mouth of Powder River in mid-August so that he could leave Terry's command behind.

A transportation issue for which the Dakota column gets poor marks is its handling of pack trains. Several military and civilian participants commented on the performance of pack trains in Crook's and Terry's commands. Although officers' opinions often reflected unit pride and loyalty, there is no doubt that General Crook's pack trains were far superior to those of the Dakota column, the first ever organized in Terry's department.[5] Col. Gibbon, commanding the Montana column, offered the following views, which were shared by many from both departments:

> Incumbered with heavily-loaded wagon-trains, our movements were necessarily slow, and when we did cut loose from these our only means of transporting supplies were the mules taken from the teams, and unbroken to packs, unsuitable pack-saddles, and inexperienced soldiers as packers. These latter soon learned to do their part tolerably well, but at the expense of the poor animals, whose festering sores after a few days' marching appealed not only to feelings of humanity, but demonstrated the false economy of the course pursued. The contrast between the mobility of our force and General Crook's was very marked, especially for rapid movements.[6]

A number of mules assigned to Major Reno's scouting mission up Powder River were unfit for further service when his 7th Cavalry wing rejoined the Dakota column on the Yellowstone. However, Terry's command anticipated that animals would likely need to be replaced in the train and sent 25 reserve mules with Custer's wing. In spite of this precaution, the poorly trained mules and soldier-packers lagged behind Custer's strike force from the time it left the Yellowstone River. On the day of the Little Bighorn fight, the train, with a substantial number of troopers assigned to keep it moving and all of the extra ammunition, was well behind the rest of the command. A professionally managed supply train would likely have been able to keep pace with the command until the 7th Cavalry battalions parted on Reno Creek to initiate the attack, and extra ammunition packs could have been sent with each battalion.

In contrast, the Wyoming column's pack train was a paragon of professional management. Many campaign participants commented on the nature of this train, and again, Col. Gibbon's report provided a good summary:

> Gen. Crook's well-organized pack-train, with trained mules and its corps of competent packers, moved almost independently of

the column of troops, and as fast as they could move. His ranks were not depleted by drafts to take charge of the packs and animals, for each mule faithfully followed the sound of the leader's bell and needed no other guide, and his pack-mules were neither worn out nor torn to pieces by bad saddles and worse packing.[7]

This well-managed pack train supported Col. Reynolds's movement from near old Ft. Reno on the Bozeman Trail to Otter Creek, from which his cavalry battalion struck a village on Powder River in March. The only significant supply issue was a shortage of forage, which resulted in the loss of 90 animals. This loss was exacerbated by winter conditions that made grazing difficult and stressed the livestock. Three months later, Crook's pack train supported another strike force from a supply depot on Goose Creek to the Rosebud battlefield. The pack animals performed well, and 200 mules, hastily broken to the saddle, served as mounts for infantry.

Crook set out in August with a reinforced command, again supported only by his pack train. After meeting Terry on Rosebud Creek, Gen. Crook's cavalry had to abandon a number of horses on the trek to the Powder, and the surviving animals badly needed rest and forage. The sturdy pack mules appear to have arrived at the mouth of Powder River intact, but many were to become steak dinners when the Wyoming column ran out of supplies after departing the Yellowstone.[8]

Department of Dakota Chief Commissary of Subsistence Capt. Charles McClure reported, "No complaint of want of subsistence-supplies, or that the stores furnished were not of good quality, has reached this office."[9] Indeed, Terry's contracted steamboats allowed him to furnish an abundance of subsistence stores. The foods available for purchase appear to have been as varied as those to be found at a well-supplied garrison (see appendix 11). However, access to these foods and those sold by the sutler was available only when troops were at one of the Yellowstone depots or base camps. When they were on the march, standard field rations of salt pork, hardtack, coffee, and sugar dominated the menu.

How frequently the men had access to a variety of commissary and sutler goods varied greatly, depending on unit assignments. Having reached Powder River after a month on the trail, Terry sent Reno's wing of 7th Cavalry on a scouting mission while Custer and the rest of the Dakota column enjoyed several days of R and R at the Powder River depot.

Reno's wing would remain solely on field rations until it rejoined Terry and Custer on the Yellowstone River. Col. Gibbon's Montana column was on the Yellowstone from March until it joined Terry in June. Supplied by wagon trains from Ft. Ellis during this period, these men might not have enjoyed the greatest variety of commissary goods, but hunting and fishing provided fresh meat much of the time. Bozeman traders also sold goods to this column. From mid-May until reassigned in July, Maj. Moore's 6th Infantry depot guard lived in relative luxury. This battalion moved supplies on steamboats from Ft. Buford and established the depots at Stanley's Crossing and Powder River. While at the depots, these companies had regular access to the full suite of commissary and sutler goods. They also built structures to enhance the quality of the ration, such as an ice house and baking oven. Fresh beef and fresh bread were available sporadically for several weeks.

There were a few complaints about commissary stores in the field, but most of them focused on tobacco shortages rather than inadequate rations. Most soldiers used tobacco, and many were out when they reached the mouth of Powder River on August 17. What little tobacco remained in Terry's subsistence stores could be purchased at cost, but those supplies had not yet been brought down from the Rosebud depot at Ft. Beans. Many were willing to pay the higher prices charged by the sutler and Bozeman traders, but they too could not meet the demand. Terry's Commissary Department was able to resume tobacco sales in early September, much to the relief of his men.

Late in the campaign one of Terry's subalterns groused that the Commissary Department failed to have adequate stores available for sale to officers, "a plain case of neglect on somebody's part."[10] Crook's adjutant also noted that those in charge of supply "have not particularly distinguished themselves in forwarding stores to the troops on the Yellowstone."[11] His complaint was directed at the commissary of subsistence rather than the quartermaster because, although he was not able to get tobacco, Crook's command was amply supplied with shoes.

If these complaints ever reached Terry, they did not affect his confidence in field-level Acting Commissary of Subsistence 2nd Lt. Richard E. Thompson, Co. K, 6th Infantry. During the first week of August, Subsistence Department staff officer Maj. Beekman DuBarry arrived intending to usurp the lieutenant's field assignment by arguing that the command was now so large as to require the major's services.[12] Terry responded that Lt. Thompson's performance was entirely satisfactory, and DuBarry found himself on the next eastbound steamboat. In addition to DuBarry's arrogance, Terry's response might have reflected the tension that often existed between staff and line officers.[13]

Although the Department of Dakota experienced some supply and transportation problems, only the lack of cavalry mounts and Custer's poorly managed pack train had the potential to affect how the fight at Little Bighorn unfolded. These issues diminished Custer's battle strength and delayed the arrival of ammunition packs. The combined battle strength of the attacking battalions under Custer, Reno, and Benteen was 480 men.[14] If the Quartermaster's Department had supplied enough mounts, the 124 troopers left at the Powder River depot would have added about 2.5 companies to these battalions.[15] A noncommissioned officer and at least six men from each of the 11 companies in the attack force had been detailed to move the unruly pack train along more quickly. This detail effectively reduced the attacking battalions' strength by about 1.5 companies. Professionally trained and managed pack mules, like those in Gen. Crook's command, would probably have required only civilian packers to manage them. They would also have been able to keep pace with the attacking battalions, and the ammunition packs would have been more readily available.[16]

Gen. Terry and his officers were fully aware of 7th Cavalry battle strength and knew that the pack train was slow and difficult to manage. Before Custer departed for the Little Bighorn, he discussed supply issues with his officers, and on the day of the battle he formed the pack train detail to move the ammunition and other supplies more quickly.[17] He was no doubt confident that his force was adequate and supplies would be available when needed, but events of the day proved differently. One thing is certain, the well-armed tribes responded with a determination that Custer, Terry, and Sheridan were incapable of imaging.

In spite of deficiencies, it is difficult to conclude that Terry's supply system contributed significantly to Custer's defeat.[18] In fact, the system worked reasonably well, given the environmental and technological constraints of the times. Chief Commissary of Subsistence Capt. McClure reported, "The expeditions in the field in the Yellowstone country were successfully supplied, and, notwithstanding large and unexpected issues made to General Crook's command, there was more than sufficiency of subsistence-stores furnished."[19] Terry issued rations to the Wyoming column when the two commands met on Rosebud Creek and again after they reached the mouth of Powder River. Crook's men and horses left

Powder River with new shoes as well as rations and forage. Terry also sent a steamboat with stores to Glendive Creek, should Crook chose to resupply there.

While at the Powder River confluence, both commands had to await supplies from the Rosebud before resuming their pursuit of the tribes. Some in the Wyoming column blamed the delay on Terry's organization. His decision to use a steamboat to patrol the Yellowstone for Indians crossing the river slowed transfer of stores from the Rosebud depot to Powder River. In any case, Crook's command could not have continued without resting and feeding its exhausted livestock for several days. Given that Crook left his stores at a depot far to his rear and Terry was able to provide supplies for another command as large as his own, it is hard to argue with the chief commissary's assessment of his department's performance.

Traders and Their Goods

John Smith, the field sutler Terry authorized to sell goods from the mobile supply depot, also performed reasonably well. Motivated by the prospect of an extremely profitable year, Smith assembled the capital to supply Terry's command with the merchandise desired. With steamboat transportation made available to him, he was able to provide goods similar in quantity and variety to those found at a garrison. Complaints from his customers included the usual charge that the sutler's prices were exorbitant.[20] Others, such as Dr. James DeWolf with Maj. Reno's command, complained about the havoc caused when Smith sold whiskey to the men.[21]

There were few negative comments about the variety or availability of Smith's stores until the combined forces reached the mouth of Powder River in August. Like the Commissary Department, Smith was unable to meet the demand for tobacco; alcohol, however, was readily available to officers. Smith sold his remaining stock to a trader on the *Carroll* bound for the post to be built at the mouth of the Tongue. After applying to trade at Tongue River himself, Smith returned to Ft. Buford for more goods.[22] With his partners, the Leighton brothers, Smith made $40,000 on their 1876 venture, the equivalent of almost $800,000 today. Six years later he left the Ft. Keogh trade and other Miles City interests with $100,000 to do business in Bozeman.[23]

Smith's partners, Joseph Leighton and Walter Jordan, found the wherewithal to expand their business interests, which included Ft. Buford and other upper Missouri locations, to the lower Yellowstone as well. They built steamboats for the Yellowstone trade and established a ranch near Miles City, and their lucrative general merchandise company in the town supplied the growing livestock industry in surrounding Montana and Wyoming territories.[24] By 1881 they organized the town's First National Bank; George Miles, who came to the area as an army civilian employee with his uncle's 5th Infantry, was listed as one of the bank's directors, as was Major James S. Brisbin, the 2nd Cavalry officer who "rescued" the Bozeman denizens of Ft. Pease in February 1876.[25]

The Bozeman entrepreneurs also profited in 1876 and beyond; one observer stated, "From the commencement of the Indian Wars the people of the Gallatin and upper Yellowstone valleys had been bringing provisions down the river by boat and by wagon train, and all producers and carriers were making money."[26] In the years following, some of the men connected with the Ft. Pease fiasco eagerly claimed the land they had coveted for a decade. Paul McCormick, Ft. Pease organizer and freelance trader with the Montana column, began merchandizing and freighting at Miles City; three years later he moved his business to the mouth of the Bighorn near a steamboat landing serving Fort Custer, the army's new post at the Little Bighorn confluence.[27]

Those who organized the Yellowstone Wagon Road and Prospecting Expedition and Ft. Pease venture believed that the Gallatin and Yellowstone valleys rightly belonged to those who would settle them and develop their resources, a view broadly shared in the settlements of Montana Territory. Governor Potts clearly embraced their position when he appointed an orator and resonator to speak for the territory at the Philadelphia Centennial Exposition. Given a month after Gen. Terry closed the Sioux campaign, the speech included a passage that captured perfectly one of the goals of the 1874 wagon road expedition and the ethos of its participants. Speaking of the decline in gold production since 1869, the orator, William Andrews Clark, was optimistic about the territory's economic future:

> Moreover, each year adds something by way of discovery and some of the mountainous regions have been imperfectly explored and other portions, whose physical features indicate the existence of gold, cannot be penetrated at this time owning to the presence of Indians. This applies more particularly to the southeastern portions on the tributaries of the Big Horn, Tongue, and Powder

Rivers. It is hoped that our military forces will drive the Sioux from that country and open it to the anxious miner, who will reveal its mineral character and bring under contribution to economic industry its imprisoned wealth.[28]

Archaeology and History

Results of the archaeological project at the mouth of Powder River comport with the documentary record and add some interesting details as well as a few mysteries. The historic record confirms that dogs at the Powder River depot included Custer's hunting breeds, a Newfoundland, and others kept as pets by enlisted men. Skeletal remains from Feature D verify that at least one dog, slightly smaller than a coyote, was dispatched with several blows to its neck from a sharp steel implement of some kind. There were no doubt many such implements at the depot for butchering fresh beef or buffalo, gathering wood, and other tasks. The killing tool would have to have been heavy enough to sever vertebrae with a chopping motion.[29] Why the dog was killed and who did the deed remain a mystery.

Many artifacts recovered from Feature D are the remains of items sold by sutler Smith or other traders. A few officers charged smoking pipes to their accounts. Although Smith's ledger is silent about the kind of pipes sold, the prices indicate that they were probably made of briar. Hundreds of fragments of white clay pipes from Feature D suggest that this inexpensive type was also available at the depot. There is no information regarding who might have bought clay pipes, but they seem too fragile for the campaign trail. Perhaps they were intended for a smoke at the depot with little concern for their longevity. This might explain why so few of the pipes retained visible evidence that they were actually used, but other explanations are certainly possible.[30]

Smith's ledger confirms that officers charged whiskey, ale, and wine to their accounts, and, not surprisingly, bottles for alcoholic beverages are among the most common items in the Feature D assemblage. These bottles reveal that the ale was imported from Britain and much of it was produced by Bass and Co. of Burton-on-Trent. The sutler's whiskey, with quality brands available in bottles, was served to at least some of his clientele in paneled tumblers, similar to those found in many bars today.[31] Stemware recovered from Feature D suggests that wine or champagne bought from the sutler was sipped from goblets.

Private Sanford noted on May 26 at the Stanley's Crossing depot that "the men can get sutlers checks now and the store is open."[32] Sanford's diary and other accounts confirm that, like officers, the rank and file sometimes had access to alcohol in abundance. The few entries for enlisted men in Smith's ledger included charges to three sergeants; one of them bought only a large quantity of tobacco, no doubt to share with the men in his company. The other two charged whiskey; one of them also purchased a half gallon of cheaper cask beer, and the other bought ale. Sales to privates are not included in the ledger, so either they paid with cash or "sutler's checks" or their charge accounts were kept in another book.

Do the beer, wine, and liquor bottles from Feature D represent expensive beverages more likely to have been purchased by officers than enlisted men? Sutlers sold imported ale and stout at western posts as early as 1850;[33] this was the only widely distributed bottled beer until American firms began exporting increasingly popular lager in the late 1870s.[34] Before export lager was available, it is reasonable to suggest that the lower ranks preferred locally brewed cask beer when available because it was less expensive than export ale.[35] Smith sold cask beer for $2.00 per gallon, while ale was 50 to 75 cents a bottle. Whiskey at 12.5 cents a drink or 75 cents a pint was cheaper alcohol per volume than cask beer or ale. A 50-cent purchase by a private in 1876 would be the equivalent today of paying about $10.00 from a monthly salary of $260.00. However, quantities of wine, liquor, and export ale bottles are found in the remains of western mining camps and towns at establishments serving those from the lower end of the socioeconomic scale as well as saloons that catered to the upper classes.[36] Because the military is "a microcosm of the culture it supports,"[37] some enlisted men probably enjoyed export ale even at a relatively high cost, especially when lower-cost alternatives were unavailable.

Archaeological data from Ft. Larned, Kansas (1859–1878), and other 19th-century military contexts demonstrate that cultural materials recovered from latrines can be indicators of social and economic status. For example, stemmed glassware might indicate that a latrine was used by officers with higher status, while tumblers suggest that the facility was used by those lower on the economic scale.[38] Given the frontier army's rigid stratification by rank and social class,[39] the contents of latrines and perhaps other features constructed at the Powder River depot might also be expected to reflect social status. Indeed, some facilities at the depot were clearly designated for exclusive use by officers or enlisted men. Sutler Smith's clerk recalled that he sold goods from a tent at Powder

River partitioned with canned goods to separate the officers from the enlisted ranks.[40] A few days later, Private Sanford noted that fatigue details constructed separate latrines for the officers and enlisted men in his company.[41]

Analysis of materials from Feature D suggests that they might have been used and discarded or lost by men from various economic and social affiliations including officers, enlisted men, and civilian employees. However, the data do not yet exist to confirm such a hypothesis. As noted above, we could not reliably associate beverage bottles from expensive export beers with officers alone. The trash pit contained the remains of a stemmed goblet (high status) in addition to a few tumblers (lower status), but the sample is too small to draw reliable conclusions. White clay tobacco pipes in late 19th-century nonmilitary contexts were associated with the working class and were used by some enlisted troops.[42] Although the rank and file came from a wide range of social and economic backgrounds, many were from working-class families.[43] Clay pipes might have been used more commonly by enlisted men than by officers, but again, there is not enough comparative date to reach firm conclusions.

Field sutlers often sold alcoholic beverages, but Terry's steamboats allowed Smith to transport large quantities of heavy, bulky items such as bottled soda water, ale, and liquor as well as casks of whiskey. Although he conducted business only where troops gathered on the banks of the Yellowstone River, he had no difficulty selling most of this stock by the end of August. His goods and a wide variety of commissary stores made a soldier's life at the Powder River depot in June and July more like being in garrison, but without the usual boredom.

Custer and one wing of his regiment enjoyed several days of R and R here after their march from Ft. Lincoln. Private Sanford and his comrades-in-arms who remained here had access to fresh beef, venison and other game, vegetables from the company gardens at Ft. Buford, and fresh bread baked in field ovens. Steamboats brought the mail from Ft. Buford as well. Pastimes included fishing, some hunting, collecting agates, playing games, and acquiring pets. The 7th Cavalry band was on hand for the occasional concert.

Did the soldiers play any games that would account for the marble in Feature D? Most of us think of these artifacts as children's toys, but beginning in the 16th century, there were a number of English marble games played by adults as well.[44] Marbles are often found in Revolutionary War campsites of both the British and the American armies, and it is probable that they belonged to soldiers, not children.[45] During the Civil War General Grant is said to have played marble solitaire, a board game dating to the 1700s.[46] In late 19th-century western mining towns, adults played with and gambled with marbles.[47] The marble, therefore, is not as mysterious a find in the depot trash as a ceramic doll.

It is hard to imagine why a Frozen Charlotte doll would be found among ale bottle shards and clay pipe fragments.[48] Ceramic dolls are often recovered from 19th-century army posts, where they too are interpreted as children's toys.[49] Small Frozen Charlottes were sometimes used as favors baked into cakes, and indeed, there was at least one cake eaten at the mouth of Powder River.[50] Lt. Charles Roe with the Montana column received a care package from his wife on August 17 that contained, among other things, a birthday cake.[51] He shared the cake with fellow officers, and it was on this occasion that wagon boss Matt Carroll set out the barrel of bottle ale for all to enjoy. The 2.5-inch-tall Feature D doll is larger than the Frozen Charlottes sometimes used as cake favors, but the probability of a doll in the lieutenant's cake seems remote in any case. Frozen Charlotte must remain a mystery.

Was Feature F an oven that Sgt. Gayle, Co. D, 6th Infantry, or a baker from another company at the depot used to make bread for his unit? Pvt. Sanford noted that the men of Company D constructed an oven, used it several times, and repaired it once before the depot guard departed on July 20. Located 300 meters south of the trash pit, the feature is certainly within the area the guard occupied and used in June and July. The feature's semidressed sandstone slabs, carefully placed to form a rectangular base for some kind of stone construction, clearly bear evidence that they were exposed to burned wood and high temperatures. These stones exhibit shades of pink and red typically produced when brown to buff-colored sandstone is heated sufficiently. The surface of these flat-lying slabs was also covered with a thin charcoal stain. Additional sandstone slabs scattered west of the rectangle and heavy charcoal deposits in the soil here suggest that Feature F might be the remains of a stone oven (see appendix 1).

Guidance regarding the construction of baking ovens both in garrison and during field operations first became available during the War of the Rebellion, and little new information was published until after the 1876 Indian War. One such source noted the importance of providing troops soft bread instead of biscuits or hardbread whenever possible to improve heath, citing incidents from imperial Rome to the Crimean

War.[52] Indeed, the Union army took this issue seriously and quickly developed the capacity to provide soft bread to thousands of soldiers. It built large bakeries to supply troops in winter quarters or extended camps and encouraged the use of field ovens in other situations.[53]

While I found no other archaeological examples of field baking ovens from a U.S. military context, several Civil War–era publications describe their construction using a variety of materials. These guidelines note that the type of field oven built depended on how long the camp would be occupied. Brick construction might be appropriate for a more permanent camp, while a simple earth-covered trench would suffice for baking bread at an ephemeral field location.[54] The ovens described range from a large 14-square-meter brick model capable of baking 500 rations to trench models covered with wood or gabions that could produce 100 to 250 rations. The superstructure of most examples consisted of materials that would support an insulating cover of soil or sod.[55] Stone construction was not among those illustrated in the guides, but it would be among the "any material available" as suggested.[56] An estimated 24 hours was needed to construct the brick model, while the one-square-meter "rapid earth" oven could be built in an hour or two.

If Feature F's rectangular area is the base of an oven, at 1.87 square meters it would have had a capacity comparable to the smaller field ovens described in Civil War–era guides. The length, width, and surface area of the feature base are almost identical to those recommended for a 100-ration field oven in the third edition of the *Manual for Army Cooks*. Although its construction preceded the publication of this manual, the feature might have been constructed to dimensions commonly known by experienced bakers to accommodate a specific number of bread rations. It certainly would have been big enough to supply a daily bread ration to any one of the depot guard companies, as none of them exceeded 50 men on duty.[57]

Private Sanford noted that Sgt. Gayle baked 40 loaves in his first batch, the number of rations needed for the men of Company D assigned to the depot.[58] The sergeant baked bread every day from July 5 to July 9, indicating that one baking was intended to supply a single day's ration for one company.[59] If other depot guard companies were baking bread, they also must have constructed ovens or arranged to use one made by another unit.

The size, structure, and appearance of Feature F's rectangular area as well as its location suggest that it was a field oven. However, the excavation failed to yield datable artifacts that would strengthen its association with 1876 events. Data do not yet exist to determine if the feature is associated with a specific company or kitchen activities other than baking bread.

Supply Depot and Battlefield Archaeology

Extensive archaeological research at the Little Bighorn Battlefield produced an archaeological assemblage that would be expected of a 19th-century fight, and it too generated a few mysteries. Cultural materials remaining on a battlefield are expected to be different from those discarded, lost, or abandoned at a supply depot, although some items might differ only in the frequency with which they occur in both types of sites. Combat-related items would certainly dominate the battlefield, but similar clothing and other personal items would not be unusual at a depot or field camp. The following comparison of the Feature D assemblage with archaeological materials recovered from the Little Bighorn Battlefield provides additional confirmation that the depot artifacts are associated with the 1876 campaign. It also provides a forum for reaching some conclusions not discussed elsewhere.[60]

Archaeology at the national monument included an investigation of the area where Custer's battalion fought as well as where Reno and Benteen waged their defensive battle. The Reno–Benteen equipment disposal site, where soldiers destroyed military equipment after the battle, was also investigated. This area contained the burned remains of equipment and supplies deemed unworthy of transport from the battlefield but then rendered totally unusable to the tribes.[61]

Light horseshoes and horseshoe nails were found across the battlefield, and a few were recovered from the equipment dump; some unused nails were probably from soldiers' saddlebags. The horseshoes and nails are types common for the period, as are those found in Feature D. The battlefield assemblage includes many items of horse equipment. The equipment dump also contained several pieces of wagon harness, perhaps modified for use on the wagon mules that were pressed into service for the Dakota column pack train. Fragments of tack from Feature D represent different parts of the wagon harness than those recovered from the equipment dump.

The remains of many horses were collected from the battlefield in the years following the battle and placed in a common location. Archaeologists found the bones of perhaps 10 different horses on the Custer battlefield and Reno–Benteen defensive site, but none were found at the equipment dump. None of the battlefield specimens identified thus far was from a fetus or foal such as those recovered from Feature D.

Documentary accounts confirm that some soldiers carried pocket watches into battle. Cheyenne warrior Wooden Leg recalled that one of his comrades took a mysterious object from a dead soldier that made a ticking noise.[62] They concluded that the timepiece was the soldier's medicine or spiritual power. The warrior added it to his own medicine objects but threw it away when it stopped ticking. Overlooked by warriors on the battlefield, Lt. Algernon Smith's gold watch fob was retrieved from his clothing by a fellow officer.[63] The empty case for another fallen officer's watch was later found in the possession of an Indian woman. The battlefield archaeological assemblage includes a badly damaged pocket watch, and its context suggests that it might be related to the battle. This lever-set and stem-wound watch did not require a watch key such as found in Feature D. The battlefield watch and key-wind models were both produced in the 1870s.

Tribesmen also recalled finding tobacco among the soldiers' possessions after the battle. However, archaeologists recovered no smoking pipes at the battlefield, and because ceramic materials preserve well in the soil, clay pipes like those from Feature D should have been found if they were present here. The only artifacts that evidence tobacco at the battlefield are three metal tags that retailers used to identify their brands. Analysis of human remains from the battlefield identified two pipe smokers among several tobacco users; one exhibited tooth wear caused by frequent use of a clay pipe.[64]

Of course many cartridges, cases, and bullets were recovered from the battlefield, including those for soldiers' sidearms. Most of the army revolver ammunition represented in the assemblage is for the Colt .45. One cartridge and a spent case are the only specimens that could be used in both the Colt and the Smith and Wesson Schofield, like the .45 cartridge from Feature D.[65] The spent case had been fired from a Colt. Although there is no direct evidence for the Schofield, it might have been carried by a few soldiers. Four brass cases for the .44 Smith and Wesson American were recovered from the battlefield, and ballistics analysis confirmed that these cases were fired from three different revolvers.[66] These .44 cases are identical to one from Feature D.

No specimens of the three types of military general-service brass buttons found on the battlefield were recovered from Feature D. Other military buttons and buttons for nonmilitary clothing were found at both sites. Three iron buttons from the Powder River depot are typical army suspender and trouser fly buttons found in quantity at the battlefield. A white porcelain specimen from the depot, commonly used on shirts and underdrawers, is also identical to a few battlefield examples.

Archaeologists concluded that none of the nails found at the battlefield and Reno–Benteen defensive site were associated with the battle. However, cut nails from the equipment disposal site are assumed to be the only surviving remnants of ammunition and hardbread boxes, items carried on the pack train and later burned. The dimensions of these boxes are known, as are the number and sizes of nails used in their construction. Ammunition boxes were made of heavier materials and assembled with larger nails than were boxes designed to carry the lighter hardbread. Screws were also used to secure the lids of ammunition boxes. This information allowed the archaeologists to calculate how many of each type of box were destroyed at the dump.

Many nails in the sizes associated with hardbread and ammunition boxes were recovered from Feature D, but the data are too incomplete to conclude whether either box type was destroyed here. The deteriorated crate from Powder River depot was clearly not a hardbread box or ammunition box; the depot crate was smaller and more lightly constructed. Shipping crates were built to accommodate the size and weight of commercial products such as those sold by the sutlers and traders or purchased by the Commissary Department.[67] Because so many different products were available at the depot site, an analysis of the nails cannot begin with the assumption that all or most of them were from hardbread and ammunition boxes, as was possible at the battlefield. Neither can the minimum number of boxes be calculated for Feature D because the nails are associated with boxes of unknown size and construction. The nail data suggest that more lightly constructed boxes are represented in the depot assemblage than those of heavier construction.

Both the crate and nail data suggest that the boxes burned in Feature D were not as heavily constructed as containers expected to survive the rigors of a pack train. However, the presence of iron banding in the feature indicates that at least some boxes were reinforced with strapping as recommended by army sources.[68] The Commissary Department noted in 1863 that boxes of canned goods should be strapped with either wood or iron,[69] and a decade later Col. David Stanley came to the same conclusion in his report of the 1873 Northern Pacific Railroad survey.

Conclusions 125

Analysis of cans from the battlefield led archaeologists to conclude that none were related to 1876 events. However, they recovered parts of three cans in the equipment dump area that might represent some of the food items carried on the campaign. Two of these artifacts are from cans similar to Feature D specimens that use friction lids; they probably contained dry substances such as baking powder or lemonade concentrate: "Neither would be unexpected in a campaigner's kit and their presence in the archaeological record supports historical sources."[70]

Unlike the many horse bones recovered from the battlefield, most nonhuman bones recovered here were unrelated to the campaign. Small bone fragments at the equipment disposal site could be identified only as belonging to some type of large mammal, perhaps beef or bison but definitely not pork.[71] Both beef and bison bones were present in Feature D.

There is no archaeological evidence that dogs were present at the battle, but the tribes were reported to have had many canines in their camps. The Cheyenne Wooden Leg recalled that Indian dogs were with the horses of the warriors fighting Reno's troops in the valley but women and other noncombatants then took the dogs to the west, away from the battle. After Custer's battalion was destroyed, Wooden Leg saw a single dog following a Sioux woman among the dead soldiers and commented that this was the only one he saw on the battlefield during or after the fight.[72] Whether this dog belonged to the woman or to a soldier cannot be determined from the context of the recollection.

In a June letter to his wife from the Powder River depot, Custer noted that he was sharing a tent with four of his dogs.[73] Custer's orderly or striker (an enlisted man hired to help with personal duties and household chores), John Burkman, remembered that two or three of the lieutenant colonel's dogs were with the command on the morning of June 25.[74] Assigned to the pack train that day, Burkman stated that he held two of the dogs back as their master rode off at the head of the attack force.[75] The orderly arrived at the Reno–Benteen defensive site with the pack train, where he recalled caring for Custer's wounded reserve horse, but he made no further comments about the fate of the hunting dogs.[76] A year after the battle, two of Custer's staghounds were among the celebrity dogs on display at the first Westminster Kennel Club Dog Show at Madison Square Garden.[77] It is unclear if these two were with Burkman at the battlefield or if they had been left at Fort Beans or were even among an unknown number of Custer's pack that might have been left at Ft. Lincoln.

Burkman also recalled seeing a small yellow bulldog leave with the troops the morning of June 25 and seeing it again on the battlefield two days later when soldiers were burying the dead.[78] Another story about a dog on the battlefield surfaced long after the event. Rusty, "a brindle non-descript canine of no particular race, breed or utility," was adopted by Company I, wounded during the battle, captured by the Sioux, and reunited with the troop after the tribesmen surrendered to the army.[79] Rusty does not appear to have been a bulldog, but these accounts suggest that there might have been a dog with Custer's battalion during the battle. Archaeological evidence from Feature D supports numerous historic accounts that dogs were indeed with the soldiers at Powder River.

Modest Results and Promising Future

After we completed archaeological field investigations at the mouth of Powder River, the Bureau of Land Management acquired Burlington Northern property here in a land exchange. Much of the area occupied by the soldiers and civilians who remained at the depot in June and July is now under state or federal jurisdiction and subject to laws that protect significant cultural resources. Local ranchers understand the history of the area, and, where the site extends onto their property, they too want to protect the historical and archaeological values here. With good stewardship by these public agencies and private landowners, the areas occupied by Terry and Crook will retain their potential to yield more details from future archaeological investigations.

Despite previous collecting at the Powder River confluence, a carefully designed and executed research program can provide new insights into the army's 1876 activities here. Additional study of Feature F should seek to determine if it is indeed the remains of an 1876 field oven, to better understand its construction and use, and possibly to associate it with contiguous kitchen activities and a specific company. Large-scale investigations utilizing geophysical mapping methods, such as ground-penetrating radar, could perhaps reveal more ovens, trash pits, or other archaeological features that further expand our understanding of the materials used here, determine the layout of the infantry guard camp in June and July, and define where various units were located in the very large camps of mid-August. Any future fieldwork must of course be guided by additional documentary research that seeks to further connect the archaeology with depot history.[80]

Conclusions

The modest archaeological project at the depot site has provided some equally modest details about the events of 1876. The investigation is perhaps more important for its potential contribution to future archaeological studies here and at other historic sites. It provides useful baseline data to support additional archaeological research at the Powder River confluence. The data may also be useful to historic archaeologists anywhere who are studying sites dating to the last half of the 19th century. Feature D was a kind of time capsule, where its contents are known to have been deposited between June and September 1876. The assemblage can be used as a reference collection when similar materials are analyzed and provide more accurate dating than can normally be derived from the attributes of the artifacts. When a Royal Bottling Co. foil wrapper like those found on the Yellowstone River is encountered anywhere in the world, the analyst will know that a mid-1870s date is reasonable.[81]

Some of the information about Terry's supply effort revealed in the project is historical minutiae at best but interesting nonetheless. The availability of Bass ale on a major campaign is certainly one of those details. Although there is no evidence that the men of the 7th Cavalry favored ale more than their comrades in other regiments, this 15th-century brew is featured in one of Custer's favorite tunes. As his wing departed the Powder River depot on June 15, the regimental band played a farewell salute with the Irish drinking song "Garry Owen." The opening lines of the chorus are "Instead of Spa we'll drink brown ale, and pay the reckoning on the nail, no man for debt shall go to jail from Garry Owen in glory."[82] It is perhaps ironic that some of the ale bottles at the Powder River depot bore a trademark image of St. George, patron saint of soldiers and cavalry, slaying the dragon. With little knowledge of its size or location, George Custer was confident that he could defeat the leviathan he so eagerly sought on the morning of June 25, 1876. He was instead bested by a determined and well-armed foe, the masters of the plains.

APPENDIX 1

Excavation Details and Formation of Features D and F

Feature D

Feature D appeared to be a pit that had been dug very close to the Yellowstone River and then filled with soil, rock, and cultural material. It was located in an alluvial terrace and exposed in the river cutbank. The terrace here consists of a layer of silt and fine sand 1.1 meters thick, resting on coarse gravels and cobbles that extend below to the river channel. When viewed from the west, the contact between the strata is easily identified by the absence of any rocks or gravel in the upper layer, while the lower stratum is devoid of soil. Feature D interrupted the natural profile of the cutbank; soil, rocks, and cultural material were visible in a five-meter-long segment of the bank, extending from the surface into the layer of cobbles. On the terrace surface, the feature was identified by a gradual depression in the soil nearest the cutbank. There was a slightly raised area of soil and rock along the east edge of the depression. An unimproved access trail passed just east of Feature D; some artifacts similar to those seen in the feature profile were also visible in the trail ruts.

We estimated the maximum extent of the feature from surface indicators and established a rectangular excavation grid six meters long and three meters wide. Before excavating, a detailed drawing was completed showing the location of cultural material and distribution of rock and lignite in the feature profile (Figure A1.1). We then excavated within the grid, recording cultural materials by the square meter and excavation level in which they were located (Figure A1.2). Level 1 was zero to 10 centimeters below a datum point on the southeast corner of the excavation grid. All subsequent levels were to a depth of 20 centimeters below the previous level. Excavators used trowels to expose cultural materials, and the resulting loose soil was sifted through ¼-inch-mesh screens to recover objects that might have been overlooked.[1]

Care was taken to find the maximum horizontal and vertical extent of the pit as the excavation proceeded. In the upper levels, this was a relatively straightforward task of determining when the soil no longer contained artifacts, rocks, or materials other than silt. The bottom-most level of Feature D intruded into the cobble stratum of the cutbank, where the feature was easily distinguished by the cultural material and rocks mixed with soil that defined the feature fill. About 10 cubic meters of soil and cultural material were excavated from the grid.

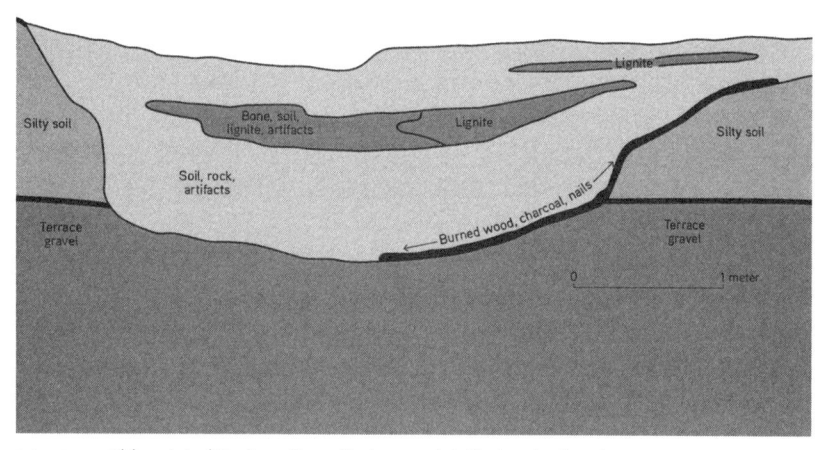

FIGURE A1.1. Abbreviated Feature D profile from a detailed scale drawing.

The pit was found to extend only about two meters east of the cutbank, and just 4.5 of the units on the west edge of the grid contained cultural deposits deeper than 30 centimeters. These units extended to about 155 centimeters below datum. The six excavation units on the east edge of the grid contained soil and artifacts among river cobbles extending a maximum of 10 centimeters below datum to undisturbed soil.

Many of the artifacts were broken, crushed, or damaged in some way and distributed throughout the feature fill. Some cultural material was concentrated in specific strata; most of the bones were in the central part of the feature, as were deposits of lignite. Charcoal, burned wood, and nails were located primarily at the bottom of the feature in the south excavation units. The south half of the excavation area generally yielded more artifacts than the north half; the density of cultural material was lowest in the north quarter of the feature.

Preservation of cultural materials after they were buried in the feature was good. Glass and ceramic materials typically preserve very well in the soil, as was the case here. Some fragments of ale bottle labels were still legible. The cans and nails were not oxidized so badly as to interfere with their analysis. Bone surfaces were in very good condition, although some wood objects such as the packing crate were badly deteriorated. There was a well-preserved layer of organic material composed mostly of fly pupae lying immediately under the dense layer of bones in the central part of the feature.

Some fragments of clay pipes, bottles, and a goblet were found to fit perfectly to other pieces in the assemblage. These fragments were parts of a single broken artifact, and some of them were found widely separated within the feature. For example, two pipe stem fragments that joined to form a longer stem were recovered from two excavation levels, and each fragment was found in a different excavation unit (see Figure A1.3). One piece was recovered from level 2 of unit 1N2W, and the second was from level 7 in 3N2W. The latter fragment was one to two meters north of and about 90 centimeters deeper in the deposit than the other piece. Likewise, 12 fragments

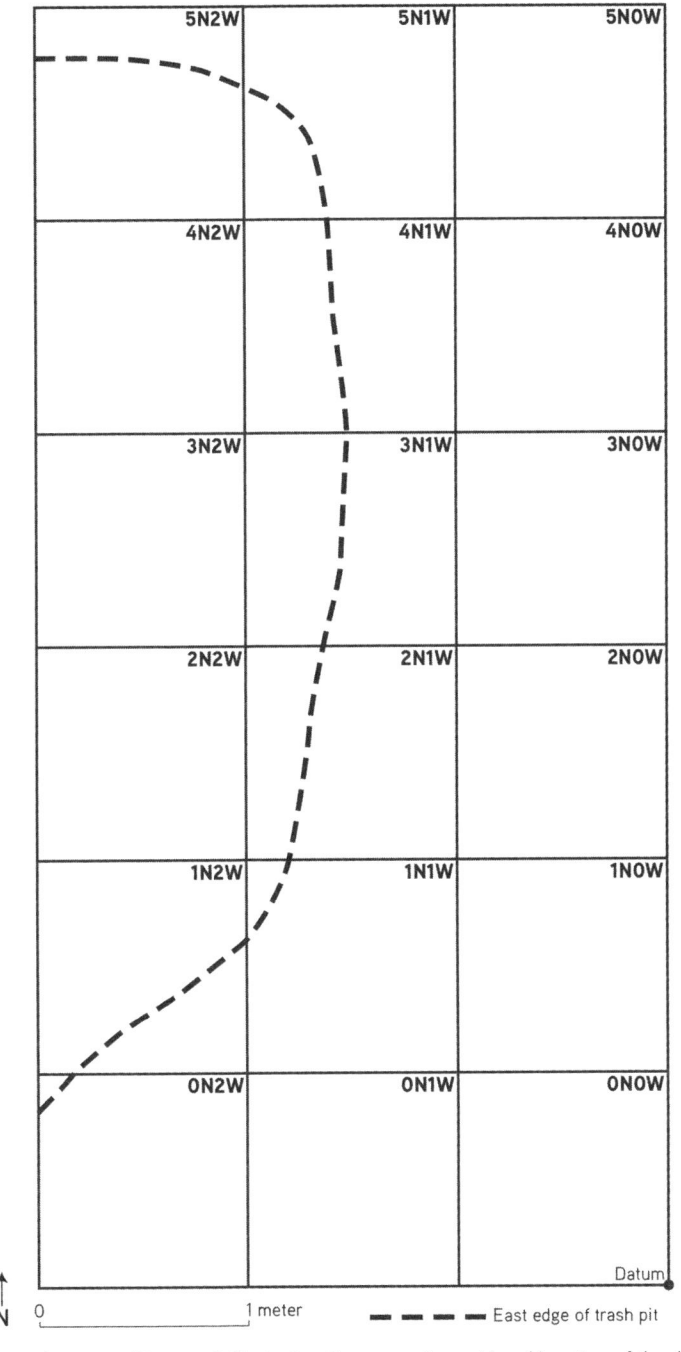

FIGURE A1.2. Plan map of Feature D illustrating the excavation grid and location of the datum. The dashed line indicates the east edge of the trash pit.

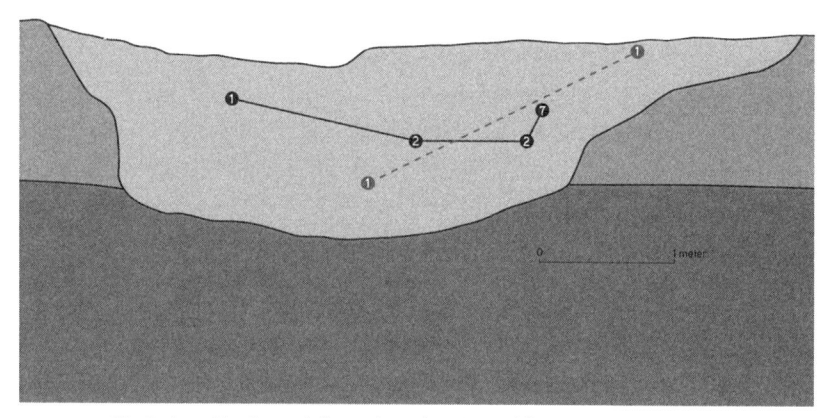

FIGURE A1.3. Vertical and horizontal dispersion of conjoined fragments from a pipe stem and champagne bottle within Feature D. The dotted line connects the locations of two pipe stem fragments (catalog number .245). The solid line connects the locations of 12 shards from a single champagne bottle (catalog number .403). Each number indicates the total from a single excavation unit and level.

of a champagne bottle were separated horizontally by as much as three meters, in 2N2W, level 4; 2N2W, level 5; 3N2W, level 5; and 4N2W, level 4.[2]

These data regarding the natural stratigraphy of the area, dimensions of Feature D, nature of the fill within it, condition of cultural materials, and horizontal and vertical dispersion of fragments from a single artifact are clues to how the feature was formed. It began as a pit excavated into the soil very near the bank of the Yellowstone River. The pit had an irregular shape, steeply sloping to vertical on the north and east with a more gradual slope on the south. The deepest part of the pit was slightly over 1.5 meters below the surface of the terrace, and its maximum length was 5.6 meters. It had a minimum width, east to west, of 1.8 meters, with the deepest part a meter wide. Only a minimum east-to-west dimension of the feature can be calculated because the feature once extended some unknown distance toward the Yellowstone as explained below.

The silty soil and river cobbles dug from the feature were thrown up on the surface and later used to fill the pit. Oxidized soil, burned wood fragments, charcoal, and nails on the bottom of the south end of the pit indicate that crates were burned here before other materials filled the pit. There was no evidence for burning in the pit bottom on the north half of the feature, where a crate, bottle fragments, cans, and other artifacts were unaltered by heat. After these items were deposited in the pit bottom, it was filled with a mix of cultural material, soil, and rock.

When it was about half filled, segments of beef and buffalo bones were thrown into the central part of the pit. With few exceptions, the bones lack evidence of butchering, and their association with a layer of fly pupae suggests that there was meat on the bones when discarded; they probably represent parts of beef and bison carcasses that were discarded for some unknown reason. The pupae also indicate that the meat remained exposed to the air long enough for flies to lay eggs and their larvae to pupate; depending on the species, this can take up to five days.[3] The dog remains were also tossed into the pit with the other bones. Lignite was placed in the pit with some of the bones; it also extended in a layer farther to the south. The lignite was not burned, and its purpose, other than disposal, is unknown.

While the layer of fly pupae suggests that carcass parts were exposed for several days, the excellent condition of the bones indicates that they were covered with soil before weathering of bone surfaces could occur. After the pupae formed, the pit continued to be filled with a mixture of silt, rocks, and cultural material until it was almost level with the ground surface. In the south third of the pit another layer of lignite was deposited, but it was much thinner than the one below. Most of the soil and rock removed to form the pit was apparently used to fill it as well. A thin mantle of river cobbles on the surface in the northeast excavation units probably contains some of the rocks initially dug from the bottom of the pit that were not later thrown back into the fill.

The horizontal and vertical separation of parts of the same artifact within the pit fill indicates that the artifacts were broken before they were deposited in the feature. Most of the glass shards, pipe fragments, and other artifacts were mixed with soil and rock throughout the pit fill, rather than being deposited in layers as were the bone deposit in the central part of the pit and the burned materials on the pit bottom. These data suggest that some of the artifacts were broken or crushed and then thrown onto the soil and rock removed from and piled next to the pit. Bits and pieces of artifacts were then indiscriminately tossed back into the pit with shovelfuls of soil and rock as the pit was gradually filled. In general, it appears that some cultural material was thrown directly into the pit and some was first deposited on the soil and rock pile. Most of the bottles were broken, and many cans were crushed, suggesting that the damage was done with purpose.

Sometime after the pit was filled, part of the feature eroded into the Yellowstone, leaving the rest of it profiled in the cutbank. The feature was probably a pit enclosed on all sides, otherwise gravity and weathering would have quickly emptied it into the river. Given this scenario, the cutbank in 1876 extended an unknown distance to the west and has since eroded eastward, a trend that continues today. Whether or not the pit served another purpose before it became a trash pit will remain a mystery, as will its east-to-west dimension.[4]

Feature F

Feature F is located 300 meters southeast of Feature D (Figure A1.4). After removal of the upper three centimeters of soil, this feature appeared to be 24 sandstone slabs, up to a meter long and a half meter wide. Four of the large sandstones were in a vertical position, while the rest were lying horizontally. The stones were unevenly distributed in an area 7 meters long by 3.5 meters wide on the fine soils common to the river terrace here. The vertical stones and those near it lay on a grassy flat contiguous to a wide, shallow depression to the west in which other stones were scattered.

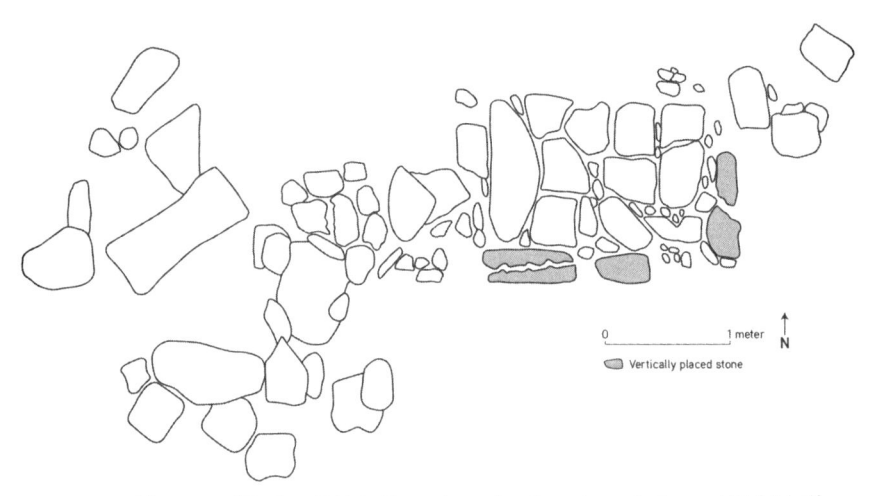

FIGURE A1.4. Plan map of Feature F. Note the rectangular-shaped area in the east (right) half of the drawing (this is the area shown in Figure 1.5).

Using a trowel to remove one to three centimeters of soil between the vertical stones, we exposed carefully laid, charcoal-stained slabs in a rectangle 1.7 meters long and 1.1 meters wide; small sandstones filled spaces between the larger stones. The vertical stones were placed tightly against the south and east edges of the rectangle. Stones in the rectangle were shades of pink and red, colors typical of normally buff to brown sandstone that has been exposed to very high temperatures; they appeared to be semidressed into rough rectangular or square shapes.

Further excavation simply involved removing soil from partially buried sandstones and those found using a metal pin to probe below the surface. We revealed eight additional stones in the rectangle and 24 more in the depression. In a space between large stones two meters west of the rectangle, we dug a 30-by-30-centimeter hole in the soil revealing a very dense, 10-centimeter-thick deposit of charcoal just below the surface of the depression but did not determine the extent of the deposit.

We terminated excavation where stones would have to be removed to reach others, therefore the total number and distribution of sandstones in the depression remain undetermined. After photographing and making a scaled drawing of the feature, we backfilled to leave the area looking as it did when we began.

Feature F might be the remains of a field oven, and the rectangular area of horizontal, dry-laid sandstones on the east end of the feature may be a largely intact oven floor or base. If the four vertical stones abutting the south and east edges of the rectangle are remnants of walls that once surrounded the base, they suggest that the oven superstructure was also made of stone. Many of the sandstones in the area surrounding the base, including the depression to the west, might once have been part of this superstructure. The steeply inclined position of stones nearest the west edge of the base suggests that much of the superstructure might have fallen or been pushed over into the depression.

Charcoal produced when the oven was heated would account for the dense carbon deposits in the soil west of the rectangle. While the stones in the rectangle were thermally altered, soil in which the charcoal was buried generally was not reddened or discolored like the soil in Feature D where the crates were burned. Differences in the thermal signature of stones in the rectangular area and in the contiguous soil might be a clue as to how an oven was constructed and operated. Additional excavation is needed to confirm whether or not the feature is an 1876 oven and get a better understanding of its form and function. Further investigation of the surrounding area is also required to determine if evidence of other kitchen activities is also preserved here.[5]

APPENDIX 2

Artifacts Associated with Beverages and Drinking

Artifacts related to drinking included bottles, bottle closures, and drinking glasses. Most bottles in the excavated assemblage were alcoholic beverage containers; a few were soda/ginger ale/sarsaparilla bottles. Complete and fragmentary remains of bottle closures included corks, wire retainers to secure corks, and foil wrappers or seals to cover the closures and bottle finishes. A single champagne/wine/ale bottle was the only complete beverage container in the assemblage. Larger bottle fragments, including finishes and bases, allowed an assessment of the minimum number of several bottle types in the assemblage, as did the aggregate weight of bottle fragments by type. Foil wrappers associated with ale/stout bottles provided another measure of the minimum number of these bottles potentially represented in the assemblage. Remnants of bottle labels as well as relief stamping on foil wrappers yielded the names of several bottlers and confirm or suggest the brands of ale or stout the bottles held. There is scant evidence of hard liquor in the assemblage. A single firm appears to be represented in a small sample of soda/ginger ale bottles; small disks recovered in the assemblage were likely part of the closures for these bottles.[1]

ALE/STOUT BOTTLES

Provenience
Slope below Feature D and throughout the excavated area. Bottle fragments for this type were recovered from all levels and most excavation units.

Description
Type 1
Glass color—dense green; closure—cork with wire retainer and foil wrapper; finish—broad collar above a narrow ring (two types) and a simple broad collar; body (two types)—cylindrical; shoulder—rounded; base—conical push-up or more shallow, rounded push-up with or without lettering; neck—regular length and slightly bulbous; mold seam—three-part dip mold with dip mold body (Figure A2.1).

Type 2
Glass color—dark green but more translucent than Type 1; closure and finish—probably same as Type 1; body—cylindrical tapering slightly from shoulder to base;

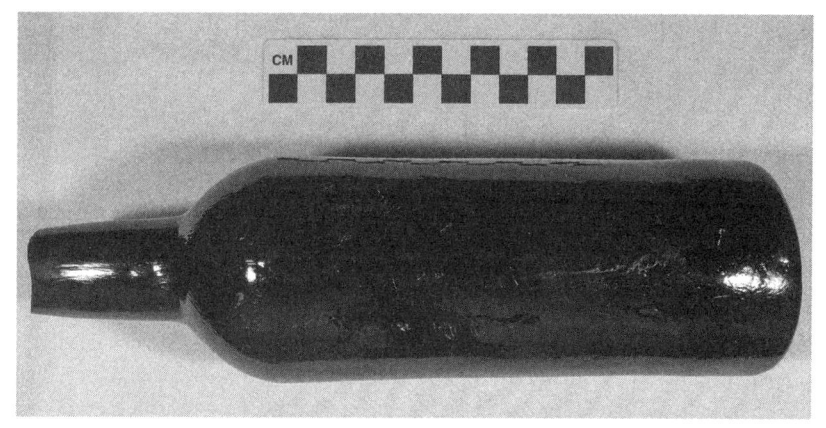

Artifacts Associated with Beverages and Drinking 137

FIGURE A2.1. Type 1 ale/stout bottle.

FIGURE A2.2. Type 2 ale/stout bottle.

shoulder—rounded; base—push-up with lettering; neck—appears slightly bulbous, but length cannot be determined; mold seam—same as Type 1 (Figure A2.2).

Measurements
Type 1 (Smaller)
Height—circa 23–24 centimeters; bore—1.7 centimeters; body—6.5 centimeters; neck—2.5 to 3.0 centimeters; base—6.4 to 6.9 centimeters; height of push-up—1.0 to 3.5 centimeters.

Type 2 (Smaller)
Height—cannot be determined from bottle fragments, but from base to neck it is slightly shorter than the smaller Type 1 bottle (15.5 centimeters); base of neck—3.65 centimeters; body—7 centimeters at upper mold seam, 6.4 centimeters at base.

Types 1 and 2 (Larger)

Lacking large fragments of this size, only incomplete description is possible. (Several larger bore finishes [1.8 centimeters] and larger bases [eight-centimeter diameter] evidence this variety.) In all other attributes such as mold type and glass color, these bottles appear to be the same as the smaller variety.

Markings

Some bases of both the smaller and larger bottles with shallow, rounded push-ups have embossed letters and numbers. Examples from two of the smaller bases are the following: "C.H./C&S/29" and "C.H./C&S/27." One of the larger bases is embossed "C.H./C&S/8." The characters circle the center of the base; the numbers are somewhat separated from the lettering.[2] The remains of a label were found on several fragments of the Type 1 ale/stout bottle. A composite sketch yielded a partial label of the Royal Bottling Company (see Figure 5.1, p. 97). The company trademark featured a representation of St. George and the dragon. The label also indicated that the bottle contained Bass Pale Ale. Most of the label was a yellow-green color, except for the Bass trademark, a prominent equilateral red triangle (one inch per side). Outlines of labels are visible on some bottles, although no fragments of the labels are present. These outlines and surviving label fragments confirm that the oval-shaped Bass Ale label was applied to the bottle first and then the triangular Royal Bottling Co. label was attached below, covering the lower part of the Bass label (Figure A2.3).

Date of Manufacture

Circa 1865–1880s.

Date of Company Operations

No information was found for the Royal Bottling Company.[3]

Minimum Number of Bottles

While several of these ale/stout bottles are more than 50 percent complete, the assemblage is dominated by smaller fragments of dark green glass. The minimum number of bottles was calculated from the total of complete bases and finishes, whichever is the higher number. Since there are 16 intact bases and 16 complete finishes, the minimum number of these bottles represented in the assemblage is 16. This number does not take into account numerous fragments of bases and finishes. The actual number of bottles represented in the assemblage is probably greater because 42 foil wrappers for ale/stout bottles were recovered (see below).

Total Weight of Bottles

Ale/stout bottle fragments weighed a total of 8,783 grams, or about 19.36 pounds, more than all other bottle types combined. A specimen of the smaller Type 1 bottle missing only the finish weighs 510 grams. The smaller Type 2 bottles are somewhat lighter, and both larger varieties would have been heavier, although no examples of

Artifacts Associated with Beverages and Drinking 139

FIGURE A2.3. Ale bottle shard with partial label. Note the Bass and Company triangular trademark on the upper portion of the label.

the larger bottle were complete enough to yield a reliable weight. The total weight of ale/stout bottles would account for roughly 17 smaller Type 1 bottles in the assemblage. This figure is close to the minimum number of ale/stout bottles calculated from the number of complete finishes or bases (16).

Foil Wrappers from Ale/Stout Bottles
Provenience
Found in all levels and most excavation units of Feature D.

Description
Royal Bottling Co.
This wrapper has relief stamping with lettering and a picture of St. George and the dragon on the top (Figure A2.4). The lettering is the following: "THE ROYAL BOTTLING Co/TRADE MARK/patent trade mark capsule Betts London." Smaller lettering is displayed on the side of the wrapper: "BETTS & Co/PATENT/TRADE/PATENT/MARK/LONDON." The lettering and figures on top of the wrapper are black, and much of the rest of the seal is yellow.

Association. While no complete bottle was found with this wrapper covering the finish, evidence for its association with the Type 1 ale/stout bottle is confirmed by several bottle fragments bearing parts of a Royal Bottling Co. label from which a

FIGURE A2.4. Top of a Royal Bottling Company foil wrapper illustrating the company trademark featuring Saint George slaying the dragon.

composite was drawn. Several bottle finishes with cork, wire retainer, and this foil wrapper intact were also recovered.

Dates of Company Operations. No information was found on the Royal Bottling Co.

Number of Wrappers. Twenty-seven complete or nearly complete Royal Bottling Co. wrappers were recovered.

E&J Burke
Relief stamping on top of this wrapper exhibits a cat and raised letters as follows: "E&J BURKE/EJB/DUBLIN/TRADE MARK/patent trade mark capsule/Betts maker/London." Lettering on the side reads: "E&J BURKE/EJB/DUBLIN/TRADE MARK/BETTS & Co/PATENT TRADE/PATENT MARK/LONDON." The raised lettering and the cat figure on the top are red surrounded by yellow. The side of the wrapper is red.

Association. This wrapper is possibly associated with the Type 2 ale/stout bottle, but firm evidence is lacking.

Dates of Company Operation. 1847–1936.[4]

Number of Wrappers. Seven complete or nearly complete E&J Burke foil wrappers were recovered.

M. B. Foster and Sons

Relief stamping includes lettering along the margins of the top of the wrapper and in the center of the seal. Along the edge of the top is "M.B.FOSTER&SONS/27 BROOK St BOND St LONDON"; the lettering at top-center is "MBFOSTER&-SONS"; on the very outer edge of the top is "patent capsule/Betts maker."

Association. This wrapper cannot be associated with a specific bottle type or bottle color. However, documentary evidence confirms that M. B. Foster and Sons distributed ale and stout, and this wrapper might be associated with the wine/champagne/ale bottle described below.

Dates of Company Operation. 1829–1936.[5]

Number of Wrappers. Eight complete or nearly complete M. B. Foster and Sons wrappers were recovered.

Fragments of Two Foil Wrappers

Two foil wrappers represent additional types that cannot be fully reconstructed. Relief stamping on one fragment from the top of a wrapper is the following: "E&G. HIBBERT/LONDON/Betts maker." The lettering on the second wrapper is even more fragmentary, as follows: "CR.../PURVEYORS TO HE/SO.O.../LON.../."

Association. These wrappers cannot be associated with a bottle type or bottle color.

Dates of Company Operation. E&G Hibbert operated 1767–1936.[6]

WINE/CHAMPAGNE/ALE BOTTLES

Provenience
Slope below Feature D and in the excavated area. Based primarily on glass color, fragments of this type occurred in all levels and most excavation units.

Description
Glass color—light green; closure—cork; finish—wine/the sealing surface is flat or slightly tapered upward toward the bore; body—cylindrical; shoulder—tapered to neck; base—deep kick-up (Figure A2.5).

Measurements
Height—24.8 centimeters; bore—1.6 to 1.8 centimeters; body—7.0 centimeters; neck—2.7 centimeters; height of kick-up—4.5 centimeters.

Markings
The outline of an oval-shaped label 8 centimeters high by 6 centimeters wide is visible on the body of the complete bottle, although the label is no longer present. The

FIGURE A2.5. Wine/champagne/ale bottle.

outline of a second label is centered on the opposite side of the bottle and oriented with its longer dimension perpendicular to the height of the bottle, therefore this outline is 8.7 centimeters wide and 6.5 centimeters high.[7]

Date of Manufacture

This type is typical of wine and champagne bottles circa 1865–1885. This bottle type with light green glass and a flat, sheared-looking sealing surface likely predates circa 1880.[8]

Minimum Number of Bottles

One complete bottle and three intact finishes indicate a minimum of four bottles in the assemblage.

Total Weight of Bottles

Weight of the bottles was calculated from a complete specimen of this type and numerous fragments of light green bottle glass. The total weight of 1,869 grams, or 4.12 pounds, was less than that of ale/stout bottles or soda/ginger ale/sarsaparilla bottles. The complete bottle of this type weighs 493 grams, therefore roughly four of these bottles are represented in the total assemblage; this figure agrees with the minimum number calculated from the number of intact finishes.

Remarks

It is possible that these bottles contained ale. M. B. Foster and Sons is known to have exported Bass ale in wine and champagne bottles as well as typical glass ale bottles in the late 19th century.[9]

FOIL WRAPPERS FROM WINE/CHAMPAGNE BOTTLES

Description

Grapes

Relief stamping consists of a bunch of grapes on the top of the wrapper with no lettering or other markings.

Artifacts Associated with Beverages and Drinking 143

Association. These wrappers cannot be associated with a specific bottle type. However, the relief stamping of grapes itself suggests wine or champagne.[10]

Number of Wrappers. Four complete or nearly complete wrappers.

M. B. Foster and Sons
See the remarks under "Wine/Champagne/Ale Bottles" and the description under "Foil Wrappers from Ale/Stout Bottles."

Whiskey/Brandy Bottles

Provenience
The type includes a bottle neck with attached finish from Feature D, excavation unit 3N2W, level 9 (bottom of feature), and a highly fragmented, shattered bottle in units 4N2W and 5N2W, bottom of the feature.

Description
The finish and neck are amber glass. The neck taper from shoulder to finish, and the finish is a "brandy" type; a mold seam is not visible. The shattered bottle appeared to have pieces of a label on small fragments, but reconstruction was not possible.

Date of Manufacture
Circa 1870–1885.

Soda Water/Ginger Ale/Sarsaparilla Bottles

Provenience
Slope below Feature D and in many levels and excavation units of the excavated area.

Description
Glass color—light aqua or dark aqua; closure—probably cork and wire retainer (see remarks below); finish—probably broad collar; body—cylindrical; base—rounded (Figure A2.6).

Measurements
Height—circa 21+ centimeters; bore—circa 1.8 centimeters; body—6.0 centimeters; neck—2.7 centimeters.

Markings
Type—embossing; lettering on most complete bottle—"CANTRELL &/CO-CHRANE/BELFAST&/DUBLIN"; lettering on another bottle fragment—"NTRELL&/OCHRANE/LFAST&BLIN/DICATED/RATED/ATERS"; place—body.

FIGURE A2.6. Soda water/ginger ale/sarsaparilla bottle.

Date of Manufacture
Circa 1860–1900.

Date of Company Operation
1852–present. Now operating as C&C Group PLC in the United Kingdom.

Minimum Number of Bottles
Complete basal fragments of this type indicate a minimum of one dark aqua and five light aqua bottles.

Total Weight of Bottles
Total weight of bottle glass attributable to this type was 2,243 grams, or about 4.9 pounds. A single bottle missing only the finish weighs 447.2 grams. At 450 grams per bottle, the glass from this type represents about five bottles, one fewer than the minimum number calculated from the complete basal fragments.

Remarks
Numerous fragments of these thick-walled bottles were recovered in the excavation. Some fragments bore remnants of the same lettering as appeared on the two more complete items described above.

METAL DISKS FROM SODA WATER/GINGER ALE/SARSAPARILLA BOTTLES

Provenience
Feature D, several excavation units from levels 1 through 8.

Description
Thin metal disks 2.5 centimeters in diameter with four raised bumps around the center surrounded by raised lettering—"CANTRELL&COCHRANE."

Artifacts Associated with Beverages and Drinking 145

FIGURE A2.7. Tumblers: (middle) Type 1 (six facets); (right) Type 2 (eight facets); (left) Type 3.

Association
Although no intact soda water bottle finish was recovered, these disks no doubt covered the cork stopper on Cantrell and Cochrane bottles. Similar disks were commonly used by bottlers to prevent wire retainers from cutting into cork stoppers.[11]

Number of Disks
Ten of these metal caps were recovered.

TUMBLERS (THREE TYPES)

Provenience
One complete tumbler was located in Feature D, excavation unit 2N2W, level 6; a slightly larger one was reconstructed from fragments recovered in unit 0N0W, level 1; and a third type was reconstructed from fragments in unit 2N2W, level 7 (Figure A2.7). Bases and fragments of others were found in several excavation units in levels 1, 2, 5, 6, and 7.

Description
With one exception, the tumblers are made of colorless pressed glass; one Type 2 basal fragment is dark amethyst.

Type 1
Glass color—colorless; six facets on body of glass with vertical orientation from base

to mid-body; base—push-up; interior—conical; height—6.5 centimeters; base diameter—4.8 centimeters; lip—5.9 centimeters; weight—159 grams.

Type 2
Glass color—colorless or amethyst; eight facets on body of glass with vertical orientation from base to mid-body; base—push-up; interior—conical; height—7.5 centimeters; base diameter—5.4 centimeters; lip—6.7 centimeters; weight—240 grams.

Type 3
Glass color—colorless; body—cylindrical tapering from base to lip (no facets); base—push-up; height—11 centimeters; base diameter—5.1 centimeters.

Markings
None.

Minimum Number of Tumblers
The assemblage includes complete bases of three Type 1 tumblers, two Type 2 tumblers, and a single Type 3 tumbler, yielding a minimum of six tumblers.

Total Weight of Tumblers
Tumblers and fragments totaled 765 grams, or about 1.7 pounds.

Date of Manufacture
Circa 1850–1910 but fit well in the 1860–1880 period.[12]

GOBLET

Provenience
Feature D, excavation units 5N2W, levels 2 and 3, and unit 4N2W, level 4.

Description
Basal portion of a stemmed, pressed glass goblet reconstructed from eight fragments; glass color—very light pink; 10 facets on a very short stem and lower body; no facets on base; height of fragment—7.1 centimeters; base diameter—7.0 centimeters; stem thickness—1.2 centimeters (Figure A2.8).

Minimum Number of Goblets
All fragments in the assemblage were refit to form a single specimen.

Date of Manufacture
Circa 1850–1910.

FIGURE A2.8. Goblet.

Remarks
The specimen from Feature D is too small to determine if it is one of the many named pressed glass goblet patterns. The very short, faceted stem and plain base are most similar to a half dozen of 710 goblet patterns described by Millard. He claimed that these six patterns were for goblets manufactured in the 1860s and 1870s.[13]

APPENDIX 3

Artifacts and Organic Materials Related to Food

Artifacts related to food include cans, a condiment bottle fragment, and closures from both jars and condiment bottles. Eggshells and food bones evidence the use of chicken eggs, beef, buffalo meat, and fish.

Cans

Of the 31 cans associated with Feature D, 11 were recovered from the slope below the feature, and 16 complete or nearly complete specimens and four fragments came from the excavation. The 20 cans recovered during excavation were distributed among six of nine levels, and most were found in excavation units 2N2W and 3N2W. A subsample of 14 complete cans from the excavated area was analyzed in detail. Following are descriptions of can morphology and manufacturing techniques with comments regarding what the cans most likely contained and the probable range of dates for their manufacture.[1] Each can is identified by the Billings Curation Center catalog number assigned to the artifact.

.770, .671, .421(b), .20, and .29
Description
These five specimens are hole-in-cap cans (Figure A3.1). They have lap side seams and machine-stamped can ends. The solder on the side seam terminates before reaching the can end. It appears that a precut piece of solder was attached to the side seam before a soldering iron made contact with it. The cap and its vent hole were also sealed by hand, and the cap's sealing solder also appears to have been a preshaped solder ring. Can .20 bears clear evidence of having had solder on the inside as well as the can exterior.

Measurements
Specimen .421(b) is 3⅝ inches in diameter and 4⅞ inches tall. All other specimens in this group are 3⅞ inches in diameter.

Other Observations
The cans were opened by cutting their top with a knife such that triangular pieces of the top could be folded back away from the center of the top. This technique of

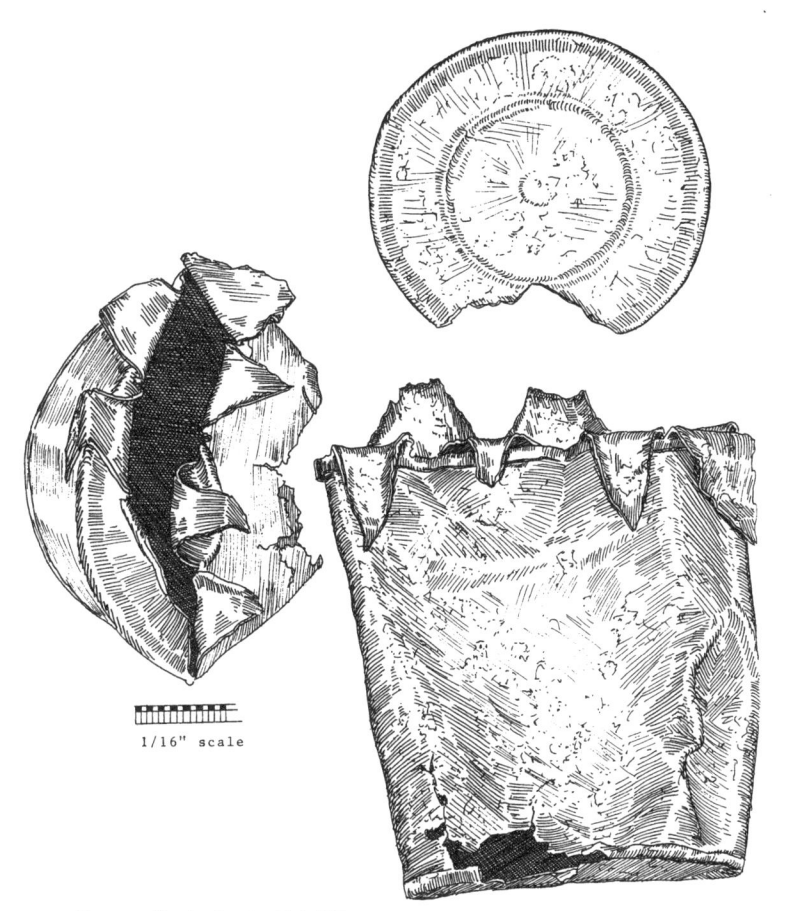

Artifacts and Organic Materials Related to Food 149

FIGURE A3.1. Can .29. Illustration by Rick Hill.

opening a can with a knife is typical for fruit and vegetable cans and possibly preserve cans.

.536
Description
Same as .770, .671, .421(b), .20, and .29 except that this is the only can with the sealer cap placed off-center (Figure A3.2).

Measurements
Can diameter is 3⅝ inches, and height is 4⅝ inches.

Other Observations
The can was opened by cutting slits into the top and then folding triangular sections of the top outward. The can likely held fruits, vegetables, or preserves.

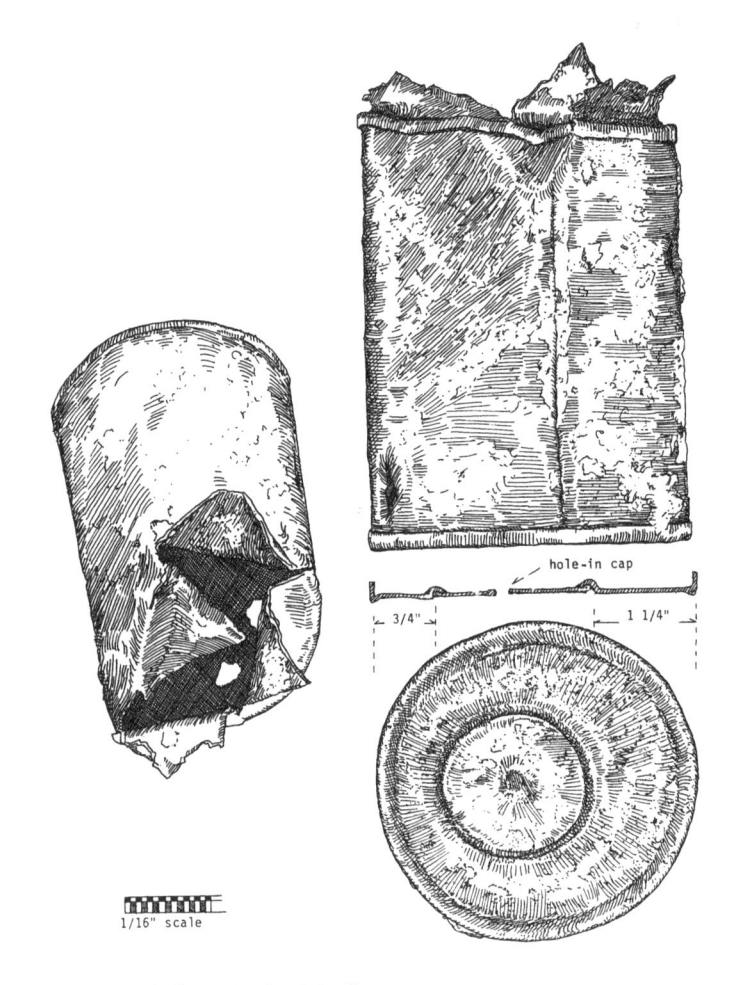

FIGURE A3.2. Can .536. Illustration by Rick Hill.

.672

Description

In most respects specimen .672 is the same as .770, .671, .421(b), .20, and .29. Like .20, this specimen was sealed in a manner that allowed solder to get within the can.

Measurements

Can height is four inches, and the filler cap diameter is 1¾ inches.

Other Observations

The specimen was opened by inserting a knife blade repeatedly around the internal edge of the can top. Once the top was cut around three-quarters of the top edge, it was folded back to extract the contents. Based on the large size of the filler cap, the

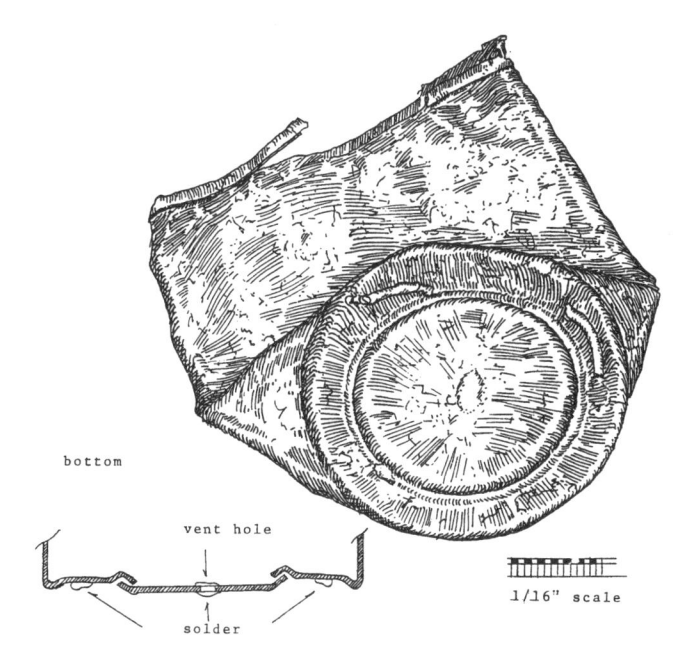

Artifacts and Organic Materials Related to Food 151

FIGURE A3.3. Can .675. Illustration by Rick Hill.

can probably held peach halves or something similar. The way the can was opened would have allowed relatively large pieces of food to be removed intact.

.675
Description
In most respects this can exhibits manufacturing techniques similar to .770, .671, .421(b), .20, and .29 (Figure A3.3). The solder around the cap appears to be a prepared ring. When the soldering iron was applied, part of this ring broke away and attached well beyond the cap depression.

Measurements
Can diameter is 3⅜ inches, and height is 4½ inches. The filler cap diameter is 2¼ inches.

Other Observations
The can was opened by cutting slashes in the top and folding back triangular-shaped sections of the top. It likely held fruit, vegetables, or preserves.

.505(a)
Description
Like .770, .671, .421(b), .20, and .29, this is a hole-in-cap can with a lap side seam.

Measurements
Can diameter is 3½ inches, and height is 4⅝ inches. The filler cap diameter is 2¼ inches.

Other Observations
Like several other specimens, the can was opened by cutting triangular sections of the top and folding them outward and back. It probably held fruit, vegetables, or preserves.

.505(b) and .673 and Lids
Description
These specimens have a lap side seam and an external ridge on the body of the can stamped ⅜ inch below the can's top. This stamped ridge protrudes outward from the can body to hold a friction lid securely in place.

Measurements
Due to the condition of these cans, only .505(b) was measured. The can is approximately two inches in diameter and three inches tall.

Other Observations
Several metal friction lids recovered from Feature D were designed to fit on the type of stamped ridge exhibited on specimens .505(b) and .673. Lid specimens .26 and .533 are 3 1/16 inches in diameter and 7/16 inch deep. Specimen .476 is a friction lid 2⅜ inches in diameter and ⅜ inch deep. The smaller lid appears to be ⅜ inch larger in diameter than can .505(b), but the can dimensions are approximate at best. However, there is no clear association between .505(b) and the smaller friction lid. While the contents of cans associated with friction lids from Feature D cannot be determined with the data available, these lids were often used for cans containing dry products such as baking powder, yeast, and powdered lemonade.[2]

.419 and .852
Description
The body of these cans as well as the top and bottom are each single pieces of stamped metal. The body piece has a lap seam at one end. Stamping of the can body resulted in a narrow ledge within the can interior to which the top and bottom pieces were soldered; solder was applied by hand to the body lap seam and the edges where the top and bottom meet the body.

Measurements
The top and bottom of the can are each about four by three inches. Height of the can body is one inch.

Other Observations
This can type held sardines.[3]

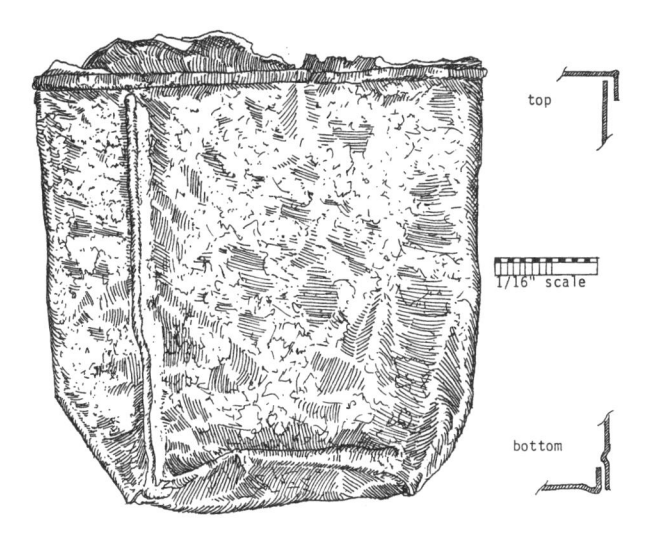

Artifacts and Organic Materials Related to Food 153

FIGURE A3.4. Can .420. Illustration by Rick Hill.

.420
Description
Most of the specimens in the subsample are hole-in-cap cans. Can .420 exhibits a different structure and technique for filling (Figure A3.4). While it has a lap side seam, the body is stamped with a narrow ridge approximately ⅜ inch below an open end of the body and inside of the can. A stamped end piece has only a vent hole and a second hole made to test the seal of the can. The entire end piece served as a cap, which was put in place after the can was filled; it was then soldered to the body after resting on the internal ridge in the can's body.

Measurements
The can is too deformed to determine its diameter. The can height is 4½ inches.

Other Observations
This specimen is not described in other published reports. Similar cans have been identified at Ft. Stambaugh, Wyoming Territory.

Dating the Cans
The morphology and manufacturing techniques exhibited by the subsample from Feature D are consistent with cans produced in the 1870s. The sardine cans likely predate 1880, and cans similar to .420 were identified at Ft. Stambaugh, Wyoming Territory, a military camp occupied from 1870 to 1878.

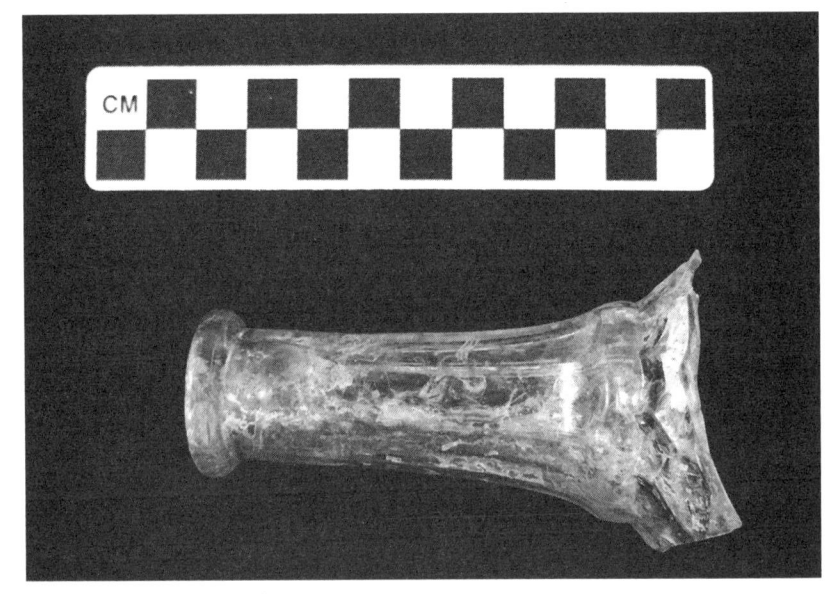

FIGURE A3.5. Condiment bottle.

Condiment Bottle, Bottle Stoppers, and Jar Closures

Condiment Bottle[4]

Provenience
Slope below Feature D.

Description
Glass color—colorless; neck—eight facets in a vertical arrangement from the shoulder to 1.6 centimeters below the finish; finish—simple "extract"; closure—probably cork; two mold seams terminate at the finish; shoulder—decorated by a checkerboard pattern of facets (Figure A3.5).

Measurements
Bore diameter—1.9 centimeters; height of specimen—9.3 centimeters.

Remarks
This is probably a ketchup bottle.

Date of Manufacture
Circa 1875–1885.

Number of Bottles
This is the only specimen of a condiment bottle.

Bottle Stoppers (Two Types)[5]
Provenience
Surface north of Feature D and Feature D excavation unit 2N0W, level 1.

Description
Glass color—light green; finial—flat, circular, horizontal; shank—tapered; neck—none.

Measurements
Type 1. Height—2.9 centimeters; finial diameter—2.6 centimeters; largest shank diameter—1.3 centimeters.
Type 2. Height—3.3 centimeters; finial diameter—2.6 centimeters; largest shank diameter—1.3 centimeters.

Markings
Type 1 is unmarked. Type 2 has embossed lettering on the finial—"LEA & PERRINS."

Remarks
These are "club sauce" bottle stoppers, which utilized both glass and cork to form the closure. Lea and Perrins was a British firm that began exporting Worcestershire sauce in 1849.[6]

Date of Manufacture
Lacking the more temporally diagnostic bottles associated with the stoppers, the range of potential dates of manufacture is very broad: 1850–?

Number of Stoppers
One stopper of each type was recovered.

Jar Closure
Provenience
A fragment of a glass fruit jar lid was recovered from the Feature D excavation (Figure A3.6). This fragment was identical to two more-complete closures located on the surface of the site.

Description
The upper surface (top) of this aqua-colored lid is embossed with a series of patent dates as follows: "PATd. Feb. 12, 56"; "Nov. 4, 62"; "Dec. 6, 64"; "June 9, 68"; "Sep. 8, 68"; "Dec. 22, 68"; "Jan. 19, 69." Five dates are arranged in a circle around the outer circumference of the lid, and four dates circle the lid more toward the center of the closure. What appears to be the number 1 is embossed on a flat, circular raised area

FIGURE A3.6. Jar closure (lid).

at the center of the lid. The outer circumference of the inner (bottom) surface of the closure is grooved to fit over the lip of a jar.

Measurements
The diameter of the most complete lid is 10.3 centimeters, and it is 1.4 centimeters thick. The lid fragment recovered from Feature D is a 5.9-centimeter-long segment of the outer rim embossed "68 Sep 8."

Remarks
All of the patents on this lid are associated with jars produced by the Hero Glass Works, Philadelphia, Pennsylvania (1856–1882). These jars included Gem, Pearl, Crystal, and others in addition to Hero. Patent dates sometimes appear on closures that do not apply to the lid on which they are embossed.[7]

Date of Manufacture
Based on the patent dates, the closure would not have been produced before 1869.

Minimum Number of Closures
Fragments of three specimens were recovered.

Organic Materials
Bones
Buffalo and Beef
Small bone fragments from which species could not be determined were recovered in 50 to 80 percent of the excavation units in all levels of Feature D.[8] Levels 4 and 5 in excavation units 2N2W, 3N2W, and 4N2W contained a layer of 241 complete bones determined to be those of beef (*Bos taurus*) and buffalo (*Bison bison*).[9] These bones and those of a dog and horse (see appendixes 9 and 10) were contained in an area about 150 by 50 centimeters and 25 centimeters deep. Based on the highest number of any complete right or left appendicular bone, there are a minimum of three individuals represented in the assemblage, parts of two bison and at least one beef (Table A3.1). The largest articulated segment of bones is the hind quarters of a buffalo that includes a lumbar vertebra, sacrum, femurs, tibiae, tali, calcanei, and fused central and fourth tarsals. Based on epiphyseal closure, these bones are from a five- or six-year-old animal.[10]

The surfaces of most bones are in good condition, exhibiting little or no deterioration from weathering. Likewise, there are almost no tooth marks or other indicators that the bones were altered by scavengers. A layer of fly pupae at the base of the bone concentration in the central part of Feature D suggests that there was enough meat to support a colony of maggots.

Cut Bone
A single cut bone was recovered from level 6 of excavation unit 1N2W. It is a buffalo or beef-size lumbar vertebra that had pieces of both the anterior and the posterior ends of the vertebra body or centrum cut off with a saw. The spinous process, one transverse process, and a piece of the vertebra body are missing and appear to have been broken off rather than cut. Part of the other transverse process is also missing, and the remaining piece exhibits chop marks from a sharp implement. The specimen resulted from butchering a buffalo or beef to produce a cut of meat from the sirloin area of the animal, perhaps a thick sirloin steak.

Fish
Three fish bones were recovered from Feature D, excavation units 3N2W and 4N2W, levels 6 and 7. Species is undermined.

Eggshells
Hundreds of eggshells were recovered from Feature D, often in clusters of small fragments. They occurred in all levels except number 9, the bottom of the feature. Eggshells were present in seven of eight excavation units in level 2 and in all units of level 6. They were also recovered in 50 to 75 percent of excavation units in the other levels. A few larger fragments exhibit a contour that suggests the shells are the size of ordinary chicken eggs. Color varies from off-white to brown. One tiny fragment has several reversed letters on it as if the egg lay on newsprint or some other printed matter and the lettering stuck to the eggshell. No word could be distinguished.

TABLE A3.1. Feature D Bone Frequencies for *Bison* and *Bos*

BONE	BISON LEFT	BISON RIGHT	BISON NO LEFT/RIGHT	BOS LEFT	BOS RIGHT	BOS NO LEFT/RIGHT	BISON/BOS LEFT	BISON/BOS RIGHT	BISON/BOS NO LEFT/RIGHT
Appendicular Bones									
Scapula		1						2	
Humerus		1			1		1		1
Radius				1	1		2		3
Ulna				1	1			1	
Radial Carpal							2	2	
Ulnar Carpal							3	2	
Fourth Carpal								3	
Intermediate Carpal								3	
Accessory Carpal								2	2
Fused 2nd and 3rd Carpal									
Metacarpal		1		1	1		1		
5th Metacarpal									2
Femur	1	1		1	1				1
Patella							1	1	
Tibia	1	1		1	1				
Talus	2	2							2
Calcaneus	2	1							
Lateral Malleolus							1	1	

Fused Central and 4th Tarsal	2	2			
Metatarsal			1	1	
Proximal Phalanx					2	11
Medial Phalanx						9
Distal Phalanx					1	11
Axial Bones						
Skull						5 fragments
Hyoid						3
Mandible			1	1		
Rib						16 complete
						32 fragments
Costal Rib	1					15
Os Coxae		1				
Ischium						2 complete
						3 fragments
Atlas					1	
Axis					1	
Cervical Vertebra						8
Thoracic Vertebra						19
Lumbar Vertebra		1				14
Sacrum		1				1
Caudal						14

APPENDIX 4

Artifacts Related to Medicines

Feature D yielded a patent medicine bottle and the neck and finish of another. However, ginger ale, sarsaparilla, soda water, and even alcoholic beverages were also thought to have medicinal qualities in the 19th century (see appendix 2).[1]

Patent Medicine Bottle

Provenience
Middle level of Feature D.

Description
Glass color—colorless; closure—undetermined; finish—patent lip; body—rectangular; base—flat rectangular with corners cut; neck—short, straight; mold—cup bottom; shoulder—rounded; remnant of foil on neck below finish and remnant of paper on both shoulders running up neck to foil remnant (Figure A4.1).

Measurements
Height—13 centimeters; bore—2.45 centimeters; base—6.3 by 4.0 centimeters; body—9.4 by 6.0 centimeters; neck—3.35 centimeters.

Markings
Type—embossing; lettering—"TARRANT & CO/DRUGGISTS/NEW YORK"; place—body; the number 1 embossed in the center of the base.

Date of Manufacture
1859–1905.[2]

Remarks
Tarrant and Co. of New York sold Seltzer Aperient, perfume, and other products.[3]

Number of Bottles
This is the only example of the bottle type in the assemblage.

Medicine/Extract/Toiletry Bottle

Provenience
Feature D, excavation unit 3N2W, level 5.

Artifacts Related to Medicines

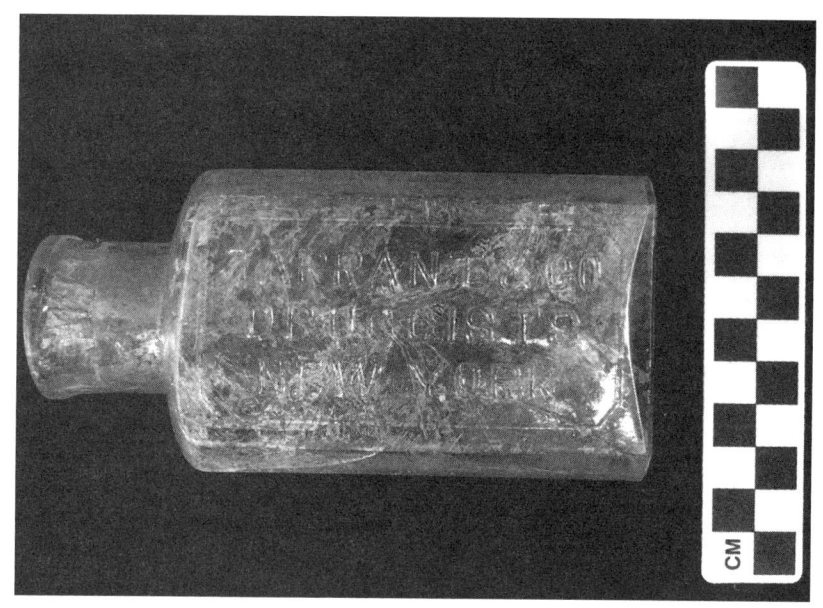

FIGURE A4.1. Patent medicine bottle.

Description
Neck and finish only; color—colorless; ball neck with "extract" finish; mold seam terminates midway between neck ring and neck finish.

Measurements
Bore—1.0 centimeter; neck diameter—1.9 centimeters.

Date of Manufacture
Circa 1860s–1910.

Remarks
The contents of the specimen are unknown; however, this neck and finish type is most often associated with patent medicine, extract, or toiletry bottles.

APPENDIX 5

Artifacts Related to Tobacco Use

Clay tobacco pipe fragments were among the most commonly occurring artifacts recovered from Feature D. No complete pipes were found, and most of the fragments are small. The 220 specimens were distributed broadly but unevenly among levels and excavation units. The top three levels yielded over 60 percent of these artifacts, while the bottom three levels contained 11 percent. More pipe fragments were found in level 2 than in levels 6 through 9 combined. Although only one of five excavation units in level 9 yielded fragments, 75 percent or more of excavation units in six other levels contained pipe fragments.

CLAY TOBACCO PIPES (TWO TYPES)

A minimum of two types of clay pipes are represented in the assemblage based on stem bore diameter (Figure A5.1).[1]

Type 1

Description[2]

This type has a 1/16-inch bore diameter, found on 101 stem fragments that are from 0.9 to 6.4 centimeters long. Thirty-seven fragments include the mouthpiece, and 64 specimens are from other parts of the stem; 34 mouthpieces are rounded, and three are flattened. As with the stems, there are no complete Type 1 bowls in the assemblage; there are a minimum of 64 Type 1 bowl fragments. Analysis of bowl and distal stem fragments confirms that the Type 1 bowl does not slant distally but, rather, is more perpendicular to the stem.

Measurements

Stem length is estimated to be about 15 centimeters, and total pipe length is about 17.5 centimeters; bowl diameter—2.09 centimeters; bowl plus spur height—4.80 centimeters; bowl height—4.13 centimeters; outside bowl diameter in the same direction as the long axis of the pipe—2.99 centimeters; stem diameter where it meets the bowl—1.09 centimeters.

Markings

The name "MCELROY" occurs on the right side of 12 fragments from the distal end of the stem; the letters are 0.22 centimeters high. There is a raised "roughead" design on both sides of the Type 1 bowl.[3]

Artifacts Related to Tobacco Use 163

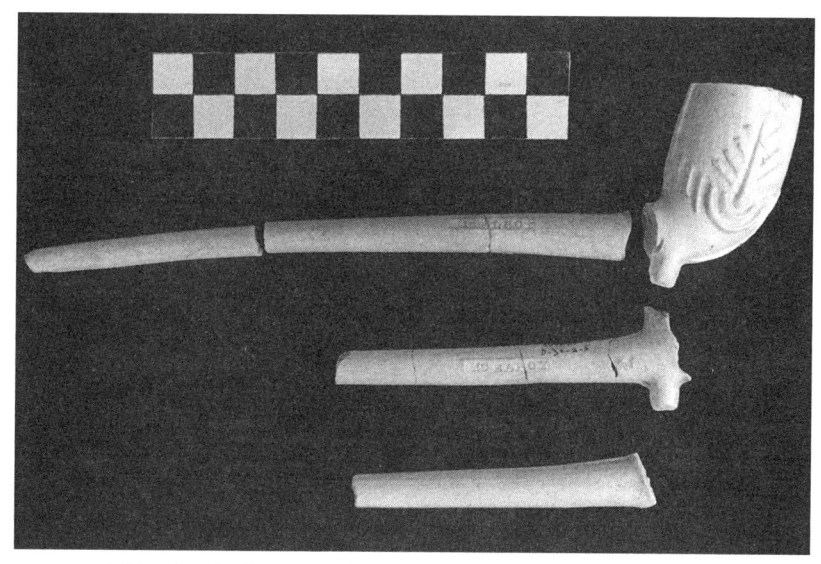

FIGURE A5.1. White clay pipe fragments: (top) Type 1 specimen composed of two conjoined stem fragments, a bowl, and a mouthpiece fragment approximating the length of a complete pipe; (middle) Type 1 specimen made of four conjoined fragments that indicate the Type 1 bowl was perpendicular to the stem (not tilted distally); (bottom) single Type 2 distal stem fragment.

Date of Manufacture
1850–? There is no known clay pipe manufacturer with the name McElroy, but the roughead design has been found on numerous pipes with no maker's mark. D. McDougall and Co. of Glasgow, Scotland, began using the roughead style about 1850, and it is probably a style used by several manufacturers during the last half of the 19th century.

Minimum Number of Pipes
There are fragments of at least 37 Type 1 pipes in the assemblage based on the number of mouthpieces with the 4/16-inch bore diameter.

Type 2
Description
The Type 2 pipe is identified by a 5/64-inch bore diameter. Fifty-five stem fragments in the assemblage exhibit this larger bore diameter; length of stem segments ranges from 1.36 to 7.24 centimeters. Twenty-one of the Type 2 stem pieces are mouthpiece fragments. No bowl fragments could be positively associated with the 5/64-inch bore stem fragments.

Measurements
Stem length is estimated to be about the same as the Type 1 pipe, 15 centimeters.

Maximum stem diameter on a distal fragment is 1.33 centimeters. Lacking associated bowl fragments, total pipe length and bowl measurements cannot be calculated.

Markings
None of the Type 2 stem segments have markings.

Date of Manufacture
Unknown.

Minimum Number of Pipes
Based on the number of mouthpieces with 5/64-inch bore diameter, there are fragments of at least 21 Type 2 pipes in the assemblage.

APPENDIX 6

Artifacts and Bones Related to Transportation

Artifacts and bones recovered from Feature D that are most likely associated with the transportation of goods and personnel include a horseshoe, horseshoe nails, horse bones, tack fragments, a packing crate, nails, boards from crates, and metal banding.

Horseshoe

Provenience
A single horseshoe was recovered from the bottom of Feature D, level 9, excavation unit 2N2W (Figure A6.1).

FIGURE A6.1. Horseshoe.

Description
The heavily oxidized horseshoe has a fuller with four nail holes on each branch. The head of a nail remains in one of the holes nearest the toe of the shoe. The configuration of the shoe is rather pointed at the toe, suggesting that it is from a rear hoof.

Measurements
The horseshoe is 5½ inches long and 4½ inches wide.

Date of Manufacture
Unknown.

Horseshoe Nails
Provenience
Three horseshoe nails were recovered from the Feature D excavation.

Description
The horseshoe nails are three different sizes with two different heads; one is a rose-head, and the other has a very short neck and longer head that tapers slightly to the crown.[1]

Measurements
The nails are in three sizes: 1¾, 2, and 2¼ inches.

Date of Manufacture
Unknown.

Horse Bones
Provenience
Three horse bones were recovered from the concentration of bones in Feature D, levels 4 and 5.

Description
A complete left humerus and a maxilla fragment are from a very young animal or animals.[2] No wear is evident on three premolars in the maxilla, indicating that the fragment belonged to a late-term fetus or foal. The humerus is 15 centimeters long. It is possible that the bones are from the same animal, but this association cannot be confirmed. There are no butcher marks on these bones, and both are in excellent condition. A distal right radius is also present, and it is from a more mature horse; the surface of this bone is also cracked and exfoliating, indicating that it was exposed to the elements for some time before burial.

Harness Fragments
Provenience
Four specimens of leather were recovered from Feature D, levels 6 and 7, and excavation units 1N2W and 2N2W; two of the specimens have metal parts as well.

Description
The largest specimen includes remnants of two leather straps fastened to an iron ring

FIGURE A6.2. Fragment of a quillor, the part of a mule harness for the hindquarters of mules closest to the wagon being pulled.

(Figure A6.2). The ends of each strap are looped over the ring, sewn together along the strap edges, and fastened with a single rivet in the center of the strap. A third piece of leather laps over the ring and portions of the straps to which it also is sewn. A second specimen is a small remnant of leather strap identical to the narrower of the two straps fastened to the ring; it has a center rivet and bears small holes where a piece of leather was sewn to it. The two smallest specimens of leather have been cut

FIGURE A6.3. Remains of a packing or shipping crate at the bottom of the trash pit. Wood boards forming the sides of the crate were too badly deteriorated to recover.

on two sides with a sharp implement, while the other two sides retain stitch marks along their edges, suggesting that they were cut from harness parts.

Measurements
The two straps attached to the ring of the largest specimen have different widths, 2¹¹⁄₁₆ inches and 1¹³⁄₁₆ inches.³ The outside diameter of the ring is four inches. The two smallest specimens are about 1¼ to 1½ inches on a side.

Date of Manufacture
Unknown.

Remarks
The largest specimen is part of a wheel mule quillor, which is a section of harness that is put on the hindquarters of the mules closest to the wagon. The leather pieces are remnants of the breech strap and hip strap.⁴

Packing Crate

Provenience
Feature D, levels 8 and 9, excavation units 2N2W and 3N2W.

Description
A wooden box or crate rested on the bottom of Feature D (Figure A6.3). It was made of ½-inch-thick boards nailed at the corners. The box was too badly deteriorated to determine the width of individual boards forming the sides and bottom or if the crate had been reinforced with metal strapping; there was no top on the crate.

Measurements
The crate was 24 inches long by 14 inches wide by 8 inches high.[5]

Date of Manufacture
Unknown.

Remarks
Fragments of wood were recovered from Feature D, including partially burned boards associated with concentrations of nails, charcoal, and ash on the bottom of the south half of the feature. A thin layer of red soil beneath some of these concentrations indicates that burning occurred in the feature; the overlying charcoal deposits were two to three centimeters thick. These deposits appear to be the remains of burned crates.

NAILS

Provenience
While nails were found in every level of the Feature D excavation area, they were more numerous and more broadly distributed in the lower levels. Fifty to 63 percent of excavation units in levels 1 through 5 yielded nails, while 60 to 100 percent of units in levels 6 through 8 contained nails.

Date of Manufacture
No specific date of manufacture can be determined for the nails. However, the assemblage contains cut nails and wire nails in a ratio of 4.3:1 (Table A6.1). The dominance of cut nails is consistent with an assemblage dating to the mid-1870s.[6]

TABLE A6.1. Feature D Nail Frequencies

Size	Cut Nails	Wire Nails
1d	1	2
2d	11	4
3d	21	3
4d	46	18
5d	32	8
6d	36	9
8d	21	
10d	3	
20d	1	
Total	172	44
Fragments	140	66
Minimum Number	234	54

Cut Nails
Description
The assemblage of cut nails, among the most numerous items recovered from Feature D, includes 172 complete specimens and 140 fragments.

Measurements
Cut nails represent 12 sizes ranging from ⅝ inch to 4 inches. The most frequently occurring size is 1½ inches, or 4d (46 specimens); smaller nails, ⅝ inch to 1⅞ inches, outnumber the larger sizes, 2 to 4 inches, by almost 2:1. The smallest and largest nails occur infrequently, with only one specimen smaller than an inch and four nails that are three inches or larger.

Minimum Number of Cut Nails
The minimum number of cut nails in the assemblage is 234, which is the sum of complete nails and fragments with heads.

Wire Nails
Description
Sixty-six wire nails were recovered from the Feature D excavation, including 44 complete nails and 22 fragments.

Measurements
Wire nails in the assemblage range from 11/16 inch to 2⅛ inches in 10 different sizes. These nails are more evenly distributed among size grades and have a narrower range of size grades than the cut nails. The most frequently occurring sizes include 1⅜ inches (3d or 4d) and 2 inches (6d), with seven nails in each. Sizes with the fewest specimens are 11/16 inch and 2⅛ inches, with two each; the low numbers in the smallest and largest size grades mirrors the distribution among cut nail sizes.

Minimum Number of Wire Nails
A minimum of 54 wire nails is the sum of complete specimens and nail points in the assemblage.

METAL STRAPPING/BANDING
Provenience
Four short pieces of iron strapping (1.38 to 4.72 inches) and one longer piece (29 inches) were recovered from levels 3 and 4 of Feature D excavation units 1N2W, 2N2W, and 4N2W (Figure A6.4).

Description
Three specimens of the thin, oxidized metal strapping have nail holes every few inches along their length. The largest specimen has no nail holes but retains a rivet

Artifacts and Bones Related to Transportation

FIGURE A6.4. Metal strapping used to reinforce shipping crates.

joining two pieces of the banding. The ends of this piece and the others appear to have been cut with shears or some other implement.

Measurements
The largest specimen and a shorter one are ⅝ inch wide; the others are ¾ inch wide.

Date of Manufacture
Unknown.

Remarks
These artifacts are the remains of metal strapping used to reinforce shipping containers. While only a few pieces were recovered from Feature D, segments up to two feet long were found on the site surface, most with nail holes along their entire length. Shipping crates recovered from the steamboat *Bertrand* were reinforced with metal strapping, mostly in ⅝- to ¾-inch widths; this strapping exhibited nail holes along its length. The *Bertrand* sank in the Missouri River with cargo bound for Montana Territory in 1865.[7]

APPENDIX 7

Artifacts Associated with Firearms

A single cartridge and cartridge case were recovered from Feature D (Figure A7.1).

REVOLVER BALL CARTRIDGE, CALIBER .45

Provenience
One .45-caliber cartridge was recovered from Feature D, level 1, excavation unit 1N0W.

Description
The specimen is a copper-cased, inside-primed .45 cartridge with no headstamp. The side of the case is cracked, exfoliating, and corroded; the bullet has a heavy white patina of oxidation.

Measurements
Cartridge length—1.45 inches; case length—1.10 inches; base diameter—0.481 inches; rim diameter—0.516 inches; neck diameter—0.478 inches; bullet diameter—0.459 inches.

Date of Manufacture
1875–1882.

Remarks
This cartridge was designed to fit the Model 1873 Colt revolver and Smith and Wesson Schofield.[1] These .45-caliber handguns were both in service with cavalry regiments in 1876, although the Colt was the dominant sidearm. By the end of 1874 the 7th Cavalry companies had been issued the Model 1873 Colt.[2] Colt also found a market for this model among civilians in 1874. Smith and Wesson produced the Schofield for the commercial market late in 1876. Two years earlier, the army's Frankford Arsenal stopped making the .45 Colt cartridge, which was too long for the Schofield, and manufactured only the shorter "Revolver Ball Cartridge, Caliber .45" for both handguns.[3]

.44 SMITH AND WESSON CARTRIDGE CASE

Provenience
One .44 cartridge case was recovered from Feature D, level 6, excavation unit 2N2W.

Artifacts Associated with Firearms 173

FIGURE A7.1. (Bottom) Revolver Ball Cartridge, Caliber .45, and (top) a .44 Smith and Wesson No. 3 cartridge case.

Description
The specimen is a brass cartridge case with Berdan primer and no headstamp. The rim is slightly distorted.

Measurements
Case length—0.886 inches; base diameter—0.449 inches; rim diameter—circa 0.517 inches.

Date of Manufacture
1870–?

Remarks
This cartridge was manufactured for the .44 Smith and Wesson No. 3 (American), a six-shot revolver. The No. 3 American was being manufactured for the commercial market in 1870 when the army ordered a number for field trials. A few of these handguns were in seven of 10 cavalry regiments in 1871, and by 1873 four regiments, including the 7th Cavalry, had a substantial number of them. The army began to distribute the Colt single-action army revolver in 1873 and the .45 Smith and Wesson Schofield in 1874. By the summer of 1875, fewer than 100 of the Smith and Wesson .44s were still being used by cavalry units. The No. 3 American sold well in the commercial market from 1870 until sometime after Smith and Wesson ceased production of this model in 1874.[4]

APPENDIX 8

Artifacts Associated with Clothing

Buttons

Several buttons were recovered from Feature D and a two-track road near the excavation grid (Figure A8.1).[1]

Provenience

Three buttons were recovered from Feature D levels 1, 3, and 5 in excavation units 0N1W, 0N2W, and 3N2W. Four buttons were also collected from the surface on a two-track road east of and contiguous to the excavation.

FIGURE A8.1. Buttons: (top) metal button for civilian work clothes (left) and iron buttons typical of military suspenders (middle) and trouser flies (right); (bottom) typical porcelain (left), glass (middle), and mother-of-pearl (right) shirt buttons.

Metal Buttons

Three buttons are iron four-hole specimens; one is 9/16 inch in diameter, and two are 11/16 inch in diameter. The larger iron buttons are typical of post-1850 army suspender buttons, and the smaller one is of a type used on trouser flies.[2] One two-piece metal button with a metal loop shank is 3/4 inch in diameter with pressed lettering around the edge of the button face as follows: "UNION/ROCKFORD." This is a work clothes button, probably manufactured sometime in the late 19th century.[3]

Porcelain and Glass Buttons

A white porcelain four-hole button and a white glass four-hole button were recovered. Both are 7/16 inch in diameter. The glass button has a radiating line pattern on its face. These are both shirt-size buttons; the porcelain type dates from circa 1835 to at least 1870, and the glass button was probably manufactured in the 19th century as well.[4]

Mother-of-Pearl Button

A single four-hole mother-of-pearl button is 5/16 inch in diameter. While small, it is considered shirt-size. This simple disc-type button was manufactured much earlier than the 19th century and is still made today.[5]

APPENDIX 9

Miscellaneous Artifacts and Minerals

Several items recovered from Feature D are single artifacts or a few specimens of a class of artifacts, including equipment and personal items. A ceramic item cannot be identified, and a glass container does not appear to be an ordinary tumbler. Two other specimens, a marble and a doll, seem incongruous in the context of a military supply depot. Agate, lead, and lignite recovered from the feature are also described here.

Ratchet Burner

Provenience
Part of a burner for a kerosene lamp was recovered from Feature D, level 5, excavation unit 4N2W (Figure A9.1).

Description
The flat-wick burner consists of a wick wheel (cric) with thumbwheel attached and wick tube; it is made of brown metal that scratches to a brass color. The outside diameter is three inches.

Markings
The end of the thumbwheel is embossed as follows: "M.L.COLLINS PAT. FEB. 4. 1866."

Remarks
Various Web sites identify Michael Collins as holding lamp patents dated September 19, 1865, and February 4, 1866. Some attribute these patents to M. H. Collins, and others, to M. L. Collins. I located several lamp patents by M. H. Collin, who also patented a paddle wheel design for steamboats and an improved gun turret for Monitor ironclad boats. However, I was unable to find any lamp patents dated February 4, 1866. The firm Holmes, Booth and Haydens of Waterbury, Connecticut, apparently made lamps patented by Michael Henry Collins of Chelsea, Massachusetts. It remains unclear whether M. L. Collins and M. H. Collins were the same person.[1]

Watch Key

Provenience
Feature D, level 1, excavation unit 0N2W.

Miscellaneous Artifacts and Minerals 177

FIGURE A9.1. Kerosene lamp burner.

Description
The specimen is the key for a key-wind watch (Figure A9.2). Scratching the gray surface of the upper two-thirds of the key reveals a brass color. The portion of the key that is inserted into a watch is heavily oxidized.

Measurements
The key is 3.7 centimeters long, with a maximum width of 1.2 centimeters.

Date of Manufacture
Circa 1850–1880.

Remarks
A number of American firms began manufacturing pocket watches in the 1850s and later, as technological changes made these timepieces more affordable. From circa 1850 to 1885 most of these companies produced key-wind and key-set watches. Manufacture of pendant wind and set watches began to increase in the 1860s, and by 1885 most companies had ceased making key-wind models. Both types of watches were sold in the 1870s.[2]

Marble
Provenience
Feature D, level 2, excavation unit 1N1W.

FIGURE A9.2. Watch key.

Description
The marble is made of a gray stone with purple tones and very small tan-colored inclusions.

Measurements
The specimen is 1.8 centimeters in diameter and weighs 9.5 grams.

Date of Manufacture
Seventeenth century to circa 1915.

Remarks
Most stone marbles were produced in Germany during the 18th and 19th centuries. Production of stone varieties declined in the 1870s as clay, porcelain, and glass marbles came to dominate the market.[3]

PORCELAIN DOLL

Provenience
A glazed-porcelain doll was recovered from the profile of Feature D before the feature was excavated (Figure A9.3). There is no question that it was within the feature fill.

Description
The doll fragment consists of the torso, legs, and feet; the head and arms are missing. The fragment is 2 inches tall, ¾ inch wide at the shoulder, and ½ inch wide at the feet. It has a glossy white, glazed finish front and back; some black material adheres to the bottom of the feet, with a few specks up to 0.1 inch up the sides of the feet. Unless arms were molded to the sides of these dolls, all or part of the arms were applied, usually at the shoulder or short of the elbow.[4] A mold seam is visible on both sides of the torso, but none is apparent on the remains of the right arm.

Miscellaneous Artifacts and Minerals 179

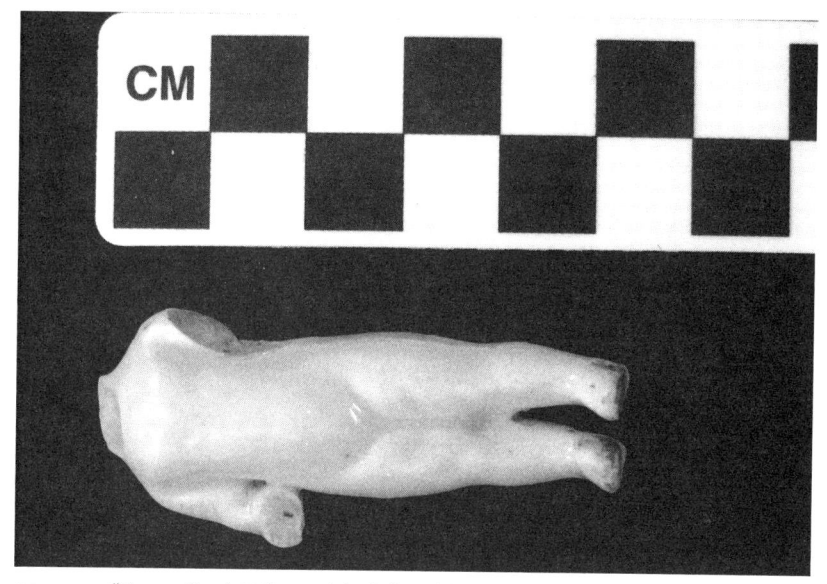

FIGURE A9.3. "Frozen Charlotte" porcelain doll, with black marks on the feet that might be remnants of paint.

Date of Manufacture
Circa 1850–1914.[5]

Remarks
The specimen is an example of a "Frozen Charlotte." These solid porcelain dolls were produced in sizes ranging from 1 to 18 inches, with most in the 1 to 4 inch range. Comparison with other Frozen Charlottes is difficult without the head. Some with similar white torsos and shoulders have painted shoes.[6] The black material on the feet of this specimen could be remnants of paint.

Glass Container

Provenience
Feature D, level 1, excavation unit 1NoW.

Description
This colorless glass container looks like a small tumbler, but the interior body wall is covered with vertically oriented facets that run from the base to 1.7 centimeters below the lip. The exterior of the container bears the remains of a paper label with green, illegible markings.

Measurements
Container height—7.3 centimeters; base diameter—5.1 centimeters; lip diameter—6.6 centimeters. The label is 3 by 5 centimeters.

Markings
The base of the container is lightly embossed with the mirror image of the following markings circling about half of the circumference of the base: "A. ISC R & Co." Horizontally across the center of the base is embossed "CIN.O."

Remarks
What the specimen contained is unknown.

CERAMIC ARTIFACT
Provenience
Four fragments of a ceramic artifact were recovered from Feature D levels 2, 6, and 7 in excavation units 1N2W, 2N2W, and 3N2W. One fragment was also recovered on the surface of a two-track trail contiguous to the excavation.

Description
The description of this artifact is derived from a fragment that appears to be about half complete. The body of the artifact is cylindrical, with one closed end that is convex and rounded and another end that is open. The exterior is a reddish brown or brick color, while the interior is gray; the lip of the open end is finished with the brick color. There are mold seams on the body.

Measurements
The artifact is 4.0 centimeters long, with a diameter of 2.0 centimeters.

Remarks
The function of this artifact is undetermined. There is more than one specimen represented in the assemblage.

LEAD
Provenience
Feature D, level 7, excavation units 1N2W and 2N2W.

Description
Two small irregularly shaped pieces of lead were recovered from Feature D. One specimen is 2.4 centimeters long and 1 centimeter wide and weighs 2.5 grams. A slightly larger piece is 1.5 centimeters long and 0.9 centimeters wide and weighs 3.1 grams.

Remarks
The function of these lead specimens and their association with other artifacts are unknown; they are not fragments of foil wrappers. The larger piece appears to have been subjected to heat.

Agate

Provenience
Five fragments of agate were recovered from Feature D levels 5, 6, and 7 in excavation units 2N2W and 4N2W.

Description
If these pieces of cryptocrystalline stone were found on a precontact archaeological site, they would be classified as shatter, a by-product of stone tool manufacture.

Remarks
Gravels of the lower Yellowstone River bed and surrounding terraces are widely known among lapidaries as a source of gem-quality agate. While a collector can determine if a river cobble is an agate by examining its surface, the quality of the stone cannot be known until the interior is visible. Novice rock collectors sometimes break a cobble to see the interior, often diminishing the stone's value for cutting and polishing. Smashing an agate cobble can produce small pieces of shatter as well as larger pieces of the stone. The fragments from Feature D were probably produced by this kind of cobble testing.

Lignite

Provenience
Lignite was recovered from seven of nine levels and 10 of 18 excavation units. Most of this material was in the southern half of Feature D between 60 and 90 centimeters below datum. A lignite deposit in unit 3N2W was mixed with a dense layer of bone.

Description
The lignite is friable and occurs as relatively small pieces. Nothing in the appearance of the lignite or in the surrounding materials suggests that it was burned; there was no clinker or ash.

Remarks
Lignite occurs naturally in the region. A small seam of this low-grade coal outcrops about 100 feet south of Feature D in the bank of the Yellowstone River; it is stratigraphically below the feature. Lignite from this or any other local source would have to have been deposited in the feature by someone.

APPENDIX 10

Dog Remains

The skeletal remains of a domestic dog, *Canis familiaris*, were recovered from Feature D.[1]

Dog Skeleton

Provenience
Feature D levels 3, 4, and 5 in excavation units 2N2W, 3N2W, and 4N2W.

Description
The specimen is a nearly complete skeleton of a mature domestic dog, slightly smaller than an average-size modern male coyote.[2] Bone elements of the specimen most critical for locomotion are different than those of a coyote, suggesting that it was not built for speed like a coyote but was more muscular.[3] The exterior bone surfaces were in good condition, and an examination found no indication of pathologies. However, the second and third cervical vertebrae exhibit breakage by a sharp steel implement. This damage was caused by a minimum of three chops to the dog's neck. There is no evidence that the dog was skinned or butchered after death.[4]

Remarks
The dog's skull was represented only by eight fragments, which were refit to compose parts of the frontal, parietal, and occipital bones. Also missing was all but the ascending ramus of the right mandible.

APPENDIX 11

The Commissary Department Provision Book

The records of the Office of the Commissary General of Subsistence include "provision books" that document supplies on hand at the end of each month and when stores were transferred among commissary of subsistence officers.[1] These books applied to the entire U.S. Army and cover more than a single year. One such book includes a number of entries under titles that record subsistence data kept during the Sioux War of 1876–1877.[2] Entries under two of these titles identify stores on hand or transferred among Department of Dakota assistant commissary of subsistence officers from May 14, 1876, until General Terry closed his campaign on September 6.

The provision book is in a ledger format; it has preprinted columns with three rows of headings along the top. The headings begin with "Date" and proceed with commodities (pork, bacon, fresh beef, beef cattle, flour, etc.) across four separate pages. Each row of hand-entries made below the headings begins, left to right, with a date (month) followed by an amount under each commodity (pounds, ounces, number, weight, barrels, gallons, cans, bottles, jars) depending on the type of commodity. Nonfood items listed are forage for livestock (hay and corn), candles, oil, wicks, bluing, soap, and tobacco. The end column on the far right of the fourth page is a wide "Remarks" column.

The book lists commissary stores commonly supplied to troops. Basic rations provided to the enlisted ranks are included as well as other items that could be purchased at cost. Officers were required to buy all of their food. Enlisted men could supplement their issue ration with purchases of commissary stores.

Yellowstone Depot—Stanley's Crossing

The handwritten title for one section of the provision book is "Yellowstone Depot—Stanley's Crossing." As explained below, this section includes provisions on hand at two depots from mid-May through the end of July 1876, including the one at Powder River (Table A11.1).

General Terry's use of steamboats allowed him to move supplies to various locations on the Yellowstone River. His "Yellowstone Depot" was established successively above the mouth of Glendive Creek (May 14–June 13), at the Powder River confluence (June 6–July 20), and opposite Rosebud Creek (July 28–August 21).

183

TABLE A11.1. "Yellowstone Depot—Stanley's Crossing" Provision Book Entries

Commodity	May 1876	June 1876	July 1876
Pork	200 pounds	200 pounds	200 pounds
Bacon	2,708 pounds	42,699 pounds	4,197 pounds
Fresh Beef	378 pounds	378 pounds	No entry
Beef Cattle	7; 4,809 pounds	Check mark	No entry
Flour	No entry	85 barrels, 142 pounds	33 barrels, 108 pounds
Corn Meal	395 pounds	1,189 pounds	1,182 pounds
Hardbread	7,380 pounds	61,530 pounds	11,400 pounds
Beans	494 pounds	11,109 pounds	8,813 pounds
Peas	210 pounds	210 pounds	Check mark
Rice	223 pounds	218 pounds	172 pounds
Hominy	200 pounds	200 pounds	Check mark
Coffee, Green	785 pounds	5,513 pounds	1,461 pounds
Coffee, Roasted	No entry	No entry	No entry
Tea, Black Choice	No entry	71 pounds	69 pounds
Tea, Green Choice	60 pounds	56 pounds	38 pounds
Sugar	1,317 pounds	12,302 pounds	4,402 pounds
Vinegar	45 gallons	1,002 gallons	533 gallons
Candles	110 pounds	1,173 pounds	514 pounds
Soap	296 pounds	2,890 pounds	975 pounds
Salt	277 pounds	7,430 pounds	5,264 pounds
Pepper	48 pounds	249 pounds	131 pounds
Tobacco	406 pounds	1,771 pounds	3,217 pounds
Forage, Hay	No entry	No entry	No entry
Forage, Corn	1,536 pounds	192 pounds	Check mark
Acid, Citric	10 pounds	9 pounds	1 pound
All Spice	4 pounds	5 pounds	5 pounds
Apples, Dried	414 pounds	131 pounds	86 pounds
Asparagus	24 cans	71 cans	69 cans
Breakfast Bacon	No entry	151 pounds	48 pounds
Butter	160 pounds	485 pounds	325 pounds
Cheese, Edam	121 (number)	5 (number)	Check mark
Cheese, PA	No entry	12 (number)	2 (number)
Cinnamon	4 pounds	5 pounds	5 pounds
Clams	90 cans	81 cans	64 cans
Cloves	4 pounds	5 pounds	5 pounds
Coffee, Java	90 pounds	391 pounds	170 pounds

TABLE A11.1. (cont'd.) "Yellowstone Depot—Stanley's Crossing" Provision Book Entries

Commodity	May 1876	June 1876	July 1876
Green Corn	185 cans	121 cans	72 cans
Crackers, type 1?*	99 pounds	92 pounds	91 pounds
Crackers, type 2?*	12 paper boxes?	291 paper boxes?	176 paper boxes?
Lemon Extract	72 bottles	71 bottles	52 bottles
Family Flour	458 pounds	311 pounds	227 pounds
Ginger	No entry	2 pounds	2 pounds
Ham, Sugar Cured	152 pounds	1,349 pounds	886 pounds
Jam, Raspberry	96 cans	90 cans	47 cans
Jelly, Currant	118 cans	150 cans	97 cans
Lard	150 pounds	456 pounds	360 pounds
Lobster	No entry	115 cans	112 cans
Macaroni	22 pounds	47 pounds	47 pounds
Mackerel	29 pounds	16 pounds	Check mark
Milk	173 cans	326 cans	193 cans
Molasses	No entry	50 gallons	50 gallons
Mustard	17 pounds	19 pounds	17 pounds
Oil, Olive	No entry	11 bottles	11 bottles
Onions	120 cans	65 cans	48 cans
Oysters	42 cans	338 cans	292 cans
Peaches	276 cans	411 cans	192 cans
Pears	191 cans	186 cans	126 cans
Peas, Green, American	48 cans	192 cans	30 cans
Peas, Green, French	87 cans	358 cans	138 cans
Pepper, Red	2 pounds	4 pounds	4 pounds
Pickles, Fine, quart bottle	144 bottles	102 bottles	38 bottles
Pickles, pint bottle	No entry	21 bottles	Check mark
Pickles, bottles	No entry	96 bottles	19 bottles
Pineapples	No entry	48 cans	Check mark
Plums	139 cans	124 cans	49 cans
Potatoes	No entry	1,279 pounds	Check mark
Salmon	No entry	72 cans	16 cans
Salt, table	25 pounds	5 pounds	Check mark
Sardines, quarter	No entry	162 boxes	118 boxes
Sauce, Cranberry	No entry	24 cans	12 cans

TABLE A11.1. (cont'd.) "Yellowstone Depot—Stanley's Crossing" Provision Book Entries

Commodity	May 1876	June 1876	July 1876
Sauce, Worcestershire	24 bottles	19 bottles	9 bottles
Soap, Toilet	No entry	69 cakes	65 cakes
Soup, M J ?*	No entry	21 cans	6 cans
Soup, Tomato	No entry	24 cans	Check mark
Soup, ?*	No entry	24 cans	24 cans
Starch, Corn	No entry	39 pounds	38 pounds
Sugar, Cut Loaf	204 pounds	311 pounds	17 pounds
Sugar, Granulated	No entry	438 pounds	421 pounds
Syrup	25 gallons	25 gallons	15 gallons
Tomatoes	277 cans	557 cans	87 cans
Yeast Powder	39 cans	480 cans	384 cans
Cranberries ?*	24 cans	72 cans	7 cans
Baking Powder	97 pounds	73 pounds	62 pounds
P.A. (Prunes ?*)	No entry	91 cans	66 cans

* Some handwritten entries are difficult to decipher.

Supplies were again brought to the mouth of Powder River in late August as Terry and Crook struggled to continue their pursuit of the tribes. After Terry closed his campaign on September 6, supplies were moved from Powder River to the cantonment being built at Tongue River. At this time a cantonment was also constructed opposite the mouth of Glendive Creek to facilitate continued movement of supplies from Ft. Buford to the Tongue River post.[3]

Maj. Moore's 6th Infantry depot guard had supplies in place and waiting on the Yellowstone where the Dakota column was expected to arrive early in June. This first depot was on the right bank of the river and some distance west of the stockade where Col. Stanley located a depot for the 1873 railroad survey.[4] Moore referred to the new location as "Stanley's Crossing."[5] The Dakota column bypassed this depot, and Moore used steamboats to move freight from Stanley's Crossing to Powder River between June 5 and June 13. When this transfer was complete, the depot at Stanley's Crossing was not needed as long as river conditions allowed the steamers to reach Powder River.

As the title of this section of the provision book suggests, it documents supplies at the Stanley's Crossing depot. In the remarks column for the month of May line of entries is written, "Lt. B A Byrne 6th Inft Recd of D L Craft 6th Inft May 14th 1876." This line details the supplies transferred on May 14 from acting assistant commissary of subsistence (ACS) 2nd Lt. David Craft at Ft. Buford to 2nd Lt. Bernard Byrne, Co. C, 6th Infantry, ACS for Moore's battalion.[6]

The Commissary Department Provision Book 187

In the remarks column for the month of July line of entries is written, "Tfd to Lt. R E Thompson 6th Inft July 16th 1876." The "16th 1876" is crossed out, and what looks like a pencil entry placed to the right is "31st 1876." This line then documents the subsistence stores transferred to 2nd Lt. Richard Thompson, Co. K, 6th Infantry, ACS with Terry's headquarters command throughout the 1876 campaign.[7]

Moore's battalion left the Powder River depot in mid-July and was joined by the rest of Terry's command at the Rosebud confluence at the end of the month. Commissary stores for which Lt. Byrne was responsible were transported from Powder River to the Rosebud depot (Ft. Beans), where they were transferred to Lt. Thompson a few days before Terry's reorganized command marched up the Rosebud in pursuit of the tribes. Moore's 6th Infantry battalion depot guard was replaced by a single company of 17th Infantry under Capt. Louis Sanger, although 1st Lt. Frederick Thibaut, Co. D, 6th Infantry, assumed ACS duties at Ft. Beans. The rest of Moore's old depot guard joined Terry's command on the march that would lead them back to Powder River.[8]

While there is no section of the provision book titled "Powder River Depot," the evidence indicates that the Stanley's Crossing section includes stores transported to Powder River in June. Moore's battalion completed the transfer of commissary stores from Stanley's Crossing to Powder River on June 13, and this Glendive depot was abandoned. The Stanley's Crossing section of the book includes an entry for the end of June and the transfer to Lt. Thompson at the end of July. Lt. Byrne was ACS for Moore's battalion when it arrived at Powder River in June, and there is no indication of a transfer of stores until after the depot was moved to the Rosebud depot in July.[9] Therefore, June entries in the Stanley's Crossing section must document commissary stores at the Powder River depot at the end of that month for which Moore's ACS was responsible.

Further confusing the issue of associating the provision book with specific depots is the section titled "Depot Glendive Creek. M.T." Despite the title, this part documents supplies on hand at the Glendive Cantonment from September 1876 through April 1877. A note under the remarks indicates that Lt. William J. Campbell, 22nd Infantry, received the bulk of these stores from Capt. John F. Weston on August 30, 1876. Beginning in late August 1876, the Glendive Cantonment was garrisoned by four companies of 22nd Infantry and two companies of the 17th Infantry.[10] The November 1876 "Regimental Returns" for the 22nd Infantry note that 1st Lt. Campbell was with his company in camp near Glendive, where he was battalion acting assistant quartermaster and ACS.[11] Capt. Weston was a commissary of subsistence staff officer.[12] This section of the provision book is not connected to the earlier depot at Stanley's Crossing, where stores were managed by Moore's 6th Infantry.

Yellowstone Depot M.T.

One section of the provision book titled "Yellowstone Depot. M.T." has hand-entries for August and September 1876 (Table A11.2). "Lt. F. W. Thibaut 6th Inf. Recd. Stores Aug 4/76" is written in the remarks column for that month. As noted

TABLE A11.2. "Yellowstone Depot. M.T." Provision Book Entries, August 1876

Commodity	Amount	Commodity	Amount
Pork	600 pounds	Coffee, Java	399 pounds
Bacon	9,913 pounds	Green Corn	4 cans
F. Beef	No entry	Crackers, type 1	79 tins, 27 cartons
Beef Cattle	30; 14,712 pounds	Crackers, type 2	316 tins, 212 cartons
Flour	422 pounds		
Corn Meal	1,212 pounds	Cream of Tartar	11 pounds
Hardbread	68,720 pounds	Lemon Extract	167 bottles
Beans	7,181 pounds	Vanilla extract	64 bottles
Peas	No entry	Macaroni	37 pounds
Rice	96 pounds	Mackerel	1 unit?
Hominy	No entry	Milk	62 cans
Coffee, Green	1,132 pounds	Molasses	61 gallons
Coffee, Roasted	No entry	Mustard	5½ pounds
Tea, Black Choice	87 pounds	Oil, Olive	11 bottles
Tea, Black	71 pounds	Olives	20 bottles
Tea, Green	No entry	Onions	3 cans; 1,021 pounds
Sugar	2,862 pounds		
Vinegar	759 gallons	Oysters	189 cans
Candles	1,759 pounds	Peaches	No entry
Soap	3,090 pounds	Pears	No entry
Salt	6,129 pounds	Peas, Green, American	83 cans
Pepper	217 pounds		
Tobacco	3,008 pounds	Peas, Green, French	259 cans
Forage, Hay	No entry	Pepper, Red	No entry
Forage, Corn	No entry	Pickles, quart jars	38 jars
Acid, Acetic	No entry	Pickles, pint bottles	34 bottles
All Spice	No entry	Pineapples	41 cans
Apples, Dried	No entry	Plums	1 can
Asparagus	59 cans	Potatoes	5,010 pounds
Breakfast Bacon	No entry	Raisins	5 boxes
Butter	676 pounds	Salmon	No entry
Cheese, Edam	50 (number)	Salt, table	25 pounds
Cheese, PA	2 (number)	Sardines, quarter	69 boxes
Cinnamon	No entry	Sauce, Cranberry	43 cans
Clams	1 can	Sauce, Worcestershire	No entry
Cloves	No entry		

TABLE A11.2. (cont'd.) "Yellowstone Depot. M.T." Provision Book Entries, August 1876

Commodity	Amount	Commodity	Amount
Soap, Toilet	161 cakes	Beef, Corned	204 cans; 408 pounds
Soup, 1 type?	105 cans		
Starch, Corn	37 pounds	Beef, Roast	168 cans
Sugar, Cut Loaf	814 pounds	Beef Tongue	108 cans
Sugar, Granulated	1,091 pounds	Ginger	3 pounds
Syrup	9 gallons; 1 quart	Ham, Sugar Cured	204 pounds
Tomatoes	20 cans	Jam, Raspberry	No entry
Wheat, Cracked	48 pounds	Jelly, Currant	1 can
Yeast Powder	62 pounds	Lard	1,000 pounds
		Lobster	213 cans

above, Lt. Thibaut assumed ACS duties at the Rosebud depot, and this document notes the stores transferred to him. It also provides some continuity in tracking stores associated with the Yellowstone depot after Moore's command was replaced as depot guard by Capt. Sanger's company of 17th Infantry.

While there are no entries for any commodities on the September line, "Closed by transfer to various officers Sept. 6th 1876, being date of last receipt" is written here in red ink. No individuals are noted as having received the stores. The date is significant as it is a day after Gen. Terry closed the campaign and the focus of his supply officers turned to construction and provisioning of the cantonment at Tongue River. Indeed, one section of the provision book is titled "On Board Steamer—Cantonment on Tongue River M.T."

Conclusion

The "Yellowstone Depot—Stanley's Crossing" section of the provision book documents stores managed by Maj. Moore's depot guard at Stanley's Crossing and at Powder River. The June line of entries in the Stanley's Crossing provision book section are probably commissary stores on hand at the end of that month and are those most clearly associated with the Powder River depot. At a minimum, this section documents the foods issued to enlisted men and those available for purchase. The section titled "Yellowstone Depot. M.T." is most clearly associated with the Rosebud depot. However, some of these stores might have been taken back to Powder River to support the forces of Terry and Crook in the latter half of August 1876.

Notes

CHAPTER 1

1. The state of Montana owns 320 acres at the Powder River confluence, and the Department of Fish, Wildlife, and Parks held rights-of-way agreements with adjacent landowners to construct a new access road.
2. An archaeological "feature" is something created by human activity but which cannot be removed from an archaeological site; examples include house floors, fire hearths, and postholes. Estimating the rate of riverbank loss was difficult, and determining the width of the historic feature exposed in the bank would require test excavations. What was thought to be the grave of an army private was recorded in the vicinity in 1975.
3. The work was conducted under Glacier Park Company Letter Permit No. AR178. Glacier Park Company was the land management subsidiary of Burlington Northern, Inc.
4. Burlington Northern owned the parcel of land on which the archaeological feature was located; the parcel was initially part of the federal land grant given the Northern Pacific Railroad. "Feature D" is the arbitrary designation given this feature. The number 24PE271 was assigned by the Department of Anthropology, University of Montana.
5. Also located on Burlington Northern land, Feature F was shown to me by the lessee, Lester Jens. Much of the feature was covered with a thin layer of fine soil, but several upright sandstone slabs were clearly visible. Mr. Jens stated that these stones had been in place since he first moved to the area many years before and he believed they were grave markers. The stones had characteristics indicating that they had been exposed to very high temperatures, and lacking other markings, they seemed unlikely to be grave markers.
6. Douglas D. Scott, "Euro-American Archaeology," in *Archaeology on the Great Plains*, ed. W. Raymond Wood (Lawrence: University Press of Kansas, 1998), 498.
7. *New World Dictionary of the American Language*, 2nd ed., s.v. "logistics."
8. Paul A. Hutton, *Phil Sheridan and His Army* (Lincoln: University of Nebraska Press, 1985), 117.

9. Robert M. Utley, *Frontier Regulars: The United States Army and the Indian, 1866–1891* (Bloomington: Indiana University Press, 1977), 15–16.
10. Ibid. Infantry regiments had only one major.
11. Ibid., 16–17. Utley gives the company strength figures for 1881 as a typical year. He notes that the 7th Cavalry fought the battle at Little Bighorn with 15 of its 43 officers absent, including the colonel, two majors, and four captains.
12. Jeremy Agnew, *Life of a Soldier on the Western Frontier* (Missoula: Mountain Press, 2008), 85.
13. Utley, *Frontier Regulars*, 28, 31. Utley notes that almost half of colonels and lieutenant colonels and more than half of the brigadiers and majors were staff officers.
14. Agnew, *Life of a Solder on the Western Frontier*, 83–84; Utley, *Frontier Regulars*, 11–12.
15. U.S. War Department, Adjutant General's Office, *Official Army Register for January, 1876*, http://archive.org/details/officialarmyregi1876unit.
16. Erna Risch, *Quartermaster Support of the Army: A History of the Corps 1775–1939* (Washington, D.C.: Center of Military History, U.S. Army, 1989), 492.
17. Agnew, *Life of a Soldier on the Western Frontier*, 90; Risch, *Quartermaster Support of the Army*, 509, 511. Turnover among acting quartermaster and commissary officers was high.
18. Utley, *Frontier Regulars*, 31.
19. Agnew, *Life of a Soldier on the Western Frontier*, 124–126; "Report of the Commissary General of Subsistence," in U.S. War Department, *Report of the Secretary of War 1877* (Washington, D.C.: Government Printing Office, 1877), 341.
20. Risch, *Quartermaster Support of the Army*, 505–506.
21. Ibid.
22. Ibid., 492.
23. David M. Delo, *Peddlers and Post Traders: The Army Sutler on the Frontier* (Salt Lake City: University of Utah Press, 1992), 1–4.
24. Ibid., 152–164.
25. Risch, *Quartermaster Support of the Army*, 468–472.

Chapter 2

1. Mark H. Brown, *The Plainsmen of the Yellowstone: A History of the Yellowstone Basin* (New York: G. P. Putnam's Sons, 1961), 16–18.
2. Pierre Jean DeSmet, "From Fort Alexander to Fort Laramie," in *Exploring the Northern Plains, 1804–1876*, ed. Lloyd McFarling (Caldwell: Caxton Printers, 1955), 216.
3. Francois-Antoine Larocque, "Francois-Antoine Larocque's 'Yellowstone Journal,'" in *Early Fur Trade on the Northern Plains: Canadian Traders among the Mandan and Hidatsa Indians, 1738–1818*, ed. W. Raymond Wood and Thomas D. Thiessen (Norman: University of Oklahoma Press, 1985), 156–220.

4. Meriwether Lewis, *The Lewis and Clark Expedition*, 3 vols., 1814 ed., ed. Archibald Hanna and William H. Goetzmann (Philadelphia: J. B. Lippincott, 1961), 3:765.
5. Brown, *Plainsmen of the Yellowstone*, 111.
6. Fort Union was a trading post of the American Fur Company. Established in 1827, it was the primary American Fur Company post in the upper Missouri country, including the Yellowstone. Ft. Union was sold to the government, and its materials were used to construct the army post Ft. Buford in 1866.
7. John S. Gray, *Custer's Last Campaign: Mitch Boyer and the Little Bighorn Reconstructed* (Lincoln: University of Nebraska Press, 1991), 14–15. Mitch Boyer, a mixed-blood Sioux who scouted for the army in the 1876 Indian War, was one of Gore's guides in 1855.
8. W. F. Raynolds, *Report of the Exploration of the Yellowstone River* (Washington, D.C.: Government Printing Office, 1868). Raynolds was a captain in the Corps of Topographic Engineers. His mission was to explore the main tributaries of the Yellowstone and mountain sources of the Gallatin and Madison forks of the Missouri River. He was to gather information on topographic features, the navigability of streams, numbers and distribution of Indians, climate, and agricultural and mineral potential and to evaluate the potential for road and railroad development for future military or emigration needs.
9. Ibid., 8, 38. Raynolds states that the Powder River was named for the "sulphurous vapors rising from burning beds of lignite in its vicinity," but most sources agree with Larocque's source of the name (see note 3).
10. Robert M. Utley, "The Bozeman Trail before John Bozeman: A Busy Land," *Montana the Magazine of Western History* 53, no. 2 (2003): 20–31. Crow Indians controlled the land between Powder River and the upper Yellowstone long before it was recognized as their territory in the Ft. Laramie Treaty of 1851. In the years following the treaty, Sioux and Cheyenne tribes contested Crow control of the Powder River and lower Yellowstone country. The 1851 treaty identified no land in the lower Yellowstone and Powder River country as Sioux or Cheyenne territory.
11. Ibid., 29–31. With other trappers, Bridger spent the winter of 1829–1830 on the Powder River. He was very familiar with this country and led both the Gore and Raynolds parties over what later became known as part of the Bozeman Trail. Raynolds followed this trail from near the mouth of Bighorn Canyon to Crazy Woman Creek, a tributary of the Upper Powder. Beginning in 1863, a number of immigrant parties used the route as a short cut from the Platte River Road (Oregon Trail) to the gold fields of Montana Territory.
12. Raynolds, *Exploration of the Yellowstone River*, 145. "Left bank" refers to the left-hand bank of a stream when one is facing downriver or in the direction the stream is flowing. Most military personnel understood this way of designating a riverbank, but accounts by civilians indicate that they sometimes got it backward.

13. Ibid., 54.
14. In 1862, conflicts between woodland Sioux bands and white settlers in the upper Mississippi country erupted into full-scale war, with many farm families killed. The U.S. military response set off a chain reaction that spread quickly across the northern plains and beyond.
15. Louis Pfaller, *Father De Smet in Dakota* (Richardson, N.D.: Assumption Abby Press, 1962), 50–52.
16. Robert W. Larson, *Gall: Lakota War Chief* (Norman: University of Oklahoma Press, 2007), 45, 113. Warriors from the Hunkpapa band of Lakota Sioux in this conflict included Sitting Bull and Gall. They became prominent figures in subsequent conflicts with the U.S. Army and figured significantly in the 1876 Sioux War.
17. Robert M. Utley, *Frontiersmen in Blue: The United States Army and the Indian, 1848–1865* (Lincoln: University of Nebraska Press, 1967), 277–278. The village of 1,400 lodges that Sully attacked at Killdeer Mountain was larger than the one Custer encountered at the Little Bighorn in 1876. Indian accounts indicate that 31 of their people were killed at Killdeer Mountain.
18. John Barsness and William Dickinson, "Cannoneer's Hop: The Sully Campaign 1864," *Montana the Magazine of Western History* 16, no. 3 (1966): 25.
19. Utley, *Frontiersmen in Blue*, 261–280.
20. David E. Wagner, *Powder River Odyssey, Nelson Cole's Western Campaign of 1865: The Journals of Lyman G. Bennett and Other Eyewitness Accounts* (Norman: Arthur H. Clark Company, 2009), 248.
21. Utley, *Frontiersmen in Blue*, 308, 323–333.
22. Ibid.; LeRoy R. Hafen and Ann W. Hafen, *Powder River Campaigns and Sawyers Expedition of 1865* (Glendale, Calif.: Arthur H. Clark, 1961), 24–25, 40–41, 60–62, 92, 108–109.
23. Utley, "Bozeman Trail before John Bozeman," 23. Several tribes of Teton Lakota (Sioux) made up most of the population in the Powder River country. By 1863 they controlled former Crow territory between the Powder and Bighorn rivers and, with their Cheyenne and Arapaho allies, continued to pressure the Crow from the east.
24. Charles H. Springer, *Soldiering in Sioux Country: 1865*, ed. Benjamin F. Cooling III (San Diego: Frontier Heritage Press, 1971), 23, 47. Soldiers, guides, and teamsters were not the only people to accompany Cole's command. The column's 1st Lt. Charles Springer kept a diary in which he documented the presence of at least three African Americans who were officers' servants, one of them his. Springer also noted that the regimental surgeon was accompanied by his wife.
25. General Connor sent maps to his subordinate commanders showing the route each column was to take and the location of a rendezvous point on the Rosebud. Cole mentions in his expedition report that he had a map prepared by Lt. G. K. Warren as well. The map on which Connor sketched the column routes probably lacked a great deal of detail between the Yellowstone River

and the headwaters of its southern tributaries. Additional geographic information about this area gathered by the Raynolds expedition was not reported until 1866 or published until 1868. Raynolds's map included information supplied by his guide, Bridger.
26. Wagner, *Powder River Odyssey*, 142. Lyman Bennett noted that Cole's livestock had been without water or feed for 32 hours in very hot weather.
27. Springer, *Soldiering in Sioux Country*, 44. By September 1, many of Cole's men were tanning buckskin to make moccasins as their shoes wore out.
28. In orders to his subordinates, Gen. Connor noted that he would communicate with them by smoke signals if he decided to change the planned rendezvous. Col. Cole stated that he interpreted the smoke as indicating the location of an Indian village or Conner trying to communicate with him so he decided to move to the mouth of Powder River. At the very least, Cole hoped to find game in the Yellowstone valley to feed his command.
29. Wagner, *Powder River Odyssey*, 248: General Sully prophetically observed from his 1864 experience on the Little Missouri, "By the time you overtake them [the Indians] your animals are reduced for want of forage, your rations are run out, and you have to fall back. The only way to finish up these Indians is to establish depots of provisions at points in their country, and keep after them until you run them down."
30. Ibid., 28; Robert M. Utley, *Sitting Bull: The Life and Times of an American Patriot* (New York: Henry Holt and Company, 1993), 67–70.
31. George B. Grinnell, *The Fighting Cheyennes*, Civilization of the American Indian Series (Norman: University of Oklahoma, 1977), 214; Wagner, *Powder River Odyssey*, 246. Cheyenne accounts indicate that an elderly Lakota, Black Whetstone, was killed by artillery while sitting a half mile from the fight. Col. Cole estimated that 200 to 500 warriors were killed or wounded in the action on Powder River. Walker, on the other hand, wrote, "As to the number of Indians killed in our long fight with them I cannot say as we killed one" (Hafen and Hafen, *Powder River Campaigns*, 100). Wagner's review of all the evidence suggests that 25–50 Indians were killed.
32. David E. Wagner, *Patrick Connor's War: The 1865 Powder River Indian Expedition* (Norman: Arthur H. Clark Company, 2010), 37–38, 70–71, 263–264. In May Connor needed an additional 800 horses, and there was little forage available at Ft. Laramie. What grain trickled into the fort was consumed by the livestock already assembled. The supply problem was exacerbated when officers at other posts along the supply line confiscated grain from wagon trains taking supplies to Connor at Ft. Laramie. Livestock was also lost to Indian horse-stealing raids.
33. H. D. Hampton, "Powder River Indian Expedition of 1865," *Montana the Magazine of Western History* 14, no. 4 (1964): 6.
34. James A. Houston, *The Sinews of War: Army Logistics 1775–1953*, Army Historic Series, Office of the Chief of Military History, U.S. Army (Washington, D.C.: Government Printing Office, 1966), 261. The 130 wagons pressed into

service belonged to civilian businessman Alvin C. Leighton. Leighton's teamsters quit briefly when he refused to meet their demands for higher pay.
35. Hafen and Hafen, *Powder River Campaigns*, 108, 206.
36. A comment by Lt. Charles Springer when Cole's column reached Ft. Connor on September 19 suggests that Leighton began operating a sutler's store at the newly constructed fort: "The cherry brandy and cigars commenced circulating very freely" (*Soldiering in Sioux Country*, 61).
37. Wagner, *Patrick Connor's War*, 159–160.
38. Ibid., 150. In one incident, a man was shot through both thighs by someone in his own unit who was drunk.
39. Col. James H. Kidd in a letter from Ft. Connor commented on the arrival of a wagon train, "The Sutler's wagons loaded with goods to swindle any of us who find it necessary to submit to the process." He did not want to patronize the sutler, as he and another officer vowed not to drink alcohol for 10 years, but Kidd added, "ale excepted." Ibid., 103.
40. Hafen and Hafen, *Powder River Campaigns*, 96.
41. Ibid., 99.
42. Springer, *Soldiering in Sioux Country*. First Lt. Springer noted that, contrary to Cole's orders, he and others in his company hunted and fished extensively and with considerable success until the final days of the expedition on Powder River. Cole's expedition report states, "The route traveled…is destitute of wild game, hence no addition from this source could be made to husband the rations whilst they ran their natural course nor substituted for them when exhausted" (Hafen and Hafen, *Powder River Campaigns*, 88). Only when rations were critically short did Cole authorize hunting, but game might have been scarce in the Powder River valley because the tribes had camped in this vicinity for some time. Hunting parties were also subject to attack here.
43. Hafen and Hafen, *Powder River Campaigns*, 61.
44. Houston, *Sinews of War*, 215; Robert A. Murray, "Wagons on the Plains," *By Valor and Arms: The Journal of American Military History* 2, no. 4 (1976): 37–40.
45. Emmett M. Essin, "Army Mule," *Montana the Magazine of Western History* 44, no. 2 (1994): 34; Lawrence A. Frost, *Custer's 7th Cav and the Campaign of 1873* (El Segundo, Calif.: Upton and Sons, 1986), 103; Murray, "Wagons on the Plains," 38. These calculations are based on the six-mule wagon. The six-mule army wagon predates the Civil War and was the primary supply wagon though the late 1870s. There were several models developed, and the figures reported for net payload vary considerably. Some sources state that the payload on rough terrain was 1,800 to 2,500 pounds. Other sources report the payload as 2,000 or 4,000 pounds. One source indicates that a 5,400-pound payload was possible with good six-year-old stock. A diarist with Connor's expedition reported that a teamster was run over with a six-mule wagon weighing 4,000 pounds. Wagner, *Patrick Connor's War*, 81.
46. Utley, *Frontier Regulars*, 158–159. Supplying cavalry units with enough forage

continued to be a problem on the western plains. Army livestock could rarely subsist on grass alone for the length of a campaign. Grass was often depleted in many areas during late summer and inaccessible in winter. However, the army typically could not carry enough forage to avoid high mortality among horses and mules.

47. Hafen and Hafen, *Powder River Campaigns*, 37, 62. Connor instructed Cole to hire Pawnee guides if possible. Whoever he used for guides, Cole reported that they knew little of the country but were useful for finding routes for the train and camping grounds.
48. Brigham D. Madsen, *Glory Hunter: A Biography of Patrick Edward Connor* (Salt Lake City: University of Utah Press, 1990), 153.
49. Hampton, "Powder River Indian Expedition of 1865," 14. Although the Powder River Expedition failed to accomplish the army's goals, Gen. Connor was a hero among many western communities. Some citizens of Virginia City, Montana Territory, adopted a resolution expressing "sincere esteem and admiration for Brigadier General P. E. Connor" and dubbed his campaign "brilliant and successful" (ibid., 14–15).
50. Frank Rzeczkowski, "The Crow Indians and the Bozeman Trail," *Montana the Magazine of Western History* 49, no. 4 (1999): 32–34. Most of the Bozeman Trail crossed Crow territory as defined by the Treaty of 1851. Lakota Sioux tribes and the Cheyenne had usurped much of the Powder River country by the 1860s, cutting off Crow access to the Missouri River fur trade.
51. Utley, *Frontier Regulars*, 93–107.
52. Larson, *Gall*, 66–72; Utley, *Sitting Bull*, 81–82. At the time of Fr. DeSmet's visit, Sitting Bull had only recently returned from leading a number of attacks on military posts near the Canadian border and on the Missouri River, including Ft. Buford near the mouth of the Yellowstone. He was among the Lakota leaders most concerned with maintaining their traditional ways by stopping white settlement and incursions into important hunting territory. Gall attended the peace conference as head of a delegation of lesser chiefs.
53. Rzeczkowski, "Crow Indians and the Bozeman Trail," 45. The 38 million acres designated Crow territory in 1851 was reduced to eight million in the 1868 treaty. Their former territory in the Powder River country became part of the unceded hunting grounds accessible to the Sioux and Cheyenne. The east boundary of the Crow reservation was established between Sarpy Creek and the Rosebud River, but the Sioux controlled Crow lands east of the Bighorn River. Therefore, all of the lower Yellowstone and Powder River country was controlled by the Sioux and their allies.
54. Robert M. Utley, *Cavalier in Buckskin: George Armstrong Custer and the Western Military Frontier* (Norman: University of Oklahoma Press, 1988), 114.
55. Raynolds, *Exploration of the Yellowstone River*, 13.
56. Hutton, *Phil Sheridan and His Army*, 170. Citizens in the West saw railroads as a major factor in economic prosperity for their fledgling communities. The

editor of Bozeman's newspaper, the *Avant Courier*, published this comment on the issue of allowing the Northern Pacific to be built across Crow land on the upper Yellowstone: "We deprecate any policy towards Indians which deprives the whites of any rights, or that retards the progress of civilization" (Brown, *Plainsmen of the Yellowstone*, 196).

57. Roy Morris Jr., *Sheridan: The Life and Wars of General Phil Sheridan* (New York: Crown Publishers, 1992), 348.
58. M. John Lubetkin, "The Forgotten Yellowstone Surveying Expeditions of 1871: W. Milnor Roberts and the Northern Pacific Railroad in Montana," *Montana the Magazine of Western History* 52, no. 4 (2002): 38, 44–45. Mitch Boyer was among the guides with the army escort. With Jim Bridger, he was also one of George Gore's guides on the extravagant hunt of 1854–1855.
59. Francis B. Robertson, "We Are Going to Have a Big Sioux War: Colonel David S. Stanley's Yellowstone Expedition, 1872," *Montana the Magazine of Western History* 34, no. 4 (1984): 11.
60. Jack Coggins, *Arms and Equipment of the Civil War* (New York: Fairfax Press, 1983), 61–66. The 12-pounder Napoleon gun was a smoothbore, muzzle-loading field artillery piece commonly used in the Civil War. It fired explosive shells and cases, including canisters full of musket balls or shot. It could deliver a 12-pound projectile up to 2,000 feet.
61. Larson, *Gall*, 83–85.
62. M. John Lubetkin, "'No Fighting Is to Be Apprehended': Major Eugene M. Baker, Sitting Bull, and the Northern Pacific Railroad's 1872 Western Yellowstone Surveying Expedition," *Montana the Magazine of Western History* 56, no. 2 (2006): 28–41. Having progressed from Ft. Ellis, located near Bozeman, to the Yellowstone River just east of present-day Billings, Montana, the western party was attacked by Lakota and Arapaho warriors with a loss of two killed and two wounded. The party cut short its eastward advance down the Yellowstone in favor of returning to Ft. Ellis and Ft. Shaw via the Musselshell River.
63. Larson, *Gall*, 83–86. The engineers surveyed several additional areas on their return trip. Before this work was complete, Stanley had lost two officers and his black servant to Lakota attacks on small parties that ventured from the main body of troops. One of the fallen officers was a cousin of President Grant's wife, Julia.
64. Lubetkin, "No Fighting Is to Be Apprehended," 31. The Hunkpapa and other Lakota tribes were well aware of the railroad surveys and clearly understood the consequences of railroad development for their way of life. In April 1872, Sitting Bull sent Spotted Eagle, a Sans Arc Lakota, to Ft. Sully with a message for Col. Stanley that he and his followers "would tear up the road and kill its builders" (ibid.).
65. Hutton, *Phil Sheridan and His Army*, 171. For several years, most operations within Sheridan's Division of the Missouri were related to supporting Northern Pacific Railroad survey and construction plans. Sheridan used railroad

planning reports from Northern Pacific officials to plan new army posts, adjust troop placement, and request funding for his division. Because military resources were typically inadequate at this time, support for the Northern Pacific was accomplished to the detriment of other obligations.

66. Houston, *Sinews of War*, 253. Army administrative boundaries at this time followed a pattern that had evolved during the Civil War. Reorganized in 1865, the United States was divided into 19 departments distributed among five military divisions. The boundaries and organization of the Department of Dakota were specifically arranged to support railroad development.
67. Hutton, *Phil Sheridan and His Army*, 172. Like General Terry, Lt. Col. Custer and his regiment had just left reconstruction duty in the South. Custer gained experience in Indian warfare on the southern plains in 1868–1869 and was highly regarded by Sheridan, under whom Custer served during the Civil War. The lieutenant colonel shared the view of his superiors regarding the military importance of railroads: "No one measure so quickly and effectively frees a country from the horrors and devastation of Indians Wars and Indian depredations generally, as the building of a railroad through the region overrun" (Utley, *Cavalier in Buckskin*, 111).
68. Joseph M. Hanson, *The Conquest of the Missouri: Being the Story of the Life and Exploits of Captain Grant Marsh* (New York: Murray Hill, 1946), 150–167. Expedition planners scheduled a May 1873 reconnaissance of the lower Yellowstone River. One of Sheridan's aides, Major George Forsyth, led the reconnaissance on the Coulson Packet Company's *Key West* commanded by Grant Marsh. The reconnaissance turned about at Wolf Rapids, about two miles below the mouth of the Powder River. Forsyth reported the Yellowstone navigable beyond the Powder.
69. Frost, *Custer's 7th Cav and the Campaign of 1873*, 26; Hutton, *Phil Sheridan and His Army*, 172. The 1873 survey was estimated to have cost the Northern Pacific less than $5,000, including payroll, rations, and forage. Cost to the United States for the military escort was estimated at $769,000 (about $13.6 million in 2009 dollars). Hutton argues that this expenditure was a government subsidy for the railroad.
70. Brown, *Plainsmen of the Yellowstone*, 203–204; Hutton, *Phil Sheridan and His Army*, 49–55, 171–172. Some of the civilians were along for the adventure. They hunted with officers and engaged in other amusements such as running game with dogs; Custer and other officers had dogs specifically for this purpose. Col. Stanley's 22nd Infantry had a regimental pack of hunting dogs.
71. Hutton, *Phil Sheridan and His Army*, 172. To meet the overland transportation needs of the expedition, Sheridan's division headquarters staff purchased 150 new wagons in Philadelphia and 900 mules in St. Louis. Two steamboats were contracted to supply river transport.
72. David S. Stanley, *Report of the Yellowstone Expedition of 1873* (Washington, D.C.: Government Printing Office, 1874), 1–2.

73. The location of this depot later became known as "Stanley's Stockade" or "Stanley's Crossing."
74. Ibid., 5. The expedition was north of the Yellowstone opposite the mouth of Powder River when it passed the confluence of these two streams. At no time did the command pass directly through or occupy what would become the Powder River depot in 1876.
75. Frost, *Custer's 7th Cav and the Campaign of 1873*, 64. Captain William Ludlow, Corps of Engineers, delivered supplies to Stanley when conducting yet another reconnaissance of the Yellowstone River. He completed a map of the Yellowstone from the Powder River confluence to the Missouri dated December 19, 1873.
76. Ibid., 49, 77. After the skirmish at the mouth of Tongue River, troops found the bodies of the veterinarian and a sutler who had wandered away from the command in search of water. The sutler, Augustus Baliran, served in the Confederacy and was a trader with the 7th Cavalry after the Civil War. Early in the expedition, Stanley ordered Baliran's barrels of whiskey destroyed but later relented.
77. Marguerite Merrington, *The Custer Story: The Life and Intimate Letters of General George A. Custer and His Wife Elizabeth*, Bison Book reprint (Lincoln: University of Nebraska Press, 1987), 260.
78. Ibid., 262.
79. Frost, *Custer's 7th Cav and the Campaign of 1873*, 98–101.
80. Stanley, *Report of the Yellowstone Expedition of 1873*, 15.
81. Ibid. Perhaps Stanley was the officer Custer was referring to as having grossly miscalculated the amount of forage and supplies needed for the expedition. Without reference to his subordinate, Stanley's detailed report on problems with young mules and inadequate forage addressed Custer's criticisms.
82. Ibid., 8, 16.
83. U.S. War Department, Army Corps of Engineers, *Report upon United States Geographical Surveys West of the One Hundredth Meridian* (Washington, D.C.: Government Printing Office, 1889), 641, http://books.google.com/books?id=jfIgAQAAMAAJ&pg=PA601&lpg=PA601&dq=corps+of+engineers+map+of+Yellowstone+River+1873&source=bl&ots=5Smg3bDQMq&sig=yQzA9VVbDoAsKmx24lTpDZrmWs8&hl=en&sa=X&ei=5FnyUtXeLsHloATOhoG4CA&ved=0CCYQ6AEwAA#v=onepage&q=corps%20of%20engineers%20map%20of%20Yellowstone%20River%201873&f=false.
84. Lubetkin, "No Fighting Is to Be Apprehended," 41.
85. E. S. Topping, *The Chronicles of the Yellowstone*, reprint, introduction, notes, and bibliography by Robert A. Murray (Minneapolis: Ross and Haines, 1968), 104.
86. Don L. Weibert, *The 1874 Invasion of Montana: A Prelude to the Custer Disaster* (Billings: self-published, Benchmark Printers, 1993), 22. Vernon's group likely joined the larger Yellowstone Wagon Road and Prospecting Expedition at

Canyon Creek a few miles west of where Billings is now located, on the north side of the Yellowstone. The smooth talker and a companion stole away from the expedition before Vernon was confirmed to have lied about finding gold.

87. Brown, *Plainsmen of the Yellowstone*, 129–131. The 1874 expedition was not the first prospecting company to venture into the lower Yellowstone country. Eleven years earlier a small party under James Stuart traveled from the southwestern section of what would soon become Montana Territory to the Yellowstone valley. At the mouth of the Bighorn, they surveyed a townsite and established claims to some of the surrounding land. Attacked by Crow warriors in the Bighorn valley, several prospectors were killed, and the survivors retreated south to the Oregon Trail.

88. Weibert, *1874 Invasion of Montana*, 129–134. Territorial Governor Potts strongly supported development of the Northern Pacific as well as the removal of all perceived obstacles to the economic prosperity of the territory. Chief among these obstacles were the Crow reservation and the unceded hunting grounds south of the Yellowstone.

89. Ibid., 11, 25, 35, 47.

90. Ibid., 90–98. Sitting Bull and other leaders convinced their warriors to abandon the fight with the wagon road expedition.

91. Utley, "Bozeman Trail before John Bozeman," 23. The expedition entered the Crow reservation soon after it left the Rosebud valley, but Lakota tribes effectively controlled that part of the Crow reservation east of the Bighorn River.

92. Addison Quivey, "The Yellowstone Expedition of 1874," *Contributions to the Historical Society of Montana* 1 (1876): 281.

93. Weibert, *1874 Invasion of Montana*, 173–178. Weibert's catalog of artifacts recorded at Yellowstone Wagon Road and Prospecting Expedition sites identifies both expedition and Indian positions. His catalog suggests that most expedition men were armed with single-shot breech-loading .50/70-caliber rifles, while many warriors carried Spencer, Henry, or Winchester repeating rifles. An expedition participant noted from cartridge cases found in 1874 that many tribesmen had Spencer and Winchester repeaters as well as breech-loading rifles. Many carried bows and arrows in addition to firearms. The breechloaders were effective at long range, but the Lakota repeaters offered considerable close-range firepower. These warriors were much better armed than those who attacked the Powder River Expedition in 1865 primarily with bows and arrows.

94. Ibid., 54, 62–63, 85–86, 109–110. The reconnaissance confirmed that the upper Rosebud terrain was too rugged for the wagons and cannons. Expedition livestock did no grazing at all between April 12 and April 15. The party abandoned a number of sick horses before they arrived at the site of Ft. C. F. Smith on the Bighorn River, and participants reported 20 to 25 head killed by Indians. A special correspondent writing from Pryor's Gap on April 26 reported that diseased horses were still dying. Both sides in this conflict were well aware that

the expedition's survival depended on keeping its horses healthy and protecting them from being stolen or shot by warriors.
95. Ibid., 122.
96. Kim A. Scott, *Splendid on a Large Scale—The Writings of Hans Peter Gyllembourg Koch Montana Territory 1869–1974* (Helena: Bedrock Editions and Drumlummon Institute, 2010), 310. Peter Koch noted in a May 1874 letter from Bozeman to his fiancé, "The Yellowstone Expedition you have read about in the papers has proved a failure; it is now on its way back, driven in by the Indians." While Koch was not with the expedition, he was probably involved in its planning. As an experienced surveyor, he was to plat the new town established at the head of navigation on the Yellowstone River.
97. James H. Bradley, "Yellowstone Expedition of 1874," *Contributions to the Historical Society of Montana* 8 (1917): 116. Lt. Bradley states in his manuscript of interviews with expedition participants (published posthumously), "Bad weather and roads and meager grazing combined to weaken their animals and retard their progress. Several days in consequence of storm or fog, they were unable to move at all, and many began to entertain apprehension that unless they return soon their animals would be in such condition that they could not return at all."
98. Scott, *Splendid on a Large Scale*, 148. In an 1871 letter, Peter Koch echoed the view of many Gallatin valley denizens when he wrote, "You have probably read in the papers about the recent Indian raid into the Gallatin valley. It shows how little fitter the soldiers are to protect the settlers and as long as our government continues their present Indian policy, we may look for trouble on our Eastern frontier. If they could only once learn that it takes citizens, not soldiers to fight Indians, they might be taught a lesson in one season they would not forget for years to come."
99. Brown, *Plainsmen of the Yellowstone*, 218.
100. Peter Koch, "Historical Sketch: Bozeman, Gallatin Valley and Bozeman Pass," *Contributions to the Historical Society of Montana* 2 (1896): 135–137.
101. Utley, *Cavalier in Buckskin*, 133. General Terry correctly asserted that conducting military business on the Great Sioux Reservation was within the scope of the 1868 Laramie Treaty.
102. Larson, *Gall*, 93–95, 98–101.

Chapter 3

1. Hutton, *Phil Sheridan and His Army*, 166–167. Lt. Col. James W. Forsyth, with the president's brother Lt. Col. F. D. Grant, completed a reconnaissance of the Yellowstone on the Coulson steamboat *Josephine* in May and June 1875. Boat captain Grant March navigated to the future site of Billings, where low water and the swift current precluded further progress. This reconnaissance established the mouth of the Bighorn River as the head of navigation on the Yellowstone.

2. John S. Gray, *Centennial Campaign: The Sioux War of 1876* (Fort Collins: Old Army Press, 1976), 19.
3. Clark C. Spence, *Montana: A Bicentennial History* (New York: W. W. Norton and Company, 1978), 61.
4. Gray, *Centennial Campaign*, 40–41; Gray, *Custer's Last Campaign*, 117–118, 125–127.
5. Weibert, *1874 Invasion of Montana*, 124, 169. At least 13 men involved in the Yellowstone Wagon Road and Prospecting Expedition were connected to the Ft. Pease venture in some way. Of the three men who organized Ft. Pease, only Paul W. McCormick may have been involved in the 1874 event.
6. Utley, *Cavalier in Buckskin*, 145.
7. Hutton, *Phil Sheridan and His Army*, 299.
8. Gray, *Centennial Campaign*, 28. Watkins had Civil War connections to both Sheridan and Crook.
9. Utley, *Cavalier in Buckskin*, 146.
10. Roger Darling, *A Sad and Terrible Blunder, Generals Terry and Custer at the Little Big Horn: New Discoveries* (Vienna, Va.: Potomac-Western, 1990), 34. The version of Raynolds's map that General Terry would use in the 1876 Sioux War showed almost all of the major streams in his area of operations but did not provide much detail about topography.
11. Hutton, *Phil Sheridan and His Army*, 301.
12. Edgar I. Stewart, *Penny-an-Acre Empire in the West* (Norman: University of Oklahoma Press, 1968), 38. General Sheridan's stated ignorance of the climate and travel conditions on the northern plains is surprising. As commander of the Division of the Missouri since 1869, he was familiar with numerous military actions here as well as the railroad surveys. He was almost certainly aware of a debate between Custer and Col. William Hazen, commander at Ft. Buford, and others regarding the suitability of railroad grant land for homesteading on the northern plains. Hazen claimed that the land was unsuitable for agriculture and not worth a penny an acre. Custer supported the Northern Pacific's view that the land would sustain bumper crops forever. The debate began in 1874 and was carried by major newspapers as well as the *Army and Navy Journal*. Hazen often mentioned climate, including severe winter conditions in western Dakota Territory.
13. Ronald V. Rockwell, *The U.S. Army in Frontier Montana* (Helena: Sweetgrass Books, 2009), 288.
14. Gray, *Centennial Campaign*, 37.
15. Gerald M. Adams, *The Post near Cheyenne: A History of Fort D. A. Russell, 1867–1930* (Boulder: Pruett Publishing, 1989), 57; J. W. Vaughn, *The Reynolds Campaign on Powder River* (Norman: University of Oklahoma Press, 1961), 15, 18. The new bridge across the North Platte also facilitated travel for those seeking their fortune in the Black Hills. The first passenger coach launched by the Cheyenne and Black Hills Stage line left Cheyenne on February 3, 1876,

for the bustling new mining town Custer City. At this time, Cheyenne was so crowded with people bound for the Black Hills that the army had difficulty finding enough transportation.
16. Vaughn, *Reynolds Campaign on Powder River*, 15.
17. Robert A. Murray, *The Army Moves West: Supplying the Western Indian Wars Campaigns* (Fort Collins: Old Army Press, 1981), 17.
18. Vaughn, *Reynolds Campaign on Powder River*, 50. Crook had successfully used pack trains when pursuing Indians on the Pacific coast and in Arizona. When transferred to the Department of the Platte, he sent the mules to a facility near Cheyenne Depot. These professionally trained and managed mules could carry 250 pounds and cover 25 miles a day. During seasons when grass was available, the mules could maintain pace without carrying forage.
19. Jerome A. Greene, "A Battle among Skirmishes," in *Legacy: New Perspectives on the Battle of the Little Bighorn*, ed. Charles E. Rankin (Helena: Montana Historical Society Press, 1996), 85. This was primarily a Northern Cheyenne village under Old Bear.
20. Utley, *Frontier Regulars*, 251; Utley, *Sitting Bull*, 129–130. The Cheyenne and Lakota village included about 210 fighting men among a total 735 residents. Indian losses were two warriors killed and several wounded. Reynolds lost four killed and six wounded; the bodies of two soldiers were left on the battlefield.
21. Vaughn, *Reynolds Campaign on Powder River*, 157–158.
22. Utley, *Frontier Regulars*, 251.
23. Hutton, *Phil Sheridan and His Army*, 303.
24. Utley, *Sitting Bull*, 129–133.
25. Gray, *Custer's Last Campaign*, 125–127.
26. James H. Bradley, "Journal of James H. Bradley: The Sioux Campaign of 1876 under the Command of General John Gibbon," *Contributions to the Historical Society of Montana* 2 (1896): 164.
27. Gray, *Custer's Last Campaign*, 145. The column's initial transportation contractor was replaced in May by an E. G. Maclay and Co. train "consisting of fourteen teams and twenty-eight wagons, *viz*: 'Diamond R'—twelve teams; twenty-four wagons, ninety-seven mules and five horses; sub-train—two teams, four wagons and twenty mules" (Matthew Carroll, "Diary of Matthew Carroll: Master in Charge of Transportation for Colonel John Gibbon's Expedition against the Sioux Indians, 1876," *Contributions to the Historical Society of Montana* 2 [1896]: 229).
28. Bradley, "Journal of James H. Bradley," 157. The soldiers at Ft. Ellis were well aware of good fishing on the Yellowstone. When working for the post sutler in the winter of 1871, Peter Koch noted that wagonloads of frozen Yellowstone trout were brought to the post. Scott, *Splendid on a Large Scale*, 123.
29. Gray, *Custer's Last Campaign*, 148.
30. George A. Schneider, ed., *The Freeman Journal: The Infantry Campaign of 1876* (San Rafael: Presidio Press, 1977), 69. McCormick apparently sought and got

Gibbon's approval to act as a freelance trader for the column. He made two, possibly three, trips with goods in May and one on July 18. In the July instance, he was accompanied by Mr. W. Cutter, post trader at Ft. Ellis since 1871. In his diary entry of July 21, Lt. William English noted that he paid a subsistence bill, probably to the commissary, and McCormick's bill. The fact that McCormick allowed officers to charge goods on account suggests that he was indeed authorized to trade with the column. Mr. Cutter's presence suggests that McCormick might also have formed a business relationship with the post trader. McCormick's entry in Sanders's history volume indicates that he joined the campaign as a trader after the Ft. Pease affair. William L. English, "With Gibbon against the Sioux in 1876: The Field Diary of Lt. William L. English," ed. with notes and intro. by Barry C. Johnson, *English Westerners' Brand Book* 9, no. 1 (1966): 7; Helen F. Sanders, *A History of Montana* (Chicago: Lewis Publishing Company, 1913), 2:986.

31. Holmes O. Paulding, "Dr. Paulding and His Remarkable Diary," notes and intro. by Barry C. Johnson, in *Sidelights of the Sioux Wars*, ed. Francis B. Taunton, Special Publication 2 (London: English Westerners' Society, 1967), 53, 56.
32. Gray, *Custer's Last Campaign*, 16–18.
33. Weibert, *1874 Invasion of Montana*, 135–144. Veterans of the 1874 wagon road and prospecting expedition and Ft. Pease hired to serve as scouts and couriers for the Montana column or other parts of Terry's command included George Herendeen, Muggins Taylor, Henry Bostwick, Zed Daniels, and John W. Williamson.
34. Gray, *Custer's Last Campaign*, 153–154.
35. Murray, *Army Moves West*, 5.
36. Lisle G. Brown, "The Yellowstone Supply Depot," *North Dakota History* 40, no. 1 (1973): 24.
37. Ibid., 25–26. Later in the campaign, the army contracted for additional steamboats: the *Carroll*, the *E. H. Durfee*, the *Yellowstone*, the *Silver Lake*, and the *Benton*.
38. Gray, *Centennial Campaign*, 102, 104. Moore's depot is also often simply referenced as the "Glendive depot," not to be confused with the "Glendive Cantonment" later constructed in this vicinity but on the left bank of the Yellowstone.
39. Delo, *Peddlers and Post Traders*, 156–164; John S. Gray, "Sutler on Custer's Last Campaign," *North Dakota History: Journal of the Northern Plains* 43, no. 3 (1976): 15–16. As General Sheridan launched the 1876 campaign, Secretary of War William Belknap was under investigation for corruption in the appointment of post traders. Custer was subpoenaed to testify at the Belknap proceedings in March and April as Terry was struggling to get his column in the field. Displeased with the lieutenant colonel's testimony, the president removed Custer as commander of the Dakota column.

40. Gray, "Sutler on Custer's Last Campaign," 17; Ben Innis, "Bottoms Up! The Smith and Leighton Yellowstone Store Ledger of 1876," *North Dakota History: Journal of the Northern Plains* 51, no. 3 (1984): 25–26. Alvin Leighton traded in the West for many years; he was the sutler with General Patrick Conner's Powder River Expedition in 1865 and set up shop at Ft. Conner (Reno) and other Bozeman Trail posts. John Smith was his partner in this trade, and they maintained business relationships after the partnership ended. Alvin, his brothers, and his brother-in-law established the Leighton and Jordan firm, acquiring the post trader position at Ft. Buford through one of Secretary Belknap's influence men. Alvin and his brothers had other interests in the region, including the Indian trade at Ft. Peck, an upper Missouri trading post.
41. James Willert, *Little Big Horn Diary: Chronicle of the 1876 Indian War* (La Mirada: James Willert Publisher, 1982), 85.
42. Ibid., 100.
43. Brown, "Yellowstone Supply Depot," 26; Gray, *Centennial Campaign*, 104–105.
44. Richard G. Hardorff, "Packs, Packers, and Pack Details: Logistics and Custer's Pack Train," in *Custer and His Times: Bk. 3*, ed. Gregory J. W. Urwin and Roberta E. Fagan (Conway: University of Central Arkansas Press, 1987), 227. An estimated 66 mules with Reno's wing were at least somewhat trained for packing. The rest of the mules taken from wagon service had no training as pack animals.
45. Thomas M. Heski, "Camp Powell: The Powder River Supply Depot," *Research and Review: The Journal of the Little Big Horn Associates* 17, no. 1 (2003): 19; Fredrick C. Wagner III, *Participants in the Battle of the Little Big Horn: A Biographical Dictionary of Sioux, Cheyenne and United States Military Personnel* (Jefferson, N.C.: McFarland and Company, 2011), 209.
46. John G. Bourke, *On the Border with Crook* (Lincoln: University of Nebraska Press, 1972), 302–303; Utley, *Frontier Regulars*, 253.
47. Utley, *Sitting Bull*, 139–142. Crook's losses totaled nine killed and 23 wounded. His command expended thousands of rounds of ammunition in the battle, his wounded needed care, and remaining supplies were limited. These were among the factors that led Crook to withdraw rather than pursue the tribes.
48. Gray, *Centennial Campaign*, 321–334.
49. Gray, *Custer's Last Campaign*, 200–203.
50. Gray, *Centennial Campaign*, 140.
51. John S. Gray, "The Pack Train on George A. Custer's Last Campaign," *Nebraska History* 57, no. 1 (1976): 61–62; Hardorff, "Packs, Packers, and Pack Details," 232; Willert, *Little Big Horn Diary*, 204. The pack train is estimated to have included 85 regular pack mules and 90 wagon mules. Twelve mules were assigned to each company to transport rations, mess gear, and company equipment, while the remaining animals carried equipment and supplies for a headquarters detachment, medical staff, and civilian employees. The train has been calculated to have hauled 97 boxes of hardbread, 1,462 pounds of sugar,

975 pounds of coffee, and 5,823 pounds of bacon carried in sacks on 93 mules. Twelve mules were dedicated to carrying the extra ammunition. Douglas D. Scott, ed., *Papers on Little Bighorn Battlefield Archeology: The Equipment Dump, Marker 7, and the Reno Crossing*, Reprints in Anthropology 42 (Lincoln: J&L Reprint Co., 1991), 101–102.

52. In spite of his command's problems with the pack train, Custer noted in a letter to his wife from the mouth of the Rosebud on June 21, "I like campaigning with pack-mules much better than wagons, leaving out the question of luxuries" (Elizabeth B. Custer, *"Boots and Saddles" or Life in Dakota with General Custer* [Norman: University of Oklahoma Press, 1961], 275).

53. Agnew, *Life of a Soldier on the Western Frontier*, 149; Custer, *"Boots and Saddles,"* 275. While livestock was sometimes pushed too hard or even eaten to sustain a field campaign, officers and enlisted men alike understood the importance of caring for cavalry mounts as well as pack and wagon mules. Individual troopers were responsible for the health and fitness of their horses. Punishment was swift for anyone who did not feed or water his mount on schedule or did not properly care for the horse's hooves and back.

54. Willert, *Little Big Horn Diary*, 211.

55. Wagner, *Participants in the Battle of the Little Big Horn*, 5.

56. Gregory F. Michno, *Lakota Noon: The Indian Narrative of Custer's Defeat* (Missoula: Mountain Press, 1997), 9–20. Estimates of the size of the village and number of warriors at Little Bighorn vary greatly. Several authors have the number of lodges at about 1,000 and the number of warriors at 2,000. Others argue that there may have been 1,000 or fewer warriors in the counterattack. Whatever the true figures, this was a large village but probably smaller than the one Sully attacked at Killdeer Mountain in 1864.

57. Richard A. Fox Jr., "West River History: The Indian Village on Little Bighorn River, June 25–26, 1876," in *Legacy: New Perspectives on the Battle of the Little Bighorn*, ed. Charles E. Rankin (Helena: Montana Historical Society Press, 1996), 144–145. Fox uses Indian accounts of the battle to argue effectively that the village extended north only to the vicinity opposite Medicine Tail Coulee. This is the point where part of Custer's command initially descended from the east ridge, apparently to cross the stream and attack. While the village is often described as extending three miles along the river, Fox's evidence strongly suggests that it was one and a half, and certainly no more than two, miles long.

58. Gray, *Centennial Campaign*, 179.

59. Hardorff, "Packs, Packers, and Pack Details," 234; Thomas B. Marquis, *Wooden Leg: A Warrior Who Fought Custer*, Bison Book reprint (Lincoln: University of Nebraska Press, n.d.), 262–263. The pack train mules did not fare well during the siege of Reno Hill. Soldiers killed some animals to bolster makeshift defensive works. Surviving mules were without water until the evening of July 26. Ten days after the battle, 50 of the 175 mules were reported fit for service; the rest were dead or crippled. Marquis notes that the Cheyenne

Wooden Leg recalled that some Sioux caught a mule that had wandered away from the Reno–Benteen defensive site. The tribesmen removed packs of cartridges from the animal and turned the stubborn mule loose.
60. Utley, *Sitting Bull*, 160–161.
61. Ibid., 162.
62. Weibert, *1874 Invasion of Montana*, 140. Custer's scout and courier George Herendeen had traveled in the area between the Rosebud and Bighorn River with the Yellowstone Wagon Road and Prospecting Expedition two years earlier. About five miles from the Little Bighorn, Herendeen, Mitch Boyer, and other scouts reported evidence that suggested the tribes were running from the valley, reinforcing Custer's belief that his command had been discovered and his decision to strike at once.
63. Hanson, *Conquest of the Missouri*, 53–54, 301–306. Grant Marsh made his first trip to the upper Missouri as mate on the *Marcella*, one of the steamboats serving Sully's campaign of 1864. Marsh became the best-known boat captain on the upper Missouri and Yellowstone, where he served for many years.
64. Gray, *Centennial Campaign*, 212.
65. Ibid., 208–220. Terry planned to consolidate his forces at the mouth of the Bighorn and move up that stream. Leaving his wagon train at the foot of the mountains, he would then pursue the tribes with Crook's command. Falling water levels precluded navigation to the Bighorn River, leading Terry to change his base camp location east to the mouth of Rosebud Creek.
66. Gray, "Sutler on Custer's Last Campaign," 20.
67. Brown, "Yellowstone Supply Depot," 29–30.
68. Gray, *Centennial Campaign*, 214–215; Utley, *Frontier Regulars*, 269.
69. Schneider, *Freeman Journal*, 73.
70. Hutton, *Phil Sheridan and His Army*, 320–321.
71. Michael D. Hill and Ben Innis, "The Fort Buford Diary of Private Sanford, 1876–1877," *North Dakota History: Journal of the Northern Plains* 52, no. 3 (1985): 19. Private Wilmot Sanford, Co. D, 6th Infantry, with Terry's command noted that there were 16 pack mules for each infantry company. The men carried only a blanket and four days' rations, with another 13 days' rations on the train. Tents and shelter halves were taken back to Ft. Beans. Lt. Edward Godfrey, commanding Co. K, 7th Cavalry, stated that his company was "ordered to take 15 days rations on 8 pack mules, no cooking utensils, no officers' baggage except what they carry on their private horses" (Edward S. Godfrey, *The Field Diary of Lt. Edward Settle Godfrey, Commanding Co. K, 7th Cavalry Regiment under Lt. Colonel George Armstrong Custer in the Sioux Encounter at the Battle of the Little Big Horn*, ed. with notes by Edgar I. Stewart and Jane R. Stewart [Portland, Ore.: Champoeg, 1957], 34). Each man had one overcoat and blanket. Godfrey also took a comforter and shelter tent on a horse he owned in addition to his service mount.
72. Utley, *Sitting Bull*, 165. After leaving the Little Bighorn battlefield, the tribes

moved toward the Bighorn Mountains, then east to the upper Rosebud and down this stream to Greenleaf Creek, and again east to Tongue River. Here the tribes split into two groups, one going south and the other going north on Tongue River searching for game. The groups reunited on Powder River about 20 miles south of the Yellowstone. The reunited village was at this location on August 1.

73. Carroll, "Diary of Matthew Carroll," 238.
74. Gray, *Centennial Campaign*, 219.
75. Carroll, "Diary of Matthew Carroll," 239.
76. Hutton, *Phil Sheridan and His Army*, 322.
77. Jerome A. Greene, *Yellowstone Command: Colonel Nelson A. Miles and the Great Sioux War 1876–1877* (Lincoln: University of Nebraska Press, 1991), 69–70. Gen. Sheridan wanted 1,500 combined infantry and cavalry at the Tongue River post, but Col. Miles received only about a third of the planned troop strength.
78. Ibid., 56–57.
79. Gray, *Centennial Campaign*, 242.
80. Greene, *Yellowstone Command*, 61–63.
81. Ibid., 70–73.
82. Jerry Keenan, *The Life of Yellowstone Kelly* (Albuquerque: University of New Mexico Press, 2006), 137.
83. Utley, *Sitting Bull*, 201.
84. John G. MacDonald, "History of Navigation on the Yellowstone River" (M.A. thesis, Montana State University, 1950), 131–139. The Northern Pacific contracted a number of steamboats in 1882 to carry railroad construction supplies up the Yellowstone. After completion of the Northern Pacific, steamboat traffic on the Yellowstone continued between Glendive and the mouth of the river until 1910.
85. Michael P. Malone and Richard B. Roeder, *Montana: A History of Two Centuries* (Seattle: University of Washington Press, 1976), 183–184.
86. While it is possible that railroad construction camps were located at the Northern Pacific crossing of Powder River, none have yet been recorded.

Chapter 4

1. O. G. Libby, ed., *The Arikara Narrative of the Campaign against the Hostile Dakota June 1876*, North Dakota Historical Collections 6, reprint (New York: Sol Lewis, 1973), 71.
2. Willert, *Little Big Horn Diary*, 125.
3. Innis, "Bottoms Up!" 27; "The Smith and Leighton Yellowstone Store Ledger of 1876," Ben Innis Collection, Fort Union Trading Post National Historic Site, Williston, N.D. A business ledger attributed to Smith and his partners is probably one of several kept during the campaign. It documents goods sold primarily to officers at various places Smith operated on the Yellowstone

between June 10 and September 13. The August entries include charges to men in both Terry's and Crook's commands when they resupplied at the mouth of Powder River. Although it does not include entries for the period when Terry and Custer's wing arrived at the Powder River depot in June, it is reasonable to assume that similar items were sold at that time.

The first page of the ledger contains only the title "Yellowstone Store Ledger 1876" and "Club Room." The following pages are an alphabetical list of those with an account and the page on which the account is detailed. The surviving ledger might have been used for a store maintained in an area designated as a "Club Room" on a steamboat. In addition to this mobile store, Smith's clerks maintained the Powder River depot store for some period of time. A number of ledger accounts begin with "To P.R. a/c" or a similar entry, perhaps indicating that another ledger was kept at the Powder River depot. Other stores may have been established on the bank of the Yellowstone where men camped for an extended period, such as the mouth of the Rosebud (Ft. Beans). Some sales were likely made from a steamer whenever troops were near.

4. U.S. War Department, Records of the Office of the Commissary General of Subsistence, Provision Books, Entry 36, Record Group 192, National Archives, Washington, D.C. See appendix 11.

5. Don Rickey Jr., *Forty Miles a Day on Beans and Hay* (Norman: University of Oklahoma Press, 1963), 118–119. The Commissary Department was allowed to sell "small stores" of canned goods and other foods to officers and enlisted men over the objections of sutlers and post traders. A review of the department's performance in providing small stores between 1866 and 1876 concluded that the Commissary Department was more concerned about supplying goods to officers than meeting the needs of enlisted men.

6. "Report of the Commissary General of Subsistence," in U.S. War Department, *Report of the Secretary of War 1877*, 342. During the fiscal year ending June 30, 1877, the Commissary Department received $415,586.12 in sales to officers and $358,309.78 in sales to enlisted men. Purchases by the rank and file would have been for nonissue rations (small stores). The mean per capita sale can be estimated by dividing the total sales by the number of enlisted men authorized by Congress (25,000); the actual mean would be somewhat higher because army personnel numbers were always under authorized strength. The average enlisted spending for the year was about $14.00, or a little more than $1.00 per month.

7. *Mill* was the soldiers' word for "guardhouse." At this time, the mill at Powder River depot was probably as described by the scout Red Star, simply a place on the prairie where offenders were kept under guard.

8. Hill and Innis, "Fort Buford Diary of Private Sanford," 14.

9. Heski, "Camp Powell," 18.

10. Gray, "Pack Train on George A. Custer's Last Campaign," 60. Slightly different than Gray's estimated 91 mules, Hardorff puts the total number at 97, only

18 of them regular pack animals and the rest wagon mules. Hardorff, "Packs, Packers, and Pack Details," 228.
11. Heski, "Camp Powell," 19.
12. Gray, *Centennial Campaign*, 273–274, 282. Contract surgeons Dr. Isaiah Ashton and Dr. Elbert Clark established the hospital at the Powder River depot. Several patients were transferred from this hospital to the *Josephine* and taken to Ft. Lincoln on July 19, indicating that the hospital was maintained until this depot was abandoned and supplies were moved to the mouth of the Rosebud.
13. Wagner, *Participants in the Battle of the Little Big Horn*, 211.
14. Innis, "Bottoms Up!" 27; Hill and Innis, "Fort Buford Diary of Private Sanford," 14–17. Smith left James Coleman to sell goods at the Powder River depot when Terry's command arrived in June. Because the Smith and Leighton ledger records sales beginning on June 30 at places other than Powder River, just how long Coleman or other clerks stayed at the Powder River depot is uncertain. The sutler was using steamboats to get his goods to the 7th Cavalry and Montana column whenever they concentrated on the Yellowstone between the Bighorn River and the Powder. Men at the Powder River depot were still getting drunk the first week in July, but Sanford does not mention visiting the sutler until July 19, the day before the depot was abandoned. There may simply have been sutler goods on the steamer assigned to ferry the personnel at the Powder River depot across the Yellowstone for their departure.
15. Douglas C. McChristian, *The U.S. Army in the West, 1870–1880: Uniforms, Weapons and Equipment* (Norman: University of Oklahoma Press, 2006), 102–103. The "dog" or "pup" tent was constructed from two shelter halves, an eight-ounce rectangle of cotton duck 65 by 66 inches. When on the march, soldiers carried a shelter half that could be paired with another to form a small two-man tent. The tent provided shade but was not particularly good at keeping the weather at bay.
16. U.S. War Department, Records of the Office of the Commissary General of Subsistence, Provision Books. See appendix 11, Table A11.1. Commissary stores at the Powder River depot at the end of June 1876 included 85 barrels of flour and 480 cans of yeast powder.
17. Risch, *Quartermaster Support of the Army*, 505–606. The army ration did not include onions, potatoes, or other fresh vegetables, but they were often grown in post gardens. Surplus government-issued subsistence items at a post could be sold, and the proceeds could be used to purchase other items. Post bakeries often accumulated "surplus" flour to support the purchase of both food and nonfood items to benefit the troops.
18. Victor G. Smith, *The Champion Buffalo Hunter: The Frontier Memoirs of Yellowstone Vic Smith*, ed. Jeanette Prodgers (Guilford, Conn.: Globe Pequot Press, 1997), 89. Civilian scout and hunter Vic Smith recalled hunting for Major Moore's command at the Powder River depot for about a month.

19. Hill and Innis, "Fort Buford Diary of Private Sanford," 14.
20. Samuel L. Meddaugh, Diary of S. L. Meddaugh, 6th U.S. Infantry, Covering the Indian Campaign along the Yellowstone River, from May to September, 1876, Newberry Library, Chicago, 4.
21. Hill and Innis, "Fort Buford Diary of Private Sanford," 17.
22. Ibid., 14.
23. Gray, *Custer's Last Campaign*, 327–329.
24. Heski, "Camp Powell," 20.
25. Gray, *Centennial Campaign*, 282–283. Private William George was a member of Capt. Benteen's Company H. He died on July 4 at 4:00 AM on the *Far West* from a penetrating wound to the chest or abdomen.
26. Heski, "Camp Powell," 20.
27. Hill and Innis, "Fort Buford Diary of Private Sanford," 17. A vedette is a mounted sentinel in advance of an outpost.
28. Meddaugh, Diary of S. L. Meddaugh, 4.
29. Hill and Innis, "Fort Buford Diary of Private Sanford," 17.
30. Hanson, *Conquest of the Missouri*, 322. Major Moore had significantly fewer mules to outfit his wagon train because many were now being used for Terry's pack trains. Whether this shortage of teams or some other factor was responsible for the forage being left at the depot is unknown.
31. *Chicago Daily Tribune*, August 11, 1876; *New York Herald*, August 2, 1876.
32. O'Kelly reported seeing some 40 sacks of forage and a large quantity of loose grain on the ground. He interpreted moccasin tracks in a trail leading to the river as evidence that Indians had dragged sacks of grain there to be floated across the Yellowstone. Other interpretations are more plausible because the only rivercraft available to the tribes were rafts and small bull boats; the latter were made by fastening a buffalo hide to a willow frame. A Cheyenne and a Lakota warrior both recalled finding grain at the mouth of Powder River, where the Indians ate some, fed some to their captured cavalry horses, and left most on the ground after taking the sacks.
33. U.S. War Department, *Chronological List of Actions, &c., with Indians from January 15, 1837 to January, 1891*, comp. and ed. with an introduction by Dale E. Floyd (Fort Collins: Old Army Press, 1979), 62; Greene, *Yellowstone Command*, 243, note 21.
34. Gray, *Centennial Campaign*, 210.
35. George M. Miles, George M. Miles Papers 1876–1878, Small Collection 318, Montana Historical Society Archives, Helena, 16. George Miles was serving as a quartermaster clerk with his uncle's regiment.
36. Several soldiers interpreted what they observed at the depot site to mean that the Indians tried to burn the grain after removing the sacks. These men were probably unaware that Lt. Macklin's detail was ordered to destroy the forage during the 22nd Infantry's firefight on July 29. Apparently, the 75 tons of forage remained largely intact, but the sacks were indeed taken by the Indians.

37. U.S. War Department, *Report of the Secretary of War 1876* (Washington, D.C.: Government Printing Office, 1876), 480–481.
38. U.S. War Department, Quartermaster Report of Persons and Articles Hired, August 1876, Record Group 92, National Archives and Records Administration, Washington, D.C. Most accounts, including Major Moore's official report, spell this name "Brockmeyer." However, the 6th Infantry Quartermaster Report of Persons and Articles Hired, August 1876, lists the name as "Wesley Brockmire."
39. U.S. War Department, *Report of the Secretary of War 1876*, 480–481.
40. Ibid.
41. Greene, *Yellowstone Command*, 35.
42. Meddaugh, Diary of S. L. Meddaugh, 8.
43. Hill and Innis, "Fort Buford Diary of Private Sanford," 19.
44. Smith, *Champion Buffalo Hunter*, 89. Twenty-six-year-old Vic Smith was a hunter who supplied meat for Ft. Buford. He recalled being at Ft. Buford when the *Far West* came down the river with wounded from the Little Bighorn (July 5). He, Brockmeyer, and Bob Jackson, a mixed-blood Blackfoot scout, were assigned to Moore's depot command, where Smith was a hunter and scout for a month. Smith's recollection that Brockmeyer was also assigned to Moore's command is supported by the fact that Brockmeyer carried a message from the depot on July 1 informing Terry that Custer's Arikara scouts had reported at the mouth of Powder River. Gray, *Centennial Campaign*, 201.
45. Smith, *Champion Buffalo Hunter*, 89–92. Smith's account has numerous errors of fact including dates and military units, as well as a fanciful story that he watched the murder of Wild Bill Hickok in Deadwood before returning to participate in the fight at Powder River. Both events occurred on August 2, 1876, when he was undoubtedly with Moore's command. Despite unintended errors and bold fabrications, some details comport with lesser-known accounts that contradict Major Moore's report.
46. Hanson, *Conquest of the Missouri*, 329. Captain Grant Marsh mentioned field glasses as one of Brockmeyer's possessions.
47. Smith, *Champion Buffalo Hunter*, 90.
48. Ibid., 60. Smith appears to have known Major Moore well, as he tells of giving him a scalp, probably in the fall of 1875.
49. Wayne Gard, *The Great Buffalo Hunt* (New York: Alfred A. Knopf, 1960), 271. That Smith was a world-class marksman with a rifle is well documented. He became a commercial buffalo hunter and later gained a reputation in the United States and Europe as an expert guide and hunter.
50. Hanson, *Conquest of the Missouri*, 329; Smith, *Champion Buffalo Hunter*, 109. Smith's comment about the sale of the horse comports with Captain Marsh's account. At Brockmeyer's request, Marsh sold the scout's belongings, including a horse, and sent the money to Brockmeyer's sister in West Virginia. Smith recalled an earlier incident about hunting with Brockmeyer when the latter

lost a valuable saddle horse. Smith found and captured the animal in the fall of 1876 and kept it for many years as a memorial to his friend.

51. *New York Herald*, August 8, 1876.
52. Walter Clifford, Diary of Captain Walter Clifford, Co. E., 7th Infantry, Marshall University Library, Huntington.
53. Smith, *Champion Buffalo Hunter*, 92.
54. Brown, "Yellowstone Supply Depot," 30; Meddaugh, Diary of S. L. Meddaugh, 7–8.
55. Gray, *Centennial Campaign*, 211.
56. Marquis, *Wooden Leg*, 280–281; Raymond J. DeMallie, *The Sixth Grandfather: Black Elk's Teachings Given to John G. Neihardt* (Lincoln: University of Nebraska Press, 1984), 199. The accounts of Wooden Leg and Black Elk were given during extended interviews in the 1920s and 1930s.
57. DeMallie, *Sixth Grandfather*, 199.
58. Greene, *Yellowstone Command*, note 24, 244; Hill and Innis, "Fort Buford Diary of Private Sanford," 20. Only one warrior's death at the mouth of Powder River was reported by Black Elk. When Terry's command returned to the mouth of Powder River with Crook's force, Pvt. Sanford noted in his August 20 diary entry that five dead warriors were observed here by the soldiers as were fragments of artillery shells. Because he reported the dead and the shells in the same sentence, perhaps he concluded that the warriors were killed during Moore's shelling on August 2. Sanford does not indicate if the dead were interred according to tribal traditions, but it would be unusual for Indian dead to simply be left on the battlefield.
59. Greene, *Yellowstone Command*, 45.
60. Gray, *Centennial Campaign*, 222–225. Matthias "Cy" Mounts came to Montana Territory via the Bozeman Trail in 1864 and was one of the founding fathers of Bozeman. He was involved in many local business ventures, including trade with the Crows and contract work for the army. Among his partners were men who served as guides and scouts for Terry and Crook, including Mitch Boyer and the Reshaw brothers. Gray, *Custer's Last Campaign*, 25; Topping, *Chronicles of the Yellowstone*, 25.
61. William P. Clark, William Philo Clark Diary, 1876, Small Collection 538, Montana Historical Society Archives, Helena, 2.
62. Ibid., 3.
63. Clark's statement indicates that his recruits were still securing loose grain at the location of Moore's August 2 forage-recovery effort.
64. Edward J. McClernand, *With the Indian and the Buffalo in Montana 1870–1878* (Glendale, Calif.: Arthur Clark, 1969), 98.
65. Carroll, "Diary of Matthew Carroll," 238; Gerhard L. Luhn, "The Big Horn and Yellowstone Expedition of 1876 as Seen through the Letters of Captain Gerhard Luke Luhn," *Annals of Wyoming*, Spring 1973: 42.
66. Hill and Innis, "Fort Buford Diary of Private Sanford," 20.

67. Schneider, *Freeman Journal*, 75; Alfred H. Terry, *The Field Diary of General Alfred H. Terry: The Yellowstone Expedition—1876* (Fort Collins: Old Army Press, 1978), 33.
68. Charles F. Roe, Letter from 2nd Lt. Charles Francis Roe to his wife dated August 21, 1876 at Powder River, M.T., Marshall University Library, Huntington. Companies of the 2nd Cavalry were serving in both Terry's and Crook's commands. Lt. Charles Roe, whose Company F was with Terry, noted on August 21 that the 2nd Cavalry companies were camped together. He also noted that his company was three miles from Lt. Clark and the new recruits from Ft. Ellis. Roe's comments suggest that, with the exception of Clark's recruits, all of the 2nd Cavalry was camped with Crook's column west of Powder River.
69. Charles King, *Campaigning with Crook* (Norman: University of Oklahoma Press, 1964), 86.
70. Luhn, "Big Horn and Yellowstone Expedition of 1876," 42. Capt. Luhn noted that those in the Wyoming column had had nothing but coffee, bacon, and hardbread since August 5. He had few cooking or eating utensils, and his clothing was worn out. He refused to buy a much-needed undershirt at the sutler's price of $4.00.
71. Thaddeus H. Capron, *Marching with General Crook or The Big Horn and Yellowstone Expedition against Hostile Indians in the Summer of 1876*, ed. Ray Meketa (Douglas, Ala.: Cheechako Press, 1983), 49.
72. John G. Bourke, *Bourke's Diary from Journals of 1st Lt. John Gregory Bourke, June 27–Sept 15, 1876: Chronicle of the 1876 Indian War*, ed. James Willert (La Mirada: James Willert Publisher, 1986), 132.
73. "Smith and Leighton Yellowstone Store Ledger of 1876."
74. "Report of the Commissary General of Subsistence," 341. After the Civil War the Subsistence Department furnished tobacco at cost. Soldiers could purchase it for cash or have it deducted from their pay. From July 1, 1876, through June 30, 1877, the army sold more than 250,000 pounds to enlisted men and officers under various statutes. In the Department of Dakota, 7,586 pounds of chewing tobacco and 2,525 pounds of smoking tobacco were sold during this period. These figures provide a rough estimate of the relative frequency of use for chewing tobacco (75 percent) and smoking tobacco (25 percent). Chewing tobacco was about 50 cents per pound, while smoking tobacco cost between 70 and 85 cents per pound, much cheaper than tobacco sold by the sutler.
75. Godfrey, *Field Diary of Lt. Edward Settle Godfrey*, 38, 46. Godfrey reported that he was able to requisition tobacco from the commissary on September 2, much to the relief of the many men in his command who were out.
76. Bourke, *Bourke's Diary from Journals of 1st Lt. John Gregory Bourke*, 158.
77. Bruce R. Liddic, ed., *I Buried Custer: The Diary of Pvt. Thomas W. Coleman, 7th U.S. Cavalry* (College Station: Creative Publishing Co., 1979), 13.
78. James T. King, *War Eagle: A Life of General Eugene A. Carr* (Lincoln: University of Nebraska Press, 1964), 171–172.

79. Charles F. Roe, Letter from 2nd Lt. Charles Francis Roe to his wife dated August 18th, 1876 at Powder River, M.T., Marshall University Library, Huntington.
80. Carroll, "Diary of Matthew Carroll," 239; Hill and Innis, "Fort Buford Diary of Private Sanford," 20.
81. "Smith and Leighton Yellowstone Store Ledger of 1876," 24–38.
82. Ernest A. Garlington, *The Lieutenant E. A. Garlington Narrative, pt. 1*, ed. John Carroll (Bryan: John Carroll Publisher, 1978), 15.
83. Ibid.
84. Willert, *Little Big Horn Diary*, 341.
85. Rickey, *Forty Miles a Day on Beans and Hay*, 160.
86. Agnew, *Life of a Soldier in the Frontier Army*, 174–176.
87. "Smith and Leighton Yellowstone Store Ledger of 1876," 63.
88. Wagner, *Participants in the Battle of the Little Big Horn*, 101–102.
89. Hill and Innis, "Fort Buford Diary of Private Sanford," 19–20.
90. Godfrey, *Field Diary of Lt. Edward Settle Godfrey*, 40.
91. Hill and Innis, "Fort Buford Diary of Private Sanford," 21.
92. Miles, George M. Miles Papers, 43.
93. Bourke, *Bourke's Diary from Journals of 1st Lt. John Gregory Bourke*, 163; John F. Finerty, *War-Path and Bivouac or The Conquest of the Sioux*, new ed. (Norman: University of Oklahoma Press, 1961), 171–174.
94. Gray, *Centennial Campaign*, 229–230. Crook departed the mouth of Powder River with only a portion of the supplies Terry offered his command. The additional forage, subsistence, and other supplies arrived at Powder River on August 23.
95. Carroll, "Diary of Matthew Carroll," 239.
96. Greene, *Yellowstone Command*, 54–57.
97. Miles, George M. Miles Papers, 47.
98. Gray, *Centennial Campaign*, 235; Heski, "Camp Powell," 24.
99. Carroll, "Diary of Matthew Carroll," 240; Greene, *Yellowstone Command*, 54–61; U.S. War Department, *Report of the Secretary of War 1877*, 487.

CHAPTER 5

1. Ronald R. Switzer, *The Bertrand Bottles: A Study of 19th Century Glass and Ceramic Containers* (Washington, D.C.: National Park Service, 1974). Some archaeological assemblages are found in contexts that leave no question about their association with a specific time or event. The archaeological recovery of goods from the steamboat *Bertrand* is a good example of an assemblage that is securely dated to April 1, 1865, when the steamer sank in the Missouri River.
2. Hill and Innis, "Fort Buford Diary of Private Sanford," 14–15.
3. U.S. War Department, *Report of the Secretary of War 1876*, 480–481.
4. Hanson, *Conquest of the Missouri*, 325.
5. Clark, William Philo Clark Diary, 2.
6. U.S. War Department, *Report of the Secretary of War 1880* (Washington, D.C.:

Government Printing Office, 1880), 1097. The army conducted a channel survey of the Yellowstone beginning in September 1878. When surveyed, this half-mile corridor along the right bank of the Yellowstone was four to six feet deep, with shallows one to three feet deep and sandbars on both ends. Draft of the *Far West* was four feet, six inches, at capacity (400 tons) and 20 inches when empty. Hanson, *Conquest of the Missouri*, 238.

7. Agnew, *Life of a Soldier on the Western Frontier*, 124, 190; Rickey, *Forty Miles a Day on Beans and Hay*, 121. Cooking in garrison was by company, with the men cooking in rotation, and while on the march the men generally fixed their own meals.
8. James Willert, *After Little Big Horn: 1876 Campaign Rosters* (La Mirada: James Willert Publisher, 1985), 23. Sanford was referring to Sgt. William G. Gayle, Co. D, 6th Infantry.
9. Hill and Innis, "Fort Buford Diary of Private Sanford," 15–17. Private Sanford often mentions that he was second cook but never first cook and Sgt. William G. Gayle was the only baker, suggesting that there was some specialization among men assigned to cooking duties in Co. D.
10. Ibid., 20.
11. Terry, *Field Diary of General Alfred H. Terry*, 33.
12. Heski, "Camp Powell," back cover. Heski speculates about the location of the guard companies, trader's store, wagon park, and other features at the depot in June and July. Only the trash pit (Feature D) and perhaps an oven (Feature F) have been studied sufficiently to determine their association with the depot and the probable location of one of the guard companies. His mapped locations of Crook's and Terry's units in August are plausible with the exception of the Dakota column's camp of August 20–24. Terry's units were underwater following a big storm during this period, so they would not have been on a well-drained high bench or bluff as indicated on Heski's map.
13. Bass PLC librarian Elizabeth Press informed me via an e-mail message December 7, 2000, that foil wrappers used by export bottlers covered the cork closure and wire retainer but also were intended to assure customers that they were buying the brewer's product. Concerned about forgery in the late 19th century, brewers and bottlers adopted strategies to combat it. Trademarks, labels, and foil seals or "capsules" were intended to thwart forgers. Great Britain began a system of registered trademarks in 1876.
14. David Hughes, *"A Bottle of Guinness Please": The Colourful History of Guinness* (Wokingham, England: Phimboy, 2006), 90, 109. There were a number of export bottling firms, many of them located in London, Liverpool, and Dublin. Bass, for example, had authorized 17 London wholesale bottlers by 1878. While the brewers exercised considerable control over labeling of their export products, they assumed no responsibility for the quality of the product once it left the brewery and bore none of the risk associated with the export market.
15. I sought information about the Royal Bottling Company in a letter to Bass PLC; public relations manager Maurice Lovett responded with a letter dated

December 3, 1987, and librarian Elizabeth Press, with an e-mail on December 7, 2000. I also hired Steven W. Taylor, Historic Research Consultants and Genealogists of Staffordshire, England, to find information about the RBC. His response is a letter dated September 16, 1991. The Bass employees stated that their firm did no bottling in the 19th century but, rather, supplied draft beers to both domestic and export bottlers. The RBC was one of the bottlers, but Bass had no further information about the firm. Mr. Taylor found no record of the Royal Bottling Company at Companies House in London, the Public Record Office in Kew, or the British Library in London or in *London Directories 1875*.

16. Hughes, *"A Bottle of Guinness Please,"* 85.
17. Ibid., 12, 22, 27, 85. After 1823, Bass developed its India Pale Ale, a high-alcohol, heavily hopped beer that could be transported long distances without spoiling. Today Bass is one of numerous brands exported by the international firm InBev. In 1849 Guinness began brewing Foreign Extra Stout for export bottler E&J Burke. Like Bass India Pale Ale, Guinness Foreign Extra Stout had a higher alcohol and hop content to prevent spoilage. Today Guinness is brewed in 50 countries and distributed in 153 nations.
18. Ibid., 288; Press, e-mail to the author, December 7, 2000; Taylor, letter to the author, September 16, 1991. M. B. Foster and Sons was founded in 1829. It added a bugle or "Robin Hood horn" to its label as a trademark in 1875 and registered it the following year. E&G Hibbert began business in 1767 and was still operating under that name in 1875. No information was found on any trademark associated with Hibbert.
19. Hughes, *"A Bottle of Guinness Please,"* 196, 287. As the brewers began to bottle and export their own products in the 20th century, the export bottling companies began to decline. The Burke, Hibbert, and Foster firms consolidated with six other bottlers in 1936 to form Export Bottlers Ltd., London.
20. Press, e-mail to the author, December 7, 2000. Bass was the first company to register its trademark when the British Patent Office opened their system for this purpose on January 1, 1876. It is Trade Mark Number 1.
21. Hughes, *"A Bottle of Guinness Please,"* 149–150.
22. "Smith and Leighton Yellowstone Store Ledger of 1876."
23. Gray, "Sutler on Custer's Last Campaign," 18.
24. Roe, Letter from 2nd Lt. Charles Francis Roe to his wife dated August 18th, 1876.
25. Hughes, *"A Bottle of Guinness Please,"* 86. British and Irish export bottlers wrapped the conditioned bottles of ale and stout in straw jackets and packed them in flour barrels or wooden boxes with additional straw packing.
26. Bradley, "Journal of James H. Bradley," 203.
27. Smith's ledger indicates that he sold cask beer for 25 cents per pint. Because cask beer is much cheaper than the bottled ale, it was probably from domestic sources.

28. Stanley Baron, *Brewed in America: The History of Beer and Ale in the United States* (Boston: Little, Brown and Company, 1962), 251. Bozeman, population 168 in 1871, had a brewery, while Helena boasted four breweries. U.S. breweries began to produce German-style lager beers in the 1840s, and by 1870 lager dominated the American market.
29. Ibid., 245.
30. Innis, "Bottoms Up!" 29; "Smith and Leighton Yellowstone Store Ledger of 1876." Both officers and enlisted men were able to buy liquor at this time. Smith's ledger indicates that liquor could be bought by the gallon, by the canteen, or by the drink. Whiskey was $6.00 per gallon or 12.5 cents per drink. Brandy was available for $3.00 per bottle.
31. Libby, *Arikara Narrative of the Campaign against the Hostile Dakota*, 207.
32. "Smith and Leighton Yellowstone Store Ledger of 1876," 11.
33. Ibid., 84. An online inflation calculator indicates that the $48.00 ginger ale purchase cost the equivalent of $955.42 today.
34. "C&C Group," *Wikipedia*, accessed February 2014, https://en.wikipedia.org/wiki/C%26C_Group; Lennon Wylie, "Belfast/Ulster Street Directory, 1880," accessed April 22, 2012, http://www.lennonwylie.co.uk/BSD1880adverts.htm. Cantrell and Cochrane dates to 1852. Today, C&C Group is a large beverage firm owned by BC Partners. A Cantrell and Cochrane advertisement in the 1880 Belfast street directory listed 26 drinks sold by the company, including ginger ale, sarsaparilla, and supercarbonated mineral waters.
35. Agnew, *Life of a Soldier on the Western Frontier*, 131–136.
36. Wagner, *Participants in the Battle of the Little Big Horn*, 74.
37. Paulding, "Dr. Paulding and His Remarkable Diary," 56.
38. Greene, *Yellowstone Command*, 36.
39. U.S. War Department, *Report of the Medical Department, Big Horn and Yellowstone Expedition, Montana, 1876*, Dr. B. A. Clements, Surgeon, U.S.A., Medical Directory, Record Group 94, National Archives and Records Administration, Washington, D.C.
40. Roe, Letter from 2nd Lt. Charles Frances Roe to his wife dated August 18th, 1876.
41. "The Tarrant Explosion. A Million Dollars Damage," *American Druggist and Pharmaceutical Record: A Semi-monthly Illustrated Journal of Pharmacy* 37 (1900): 289, http://books.google.com/books?id=_NAAAAAYAAJ&printsec=frontcover&source=gbs_ge_summary_r&cad=0#v=onepage&q&f=false. Dates for Tarrant and Co. are most often given as 1859 to 1905 or 1906. The article in the journal cited describes an explosion at the Tarrant facilities in 1900 and states that the firm was founded in 1834 and incorporated as Tarrant and Co. in 1861.
42. *Physician and Pharmaceutist* 2, no. 7 (1870): 17, http://books.google.com/books?id=7FECAAAAYAAJ&pg=RA1-PA14&lpg=RA1PA14&dq=The+Physician+and+Pharmaceutist+August+1870&source=bl&ots=UsIVO4

_eU6&sig=ojtg3FyNqJ1rmFePpwCawMhmfdY&hl=en&sa=X&ei=HPsjU fLmPOiyigLjgIG4AQ&ved=0CDMQ6AEwAA#v=onepage&q=The%20 Physican%20and%20Pharmaceutist%20August%201870&f=false.

43. U.S. War Department, Records of the Office of the Commissary General of Subsistence, Provision Books.
44. Hill and Innis, "Fort Buford Diary of Private Sanford," 16. Sanford noted on July 1 that the steamboat escort returned from Ft. Buford with lettuce, onions, radishes, and pie. The vegetables were no doubt from the regiment's gardens at the fort.
45. Bourke, *Bourke's Diary from Journals of 1st Lt. John Gregory Bourke*, 146; Godfrey, *Field Diary of Lt. Edward Settle Godfrey*, 38–40. Smith's inventory was apparently almost depleted at this time, but several of the Bozeman traders brought goods in mackinaw boats. Additional sutler goods arrived on August 22. Lt. Godfrey commented that no commissary goods were available for sale to officers until the wagon train arrived from Ft. Beans on August 22.
46. U.S. War Department, Records of the Office of the Commissary General of Subsistence, Provision Books.
47. Hill and Innis, "Fort Buford Diary of Private Sanford," 15, 17; Smith, *Champion Buffalo Hunter*, 89. Expert marksman and acclaimed buffalo hunter Vic Smith was assigned to provide meat for the depot guard camp.
48. Danny N. Walker, "Canid Remains from the Powder River Supply Depot, Prairie County, Montana (24PE231)," *Archaeology in Montana* 36, no. 2 (1995): 67.
49. Ibid., 64.
50. James E. Potter, "The Great Source of Amusement: Hunting in the Frontier Army," *Montana the Magazine of Western History* 55, no. 3 (2005): 34–47.
51. Walker, "Canid Remains from the Powder River Supply Depot," 68.
52. Bradley, "Journal of James H. Bradley," 173.
53. Bourke, *On the Border with Crook*, 362.
54. Potter, "Great Source of Amusement," 39.
55. Hill and Innis, "Fort Buford Diary of Private Sanford," 14.
56. Walker, "Canid Remains from the Powder River Supply Depot," 72.
57. *Sturgis Weekly Record*, January 27, 1888.
58. Shannon M. Vihlene, "Custer's Last Drag: An Examination of Tobacco Use among the Seventh Cavalry during the Nineteenth Century" (M.A. thesis, University of Montana, 2008), 75–76. Fully 86 percent of Custer's regiment used tobacco in some form. Perhaps as many as 75 percent of the rank and file who used tobacco chewed, while 25 percent smoked a pipe.
59. Capron, *Marching with General Crook*, 24.
60. Douglas D. Scott, letter to the author, February 9, 1989. The March 6, 1869, issue of *Scientific American* described the manufacturing of briar smoking pipes, noting that they sold for $1.00 to $2.00 each.
61. Gerald R. Clark, "White Clay Pipes from General Alfred Terry's 1876 Powder River Supply Depot, 24PE231, Southeastern Montana" (unpublished

manuscript, 1988), 17; J. Byron Sudbury, "White Clay Pipes from the Old Connellsville Dump, 36 Fa 140," *Historic Clay Tobacco Pipe Studies* 1 (1980): 28–30. It is possible that the McElroy name does not refer to the pipe manufacturer but, rather, a distributor who ordered pipes with his name stamped on them. The D. McDougall and Co. price list ca. 1875 states, "Pipes stamped with name on the bowl or stem, 2d. per gross extra."

62. Sudbury, "White Clay Pipes from the Old Connellsville Dump," 28–31.
63. *New York Times*, September 12, 1876, 5, col. 1.
64. Bourke, *Bourke's Diary from Journals of 1st Lt. John Gregory Bourke*, 134.
65. *New York Herald*, August 7, 1876, 5.
66. Catherine M. Thuro, *Oil Lamps, the Kerosene Era in North America* (Des Moines: Wallace-Homestead Book Company, 1976), 15, 22.
67. National Park Service, "These Relics of Barbarism: A History of Furniture in Barracks and Guardhouses of the United States Army, 1800–1880" (report prepared for Harpers Ferry Center by David A. Clary and Associates, Harpers Ferry, W.V., n.d.), 170–172.
68. U.S. War Department, Records of the Office of the Commissary General of Subsistence, Provision Books.
69. Louis A. Garavaglia and Charles G. Worman, *Firearms of the American West, 1866–1894* (Albuquerque: University of New Mexico Press, 1985), 83–85.
70. F. W. Hackley, W. H. Woodin, and E. L. Scranton, *History of Modern U.S. Military Small Arms Ammunition*, vol. 1 (New York: Macmillan, 1967), 10.
71. Ernest L. Reedstrom, *Bugles, Banners and War Bonnets* (New York: Bonanza Books, 1986), 282–285. Reedstrom's book includes Ordnance Department records indicating that all 12 7th Cavalry companies had been issued .45 Colts by December 31, 1874. These records do not list any Schofield .45s for the regiment.
72. McChristian, *U.S. Army in the West*, 122.
73. Garavaglia and Worman, *Firearms of the American West*, 278.
74. Ibid., 85.
75. Reedstrom, *Bugles, Banners and War Bonnets*, 277–285.
76. Ibid.
77. Hill and Innis, "Fort Buford Diary of Private Sanford," 12, 14. Sanford noted that the wife and children of Capt. Powell, Co. C, 6th Infantry, visited him at the Stanley's Crossing depot in May. On June 15 at the Powder River depot, Sanford also stated, "Lt. Brinan and wife & children stopped here." It is remotely possible but unlikely that a brief visit by children would account for the marble and doll in Feature D.
78. Genevieve Angione, *All-Bisque and Half-Bisque Dolls* (Camden: Thomas Nelson and Sons, 1969), 87.
79. Martin S. Garretson, *The American Bison* (New York: New York Zoological Society, 1938), 152–153; Tom McHugh, *The Time of the Buffalo* (New York: Alfred Knopf, 1972), 278–279.
80. Brown, *Plainsmen of the Yellowstone*, 357, 360.

81. Paul L. Hedren, *After Custer: Loss and Transformation in the Sioux Country* (Norman: University of Oklahoma, 2011), 74–77. Hedren describes the Northern Pacific's grading, bridging, and tracklaying operations in some detail.
82. Bill Lockhart, "The Origins of Life and the Export Beer Bottle," *Bottles and Extras: The Official Publication of the Federation of Historical Bottle Collectors* 18, no. 3 (2007): 50.
83. Elliott West, *The Saloon on the Rocky Mountain Mining Frontier* (Lincoln: University of Nebraska Press, 1979), 108.

Chapter 6

1. U.S. War Department, *Report of the Secretary of War 1876*, 447.
2. Ibid., 442.
3. Ibid., 447.
4. Ibid., 442.
5. Ibid., 460. General Terry noted that mule trains had never before been organized in his department so his marching columns were dependent on supply wagons. However, his column carried about 250 pack saddles to use with mules in the train "in an emergency."
6. Ibid., 475.
7. Ibid.
8. After leaving Terry at the mouth of Powder River, Crook ran out of supplies before his command reached Deadwood in the Black Hills. Officers were often willing to sacrifice livestock if it would result in accomplishing their mission or the survival of their command. Custer was prepared to subsist on mule meat if his rations were exhausted before he made contact with the tribesmen in 1876.
9. Ibid., 308.
10. Godfrey, *Field Diary of Lt. Edward Settle Godfrey*, 46.
11. Bourke, *Bourke's Diary from Journals of 1st Lt. John Gregory Bourke*, 39, 158.
12. Hanson, *Conquest of the Missouri*, 321–322; U.S. War Department, *Report of the Secretary of War 1876*, 310–311.
13. Terry's dismissal of Maj. DuBarry may have reflected the long-standing conflict in the army's "staff and line" organization. DuBarry was a Commissary Department staff officer, while Lt. Thompson was a company-level line officer acting as commissary of subsistence for Terry's column. As a line officer on campaign, Terry might have been inclined to support his subordinates who were performing satisfactorily as assistant commissary or quartermaster.
14. Wagner, *Participants in the Battle of the Little Big Horn*, 211–213.
15. Ibid., 211, 217. Fully 80 percent of the regiment's new recruits with less than six months' service were at the Powder River depot. A few of those left here were also listed as sick.
16. Gray, "Pack Train on George A. Custer's Last Campaign," 67.
17. Ibid., 64.
18. Utley, *Frontier Regulars*, 271. Utley notes that the logistical requirements of

heavy columns in the pursuit of plains tribes seldom achieved the desired goals and often became exercises in self-preservation. While this was true of Crook's command late in the campaign, Terry's Yellowstone depot served him well until the river could no longer support steamboat traffic.

19. U.S. War Department, *Report of the Secretary of War 1876*, 308.
20. When camped at the mouth of the Bighorn River, 7th Cavalry Private Thomas Coleman stated in a diary entry, "Sutlers are a curse to the Army and they do not sell first class goods in the first place then they charge exorbitant prices for everything" (Liddic, *I Buried Custer*, 144–145).
21. In a letter to his wife written at the mouth of the Rosebud, DeWolf stated, "The Post Trader or John Smith has opened his Whiskey, etc. and of course you all know what will follow for the time we remain here" (James M. De-Wolf, "The Diary and Letters of Dr. James M. DeWolf, Acting Assistant Surgeon, U.S. Army: His Record of the Sioux Expedition of 1876 Kept until His Death," reprint, transcribed and editorial notes by Edward S. Luce [State Historic Society of North Dakotan, n.d.], 52).
22. Carroll, "Diary of Matthew Carroll," 240.
23. Libby, *Arikara Narrative of the Campaign against the Hostile Dakota*, 208. Smith's clerk, James Coleman, recalled that Smith had a liquor palace in Bozeman where a gambler's murder at a card game ruined him. John Smith died a pauper in a Billings "Sister's hospital" in 1904 or 1905.
24. Delo, *Peddlers and Post Traders*, 179–180; Michael Leeson, ed., *History of Montana* (Chicago: Warner, Beers and Company, 1885), 523, 1041.
25. *Miles City Daily Yellowstone Journal*, November 14, 1882. When I lived in Miles City in the 1970s and 1980s, many place-names and some businesses reflected the influence of the early entrepreneurs. Our home was on Jordan Avenue, not far from Leighton Boulevard. Miles and Ulmer was one of the local hardware stores.
26. Topping, *Chronicles of the Yellowstone*, 200.
27. Leeson, *History of Montana*, 619; Sanders, *History of Montana*, 986; Topping, *Chronicles of the Yellowstone*, 231.
28. William A. Clark, "Centennial Address on the Origin, Growth and Resources of Montana," *Contributions to the Historical Society of Montana* 2 (1896): 50. The speech was delivered by William Andrews Clark, an entrepreneur with transportation, merchandising, and mining interests in the western part of Montana Territory. While ultimately no gold was found in the lower Yellowstone and Powder River country, mining dominated Montana's economy and politics for the next century. Clark became one of the state's wealthy "copper kings" and ranked among its most corrupt politicians.
29. James S. Hutchins, "The Cavalry Campaign Outfit at the Little Big Horn," in *The Custer Reader*, edited by Paul A. Hutton (Lincoln: University of Nebraska Press, 1992), 328. Hutchins states that most of the 7th Cavalry carried butcher knives and presumably other soldiers carried them too. If these were

similar to a Green River Works knife with an 1872 patent found on the surface at the Powder River depot, they would have had a five- to 10-inch blade. These light knives would be fine for cutting but not very efficient for chopping tasks. Some carried heavier knives; when at the mouth of Powder River in August, 1st Lt. William P. Clark, 2nd Cavalry, had a hunting knife "as heavy as a hatchet; two or three blows from it will cut down a stout sapling" (Bourke, *Bourke's Diary from Journals of 1st Lt. John Gregory Bourke*, 163).

30. Kelly J. Dixon, *Boomtown Saloons* (Reno: University of Nevada Press, 2005), 113–114. White clay pipes are frequently found in archaeological assemblages of mid-19th-century mining town saloons. Tobacco smoking accompanied social drinking at these establishments.
31. Ibid., 100–101. Colorless tumblers with faceted bases are among the most frequently occurring drinking vessels at mid-19th-century western mining boomtowns such as Virginia City, Nevada.
32. Hill and Innis, "Fort Buford Diary of Private Sanford," 12.
33. Rex L. Wilson, *Bottles on the Western Frontier* (Tucson: University of Arizona Press, 1981), 7–8.
34. Herman Ronnenberg, *Beer and Brewing in the Inland Northwest 1850–1950* (Moscow: University of Idaho Press, 1993), 90.
35. Hughes, "A Bottle of Guinness Please," 258. British and Irish ales and stout were expensive because they required long maturation and the cost of bottling was considerable. They were a luxury item sold around the world at a relatively high price.
36. Dixon, *Boomtown Saloons*, 74–75.
37. Doulas D. Scott, "An Officer's Latrine at Fort Larned and Inferences on Status," *Plains Anthropologist* 34, no. 123 (1989): 24.
38. Ibid., 23–31. Archaeological assemblages from Virginia City, Nevada, reflect a similar pattern. They contained many paneled tumblers, but those from higher-class establishments had relatively more stemware. Dixon, *Boomtown Saloons*, 100–103.
39. Oliver Knight, *Life and Manners in the Frontier Army* (Norman: University of Oklahoma Press, 1978), 3, 76.
40. Libby, *Arikara Narrative of the Campaign against the Hostile Dakota*, 207.
41. Hill and Innis, "Fort Buford Diary of Private Sanford," 14.
42. Sean M. Rafferty and Rob Mann, eds., *Smoking and Culture: The Archaeology of Tobacco Pipes in Eastern North America* (Knoxville: University of Tennessee Press, 2004), xiv; Lauren J. Cook, "Tobacco-Related Material and the Construction of Working-Class Culture," in *Interdisciplinary Investigations of the Boott Mills, Lowell, Massachusetts, vol. 3: The Boarding House System as a Way of Life*, ed. Mary C. Beaudry and Stephen A. Mrozowski (Boston: Government Printing Office, North Atlantic Region, National Park Service, 1989), 209–229, accessed February 5, 2014, https://archive.org/details/interdisciplinaroovol3.

43. Rickey, *Forty Miles a Day on Beans and Hay*, 18–25.
44. Paul Baumann, *Collecting Antique Marbles* (Lombard: Wallace-Homestead Books, 1970).
45. Stanley South, *Method and Theory in Historical Archeology* (New York: Academic Press, 1977), 182.
46. American Toy Marble Museum, "A Glossary of Marble Players' Terms," s.v. "General Grant Board, General Grant Game," accessed February 10, 2013, http://www.americantoymarbles.com/glossary.htm.
47. Dixon, *Boomtown Saloons*, 132–133. Marbles were recovered in the remains of 19th-century saloons at Virginia City, Nevada.
48. Ibid. Porcelain dolls were also found in saloon remains in Virginia City, Nevada.
49. Robert M. Herskovitz, *Fort Bowie Material Culture*, Anthropology Papers of the University of Arizona 31 (Tucson: University of Arizona Press, 1978), 141; John D. Reynolds, "Archaeological Investigation at Old Fort Scott, 14BO302, Fort Scott, Kansas 1968 to 1972" (report submitted to the National Park Service, Omaha, 1983), 126.
50. Dorothy S. Coleman, Elizabeth A. Coleman, and Evelyn J. Coleman, *The Collector's Encyclopedia of Dolls* (New York: Crown Publications, 1968), 240.
51. Roe, Letter from 2nd Lt. Charles Francis Roe to his wife dated August 21, 1876.
52. Henry L. Scott, *Military Dictionary: Comprising Technical Definitions; Information on Raising and Keeping Troops; Actual Service, Including Makeshifts and Improved Matériel; and Law, Government, Regulation, and Administration Relating to Land Forces* (New York: D. Van Nostrand, 1861), 579–580, http://quod.lib.umich.edu/m/moa/aek7340.0001.001/1?page=root;size=100;view=image;q1=sutler.
53. William C. Davis, *A Taste for War: The Culinary History of the Blue and the Gray* (Mechanicsburg, Pa.: Stackpole, 2003), 5, 30.
54. Scott, *Military Dictionary*, 449–450.
55. William P. Craighill, *The Army Officer's Pocket Companion; Principally Designed for Staff Officers in the Field* (New York: D. Van Nostrand, 1862), 240, http://books.google.com/books?id=oAA_AAAAYAAJ&printsec=frontcover&source=gbs_ge_summary_r&cad=0#v=onepage&q&f=false.
56. U.S. War Department, *Manual for Army Cooks* (Washington, D.C.: Government Printing Office, 1896), 225, http://www.grandarmyofthefrontier.org/articles/manual_for_army_cooks-1896.pdf.
57. Ibid. The 1896 issue of the manual contains a table with the capacities and hearth dimensions for field ovens. The 100-ration oven using 30 square inches of surface per loaf must have a total surface area of 20.28 square feet, with a hearth that is 5.41 feet long and 3.75 feet wide. The Feature F rectangle or base is very close to these dimensions at 5.57 feet long by 3.6 feet wide, with surface area of just over 20 square feet.

58. Willert, *After Little Big Horn*, 22–25.
59. Hill and Innis, "Fort Buford Diary of Private Sanford," 15–17.
60. Archaeological investigations at the Little Bighorn were conducted on a vastly larger scale and with very different methods than the modest Powder River depot project. Metal-detecting surveys that guided excavation at the battlefield might have biased the archaeological samples recovered to some unknown degree, as nonmetal items would be found only if they were in close proximity to metal items. The archaeological project at Powder River depot was so small that it undoubtedly represents only a fraction of the types of materials used here.
61. Douglas D. Scott, Richard A. Fox Jr., Melissa A. Connor, and Dick Harmon, *Archaeological Perspectives on the Battle of the Little Bighorn* (Norman: University of Oklahoma Press, 1989); Scott, *Papers on Little Bighorn Battlefield Archeology*. Unless otherwise noted, all information about the archaeological assemblages from the Little Bighorn Battlefield is from these two sources.
62. Marquis, *Wooden Leg*, 264–265.
63. Katherine G. Fougera, *With Custer's Cavalry* (Caldwell: Caxton, 1940), 275–276.
64. Vihlene, "Custer's Last Drag," 50, 74. Indians took weapons, clothing, and other useful items from the battlefield, and fellow soldiers recovered personal items from the fallen that might have been overlooked. Souvenir hunters also collected material from the site for many years. Some artifacts, such as pipes, that are not represented in the archaeological assemblage might have been present on the battlefield before they were removed.
65. Most of the revolver ammunition used at the battlefield would have been produced before 1874 when the Frankford Arsenal stopped production of the Colt cartridge to produce only the Revolver Ball Cartridge, Caliber .45, which could also be used in the Smith and Wesson Schofield.
66. Liddic, *I Buried Custer*, 153–154. Private Coleman, who fought at the Reno-Benteen defensive site, might have carried a Smith and Wesson on June 25, 1876, but there is no indication whether it was a .44 American or a .45 Schofield.
67. In a June 9, 1987, letter to the author, Leslie Perry Peterson, DeSoto National Wildlife Refuge, noted that the sizes of wooden crates recovered from the steamboat *Bertrand* are as varied as the products they contained. The *Bertrand* sank in the Missouri River with cargo bound for Ft. Benton, Montana Territory, in 1865.
68. Ibid. Some of the *Bertrand* cargo was shipped in boxes reinforced with iron bands.
69. C. L. Kilburn, *Notes on Preparing Stores for the United States Army* (Cincinnati: Bradley and Webb, Steam Printers and Stationers, 1863), 42, http://books.google.com/books?id=c5syAQAAMAAJ&printsec=frontcover&source=gbs_ge_summary_r&cad=0#v=onepage&q&f=false.
70. Scott, *Papers on Little Bighorn Battlefield Archeology*, 81–82, 97.
71. The three battle-related cans are from the equipment disposal site. They are similar to cans as found in Feature D at the Powder River depot, but detailed

comparisons were not possible from descriptions alone. Archaeologists suggest that small bones from the equipment dump site might have come from freshly killed animals or from salt beef sold to officers and civilian employees from commissary stores.
72. Marquis, *Wooden Leg*, 263.
73. Custer, *"Boots and Saddles,"* 272. The dogs sharing the tent were Tuck, Swift, Lady, and Kaiser.
74. Glendolin D. Wagner, *Old Neutriment*, Bison Book edition, reprint, intro. by Brian W. Dippie (Lincoln: University of Nebraska Press, 1989), 57, 65, 104, 123, 135, 152. Burkman mentions two of Custer's dogs, Tuck and Bleuch, with the attack force in several contexts. Only once does he mention a third, unnamed dog on the march up the Rosebud to the Little Bighorn. Custer did not include Bleuch as one of the dogs sharing his tent at the Powder River depot. Custer, *"Boots and Saddles,"* 272.
75. Wagner, *Old Neutriment*, 152.
76. Ibid., 179.
77. John Homans, *What's a Dog For? The Surprising History, Science, Philosophy and Politics of Man's Best Friend* (New York: Penguin Press, 2012), 143.
78. Wagner, *Old Neutriment*, 152.
79. *Sturgis Weekly Record*, January 24, 1888.
80. Joseph Balicki, "Watch Fires of a Hundred Circling Camps: Theoretical and Practical Approaches to Investigating Civil War Campsites," in *Historical Archaeology of Military Sites: Method and Topic*, ed. Clarence R. Grier, Lawrence E. Babits, Douglas D. Scott, and David G. Orr (College Station: Texas A&M University Press, 2011), 57–73. Archaeological investigations of Civil War campsites in the past two decades suggest models, methods, and techniques that might be useful in planning future work at the Powder River confluence. Background research, informant interviews, subsurface testing, metal detection, and mechanical stripping of soil under the right circumstances have produced good results. Geophysical mapping should be attempted before more destructive methods are used. Collectors who are willing to work with archaeologists can contribute valuable information about the possible location of sites and features.
81. Scott, *Papers on Little Bighorn Battlefield Archeology*, 130. The Reno–Benteen equipment dump was also a time capsule, with its contents dated to a specific day, June 27, 1876.
82. Reedstrom, *Bugles, Banners and War Bonnets*, 190.

Appendix 1

1. After the first two levels had been excavated, a second profile of the feature was completed before proceeding. The west side of the feature exposed in the river cutbank was shaved with a shovel to better reveal its stratigraphy and content.
2. Rodents burrowing into an archaeological feature can displace cultural materials from the position in which they were first deposited. Five old rodent

burrows that had subsequently filled were recorded in the Feature D profile. All of these krotovena were small and confined to the northern 1.5 meters of the excavation grid. Rodent activity cannot account for the magnitude of vertical and horizontal dispersion of artifacts in Feature D.

3. National Integrated Pest Management Network, "Public-Health Pesticide Applicator Training Manual, Chapter 6: Flies," 6-1, accessed January 14, 2013, http://entomology.ifas.ufl.edu/fasulo/vector/chap06.pdf. The larvae of some fly species can burrow to the surface from under one to four feet of moderately packed soil. In Feature D, the pupae level is in contact with the bottom of the bone level, indicating that the larvae did not have to migrate up through soil to pupate. The bone level was therefore probably exposed for several days before it was covered.

4. When we completed the excavation of Feature D, it was of course open on the west side where it had been profiled in the cutbank. When we shoveled the soil and rock we had removed back into the pit, gravity took much of it down to the gravel slope below. With nothing to retain the fill on the west, the material we replaced was quickly eroding away, and a vertical west face like the rest of the cutbank was impossible to maintain.

5. Balicki, "Watch Fires of a Hundred Circling Camps," 71. Archaeologists have had some success inferring the function of Civil War–era hearths by examining differences in how various kinds of features alter the surrounding soil. The way field ovens were constructed and used might be found to register unique thermal signatures.

APPENDIX 2

1. Descriptions follow Dale L. Berge, *Simpson Springs Station: Historical Archaeology in Western Utah*, Cultural Resource Series No. 6 (Salt Lake City: Utah State Office Bureau of Land Management, 1980); and Herskovitz, *Fort Bowie Material Culture*. Approximate dates of manufacture for bottles are from historic archaeologist Richard E. Fike, Montrose, Colorado, letter and attachment to the author, 1986.

2. Fike, letter to the author, 1986. Base marks on bottles are often associated with specific manufacturers or bottlers. Fike was unable to find any similar base marks among U.S. firms and concluded that the marks on the Feature D specimens are probably British. Recent online searches failed to reveal any further information about these base marks.

3. Stephen W. Taylor, Historical Research Consultants and Genealogists, Barton Under Needwood, Staffordshire, England, letter to the author, September 16, 1991.

4. Hughes, *"A Bottle of Guinness Please,"* 287.

5. Ibid., 288.

6. Ibid., 125–126.

7. Images of a bottle of "old Bass Ale" posted on the Realbeer.com Beer Community Web site, August 24, 2008, depict a bottle identical in color, size, and

shape to the wine/champagne/ale bottle from Feature D. It has a Bass label on one side and an M. B. Foster and Sons label on the other. The latter is gray and white with "BASS'SINDIAPALEALE" along the top edge and "FIRST QUALITY" along the bottom edge. In the center is "M.B. FOSTER & SONS, 27 BROOK ST BOND ST, LONDON" and the Foster trademark, a green hunter's horn. The two labels are oriented in the same configuration as the label outlines on the Feature D bottle. No specific date was associated with the "old Bass Ale" bottle.

8. Fike, letter to the author, 1986.
9. U.S. Treasury Department, "Bottles—Capacity of Brandy, Ale, Beer, Porter, Treasury Department, February 21, 1884," in *Hand Book of the United States Tariff* (New York: F. B. Vandergrift and Co., 1897), 13–14, http://books.google.com/books?id=QGEuAAAAYAAJ&pg=PA13&lpg=PA13&dq=bass+ale+bottles&source=bl&ots=rB1jQG1mz9&sig=MbIXQNFnbsSAJyv_5UVoaY8qP_U&hl=en&ei=l8_iTL6mB43UtQPK7-Fm&sa=X&oi=book_result&ct=result&resnum=9&ved=0CEsQ6AEwCDgK#v=onepage&q=bass%20ale%20bottles&f=false; Hughes, *"A Bottle of Guinness Please,"* 86, 258. British and Irish bottlers used new glass bottles or recycled champagne bottles for the high-class beer trade.
10. Switzer, *The Bertrand Bottles*, 21. The steamboat *Bertrand* sank in the Missouri River on April 1, 1865, with cargo for Ft. Benton, Montana Territory. Champagne/wine bottles recovered from this cargo included foil wrappers with bunches of grapes but also company names.
11. Herskovitz, *Fort Bowie Material Culture*, 73–74.
12. Ruth W. Lee, *Early American Pressed Glass* (Wellesley Hills, Mass.: Lee Publications, 1960), 5; George L. McKearin and Helen McKearin, *American Glass* (New York: Crown Publication, 1948), 398. In classifying pressed glass of the period 1840 to 1880, Lee notes that tumblers with flutes (sometimes called panels) in an 1868 Blakewell, Pears and Co. catalog were listed by the number of flutes only for those tumblers manufactured primarily for ships, hotels, and barrooms (*Early American Pressed Glass*, 45). Interestingly, one of the tumblers illustrated in this catalog that looks much like the Type 2 specimen is called the "Montana Bar," although many companies produced similar tumblers. McKearin and McKearin state that pressed paneled tumblers were made extensively in the 1860s and 1870s in Pittsburgh and other glass houses in the Midwest. In addition to clear glass, these tumblers were made in deep blue and amethyst (McKearin and McKearin, *American Glass*, 398).
13. S. T. Millard, *Goblets* (Topeka: Central Press, 1938), plates 1, 2, 12, 72, 125.

Appendix 3

1. Historic archaeologist James T. Rock analyzed a subsample of cans from Feature D. His five-page report to the author, "The Powder River Supply Depot, Southeastern Montana, 24PE231, Cans," is dated April 1990. Illustrations by Rick Hill accompanied the report and are included in this appendix.

2. Jerome E. Petsche, *The Steamboat* Bertrand: *History, Excavation and Architecture* (Washington, D.C.: National Park Service, 1974), 60; Leslie Perry Peterson, DeSoto Wildlife Refuge, letter to the author, July 28, 1987. Both the smaller lid and can .505(b) are close to the size of yeast powder cans recovered from the steamboat *Bertrand*, which sank in 1865 with cargo consigned to Montana Territory. Yeast powder was among the canned goods available from the commissary of subsistence and the mouth of Powder River. The larger friction lids are very close to the size of those fitted to boot black cans in the *Bertrand* collection. While canned yeast powder was in the commissary of subsistence inventory and boot black was sold by the sutler, the Feature D specimens cannot be positively associated with a specific product.
3. Rock, "Powder River Supply Depot," 5. Sardines were exported from France as early as 1834, but Rock states that these are not French cans. He further states that these specimens were likely made before 1880 and predate the use of key-opened sardine cans.
4. Fike, letter to the author, 1986.
5. Ibid.
6. Dixon, *Boomtown Saloons*, 97. Lea and Perrins Worcestershire sauce was a commonly used condiment in the late 19th century. Bottles and stoppers appear in archaeological assemblages throughout the West.
7. Julian H. Toulouse, *Fruit Jars* (Camden: Thomas Nelson, 1969), 348.
8. *Bison* and *Bos* bones include those identified by Danny N. Walker, Office of the Wyoming State Archaeologist, Laramie, and Ken Deaver, Billings.
9. Stanley J. Olson, "Post-cranial Skeletal Characteristics of *Bison* and *Bos*," *Papers of the Peabody Museum of Archaeology and Ethnology* 35, no. 4 (1960), https://archive.org/details/postcranialskeleooolse.
10. Lathel F. Duffield, "Aging and Sexing the Post-cranial Skeleton of Bison," *Plains Anthropologist* 18, no. 60 (1973): 132–139.

Appendix 4

1. Wilson, *Bottles on the Western Frontier*, 39–43; Dixon, *Boomtown Saloons*, 82–28; Herskovitz, *Fort Bowie Material Culture*, 13.
2. See chapter 5, note 41.
3. Wilson, *Bottles on the Western Frontier*, 42–43; chapter 5, note 41. An 1873 advertisement for Tarrant's Effervescent Seltzer Aperient states that the product "cures dyspepsia and biliousness, restores the appetite, regulates the disordered bowels, and tones and invigorates the whole vital system."

Appendix 5

1. Clark, "White Clay Pipes from General Alfred Terry's 1876 Powder River Supply Depot."
2. Sudbury, "White Clay Pipes from the Old Connellsville Dump." Descriptive terms are derived from Sudbury.

3. Ibid., 30. The raised design on the Type 1 pipe is identical to the number 2, "roughead" style in the D. McDougall and Co. price list of ca. 1875.

Appendix 6

1. Berge, *Simpson Springs Station*, 242–244.
2. Billings Curation Center, 24PE231 collection, catalog number .927; bone sample identified by Danny N. Walker.
3. These leather items are brittle and somewhat desiccated. When in service, they might have been slightly wider.
4. U.S. War Department, Quartermaster's Department, *U.S. Army Wagon Harness (Horse and Mule)* (Washington, D.C.: Government Printing Office, 1877), 13, plates Showing Mule Harness, plate 1; U.S. War Department, *Ordnance Memoranda No. 29, Horse Equipments and Cavalry Accoutrements*, reprint, intro. by James S. Hutchins (Tucson: Westernlore Press, 1984), 27, 29. The quillor is the only piece of mule or horse harness where leather straps of different widths are attached to a ring. The 1877 quartermaster's report specifies a greater difference in the width of the breech strap and hip strap for a mule harness than for a horse harness. The difference in the width of these two straps for a horse harness is a half inch, and for a mule harness it is one inch. This difference in the Feature D specimen is much closer to that specified for a mule harness, at ⅞ inch. I also consulted *Ordnance Memoranda 29* to determine if the Feature D specimen might be a component of the McClellan saddle as described in 1885. While the saddle quarter straps attach to a metal ring, these straps are of equal width and the ring is just 2½ inches in diameter. The straps and ring of the Feature D artifact are too large to be a piece of a saddle.
5. I inquired about shipping crates recovered from the steamboat *Bertrand*. Leslie Perry Peterson, DeSoto National Wildlife Refuge, responded in a letter dated June 9, 1987. Shipping crates were recovered from the wreck of the steamboat *Bertrand*, which sank in the Missouri River in 1865 with cargo bound for Montana Territory. Many of these wooden crates were 22–26 inches long, 13–18 inches wide, and 5–13 inches deep. They contained many kinds of items including fruit, vegetables, Worcestershire sauce, boots, matches, and hardware. The Feature D specimen is within the size range of some shipping crates, but there is no way to determine specifically what it contained.
6. Berge, *Simpson Springs Station*, 256; Peter Priess, "Wire Nails in North America," *Bulletin of the Association for Preservation Technology* 5, no. 4 (1973): 87. Machine-cut nails date from ca. 1830 and were the dominate type of nail used in the United States until ca. 1890. While wire nails were invented in France in 1830, they were not used in the United States until ca. 1850. Wire nails began to be used in building construction in the United States ca. 1880 and outnumbered cut nails by ca. 1890; by 1900 use of wire nails greatly exceeded that of cut nails.
7. Peterson, letter to the author, June 9, 1987.

APPENDIX 7

1. Garavaglia and Worman, *Firearms of the American West*, 83–85; Hackley et al., *History of Modern U.S. Military Small Arms Ammunition*, 10.
2. Reedstrom, *Bugles, Banners and War Bonnets*, 282–285.
3. McChristian, *U.S. Army in the West*, 122; Scott et al., *Archaeological Perspectives on the Battle of the Little Bighorn*, 105.
4. Garavaglia and Worman, *Firearms of the American West*, 78–80, 278.

APPENDIX 8

1. Archaeologist Douglas D. Scott and his colleagues at the National Park Service Midwest Archaeological Center commented on photographs and descriptions of some of the Feature D artifacts, including buttons, in a letter to the author, March 10, 1989.
2. William J. Hunt Jr., "Fort Union Trading Post National Historic Site (32WI17) Material Culture Reports, part V: Buttons as Closures, Buttons as Decoration: A Nineteenth Century Example from Fort Union" (Lincoln: National Park Service, Midwest Archaeological Center, 1986), 32.
3. Sally C. Luscomb, *The Collector's Encyclopedia of Buttons* (Atglen, Pa.: Schiffer Publishing, 2006), 224. Quantities of work clothes buttons were being made in the late 19th century.
4. Hunt, "Fort Union Trading Post National Historic Site (32WI17) Material Culture Reports," 33; Scott, letter to the author, March 10, 1989.
5. Scott, letter to the author, March 10, 1989.

APPENDIX 9

1. Thuro, *Oil Lamps*, 15, 22.
2. Roy Ehrhardt and William Meggers, *American Pocket Watches: Identification and Price Guide Beginning to End 1830–1980* (Kansas City: Heart of America, 1987), 56–196.
3. Mark E. Randall, "Early Marbles," *Historical Archaeology* 5 (1971): 102.
4. Angione, *All-Bisque and Half-Bisque Dolls*, 79.
5. Coleman et al., *Collector's Encyclopedia of Dolls*, 240.
6. Angione, *All-Bisque and Half-Bisque Dolls*, 87.

APPENDIX 10

1. Ken Deaver, notes taken when analyzing bones from the Powder River depot excavation, 1986; Walker, "Canid Remains from the Powder River Supply Depot." Two archaeologists analyzed the canid remains and concluded independently that the skeleton is that of a dog rather than a coyote, wolf, or hybrid.
2. Walker, "Canid Remains from the Powder River Supply Depot," 64.
3. Deaver, notes, 1986.
4. Walker, "Canid Remains from the Powder River Supply Depot," 67.

APPENDIX 11

1. U.S. War Department, Records of the Office of the Commissary General of Subsistence, Provision Books.
2. Ephraim Dickson, National Museum of the U.S. Army being constructed at Ft. Belvoir, Virginia, personal communication. Mr. Dickson located the provision books in the National Archives. He explained that each line of entries documents total commodities on hand at the end of a month. Receipt of stores from one officer and transfer to another are noted in the remarks section of the book. Several titles in the book pertain to the Sioux War, but only two of these document subsistence stores with Terry's Yellowstone supply depot.
3. Greene, *Yellowstone Command*, 71–72. Low water levels in the fall precluded steamboats from reaching Tongue River. The Glendive Cantonment functioned as a supply depot from which freight could be forwarded to the Tongue River Cantonment via wagon trains. Infantry units at the Glendive facility also escorted the wagon trains.
4. Brown, "Yellowstone Supply Depot," 26.
5. Gray, *Centennial Campaign*, 103–105. Maj. Moore sent a letter to Gen. Terry on June 1, 1876, from the Glendive depot he had recently established on the Yellowstone River. He was forwarding a dispatch received from Col. Gibbon: Terry was with the Dakota column near Beaver Creek. The general concluded from this dispatch that there were no Indians in his immediate vicinity and decided to push on to Powder River, bypassing the Glendive depot. Moore noted in his letter to Terry that all of the freight except 100 tons of forage from Ft. Buford was now at the Glendive depot. In his letter heading, Moore referred to the Glendive depot as "Stanley's Crossing." Moore sent a second dispatch to Terry from Stanley's Crossing on June 5 affirming his compliance with the general's orders to send supplies to the mouth of the Powder. Terry then had Moore and his 6th Infantry guard transfer all of the supplies from Stanley's Crossing to the new Powder River depot.
6. "Post Returns Ft. Buford June, July, August 1876," in U.S. War Department, *Returns from U.S. Military Posts, 1800–1916*, Record Group 94, National Archives and Records Service, Washington, D.C., Roll 158. The post returns verify Craft's and Byrne's assignments at this time (see note 9 below).
7. Brown, "Yellowstone Supply Depot," 25.
8. Ibid., 30.
9. Ibid., 25, 27; "Post Returns, Ft. Buford, May and June 1876," in U.S. War Department, *Returns from U.S. Military Posts*; "Regimental Returns, 6th Infantry, June, July, 1876," in U.S. War Department, *Returns from the Regular Army Infantry Regiments, June 1821–December 1916*, Record Group 94, National Archives and Records Service, Washington, D.C. Citing regimental returns, Brown states that Maj. Moore assigned assistant commissary of subsistence duties at the Powder River depot to Lt. Josiah Chance, Co. G, 17th Infantry,

on June 16. Lt. Byrne was apparently acting as Moore's adjutant at that time in addition to other duties. This information is at odds with 6th Infantry regimental returns and Ft. Buford post returns for May–July indicating that Byrne remained depot assistant quartermaster and ACS during this period. Sixth Infantry regimental returns also record Byrne as ACS for the "Yellowstone Depot" in June and "Depot Commissary Powder River" in July; in August he was reported with his company supporting General Terry but was not listed as ACS. The provision book comports with the returns, as it does not show a transfer of stores from Lt. Byrne until the end of July. Regardless of who was Moore's ACS, the major was responsible for the subsistence stores until they were transferred to Lt. Thompson at the end of July; soon after the transfer, Moore's battalion was relieved as depot guard.

10. Greene, *Yellowstone Command*, 72.
11. "Regimental Returns, 22nd Infantry, November 1876," in U.S. War Department, *Returns from the Regular Army Infantry Regiments*, Roll 228.
12. U.S. War Department, Adjutant General's Office, *Official Army Register*, 21.

Bibliography

Adams, Gerald M. *The Post near Cheyenne: A History of Fort D. A. Russell, 1867–1930*. Boulder: Pruett Publishing, 1989.

Agnew, Jeremy. *Life of a Soldier on the Western Frontier*. Missoula: Mountain Press, 2008.

American Toy Marble Museum. "A Glossary of Marble Players' Terms." Accessed February 10, 2013, http://www.americantoymarbles.com/glossary.htm.

Angione, Genevieve. *All-Bisque and Half-Bisque Dolls*. Camden: Thomas Nelson and Sons, 1969.

Balicki, Joseph. "Watch Fires of a Hundred Circling Camps: Theoretical and Practical Approaches to Investigating Civil War Campsites." In *Historical Archaeology of Military Sites: Method and Topic*, edited by Clarence R. Grier, Lawrence E. Babits, Douglas D. Scott, and David G. Orr, 57–73. College Station: Texas A&M University Press, 2011.

Baron, Stanley. *Brewed in America: The History of Beer and Ale in the United States*. Boston: Little, Brown and Company, 1962.

Barsness, John, and William Dickinson. "Cannoneer's Hop: The Sully Campaign 1864." *Montana the Magazine of Western History* 16, no. 3 (1966): 23–29.

Baumann, Paul. *Collecting Antique Marbles*. Lombard: Wallace-Homestead Books, 1970.

Berge, Dale L. *Simpson Springs Station: Historical Archaeology in Western Utah*. Cultural Resource Series No. 6. Salt Lake City: Utah State Office Bureau of Land Management, 1980.

Bourke, John G. *Bourke's Diary from Journals of 1st Lt. John Gregory Bourke, June 27–Sept 15, 1876: Chronicle of the 1876 Indian War*. Edited by James Willert. La Mirada: James Willert Publisher, 1986.

———. *On the Border with Crook*. Lincoln: University of Nebraska Press, 1972. First published 1891 by Charles Scribner's Sons.

Bradley, James H. "Journal of James H. Bradley: The Sioux Campaign of 1876 under the Command of General John Gibbon." *Contributions to the Historical Society of Montana* 2 (1896): 140–226.

———. "Yellowstone Expedition of 1874." *Contributions to the Historical Society of Montana* 8 (1917): 105–125.

Brown, Lisle G. "The Yellowstone Supply Depot." *North Dakota History* 40, no. 1 (1973): 24–33.

Brown, Mark H. *The Plainsmen of the Yellowstone: A History of the Yellowstone Basin.* New York: G. P. Putnam's Sons, 1961.

"C&C Group." *Wikipedia*, accessed February 2014, https://en.wikipedia.org/wiki/C%26C_Group.

Capron, Thaddeus H. *Marching with General Crook or The Big Horn and Yellowstone Expedition against Hostile Indians in the Summer of 1876.* Edited by Ray Meketa. Douglas, Ala.: Cheechako Press, 1983.

Carroll, Matthew. "Diary of Matthew Carroll: Master in Charge of Transportation for Colonel John Gibbon's Expedition against the Sioux Indians, 1876." *Contributions to the Historical Society of Montana* 2 (1896): 229–240.

Clark, Gerald R. "White Clay Pipes from General Alfred Terry's 1876 Powder River Supply Depot, 24PE231, Southeastern Montana." Unpublished manuscript, 1988.

Clark, William A. "Centennial Address on the Origin, Growth and Resources of Montana." *Contributions to the Historical Society of Montana* 2 (1896): 45–60.

Clark, William P. William Philo Clark Diary, 1876. Small Collection 538, Montana Historical Society Archives, Helena.

Clifford, Walter. Diary of Captain Walter Clifford, Co. E., 7th Infantry. Marshall University Library, Huntington.

Coggins, Jack. *Arms and Equipment of the Civil War.* New York: Fairfax Press, 1983.

Coleman, Dorothy S., Elizabeth A. Coleman, and Evelyn J. Coleman. *The Collector's Encyclopedia of Dolls.* New York: Crown Publications, 1968.

Cook, Lauren J. "Tobacco-Related Material and the Construction of Working-Class Culture." In *Interdisciplinary Investigations of the Boott Mills, Lowell, Massachusetts, vol. 3: The Boarding House System as a Way of Life,* edited by Mary C. Beaudry and Stephen A. Mrozowski, 209–229. Boston: Government Printing Office, North Atlantic Region, National Park Service, 1989.

Craighill, William P. *The Army Officer's Pocket Companion; Principally Designed for Staff Officers in the Field.* New York: D. Van Nostrand, 1862.

Custer, Elizabeth B. *"Boots and Saddles" or Life in Dakota with General Custer.* Norman: University of Oklahoma Press, 1961.

Darling, Roger. *A Sad and Terrible Blunder, Generals Terry and Custer at the Little Big Horn: New Discoveries.* Vienna, Va.: Potomac-Western, 1990.

Davis, William C. *A Taste for War: The Culinary History of the Blue and the Gray.* Mechanicsburg, Pa.: Stackpole, 2003.

Delo, David M. *Peddlers and Post Traders: The Army Sutler on the Frontier.* Salt Lake City: University of Utah Press, 1992.

DeMallie, Raymond J. *The Sixth Grandfather: Black Elk's Teachings Given to John G. Neihardt.* Lincoln: University of Nebraska Press, 1984.

DeSmet, Pierre Jean. "From Fort Alexander to Fort Laramie." In *Exploring the Northern Plains, 1804–1876,* edited by Lloyd McFarling, 211–219. Caldwell: Caxton Printers, 1955.

DeWolf, James M. "The Diary and Letters of Dr. James M. DeWolf, Acting Assistant Surgeon, U.S. Army: His Record of the Sioux Expedition of 1876 Kept until His Death." Reprint. Transcribed and editorial notes by Edward S. Luce. State Historical Society of North Dakota, n.d. First published in *North Dakota History* 25, nos. 2–3 (April–July 1958).

Dixon, Kelly J. *Boomtown Saloons*. Reno: University of Nevada Press, 2005.

Duffield, Lathel F. "Aging and Sexing the Post-cranial Skeleton of Bison." *Plains Anthropologist* 18, no. 60 (1973): 132–139.

Ehrhardt, Roy, and William Meggers. *American Pocket Watches: Identification and Price Guide Beginning to End 1830–1980*. Kansas City: Heart of America, 1987.

English, William L. "With Gibbon against the Sioux in 1876: The Field Diary of Lt. William L. English." Edited with notes and introduction by Barry C. Johnson. *English Westerners' Brand Book* 9, no. 1 (1966): 1–10.

Essin, Emmett M. "Army Mule." *Montana the Magazine of Western History* 44, no. 2 (1994): 30–45.

Finerty, John F. *War-Path and Bivouac or The Conquest of the Sioux*. New ed. Norman: University of Oklahoma Press, 1961.

Fougera, Katherine G. *With Custer's Cavalry*. Caldwell: Caxton, 1940.

Fox, Richard A., Jr. "West River History: The Indian Village on Little Bighorn River, June 25–26, 1876." In *Legacy: New Perspectives on the Battle of the Little Bighorn*, edited by Charles E. Rankin, 139–165. Helena: Montana Historical Society Press, 1996.

Frost, Lawrence A. *Custer's 7th Cav and the Campaign of 1873*. El Segundo, Calif.: Upton and Sons, 1986.

Garavaglia, Louis A., and Charles G. Worman. *Firearms of the American West, 1866–1894*. Albuquerque: University of New Mexico Press, 1985.

Gard, Wayne. *The Great Buffalo Hunt*. New York: Alfred A. Knopf, 1960.

Garlington, Ernest A. *The Lieutenant E. A. Garlington Narrative, pt. 1*. Edited by John Carroll. Bryan: John Carroll Publisher, 1978.

Garretson, Martin S. *The American Bison*. New York: New York Zoological Society, 1938.

Godfrey, Edward S. *The Field Diary of Lt. Edward Settle Godfrey, Commanding Co. K, 7th Cavalry Regiment under Lt. Colonel George Armstrong Custer in the Sioux Encounter at the Battle of the Little Big Horn*. Edited with notes by Edgar I. Stewart and Jane R. Stewart. Portland, Ore.: Champoeg, 1957.

Gray, John S. *Centennial Campaign: The Sioux War of 1876*. Fort Collins: Old Army Press, 1976.

———. *Custer's Last Campaign: Mitch Boyer and the Little Bighorn Reconstructed*. Lincoln: University of Nebraska Press, 1991.

———. "The Pack Train on George A. Custer's Last Campaign." *Nebraska History* 57, no. 1 (1976): 53–68.

———. "Sutler on Custer's Last Campaign." *North Dakota History: Journal of the Northern Plains* 43, no. 3 (1976): 14–21.

Greene, Jerome A. "A Battle among Skirmishes." In *Legacy: New Perspectives on the Battle of the Little Bighorn*, edited by Charles E. Rankin, 83–92. Helena: Montana Historical Society Press, 1996.

———. *Yellowstone Command: Colonel Nelson A. Miles and the Great Sioux War 1876–1877*. Lincoln: University of Nebraska Press, 1991.

Grinnell, George B. *The Fighting Cheyennes*. Civilization of the American Indian Series. Norman: University of Oklahoma, 1977.

Hackley, F. W., W. H. Woodin, and E. L. Scranton. *History of Modern U.S. Military Small Arms Ammunition*, vol. 1. New York: Macmillan, 1967.

Hafen, LeRoy R., and Ann W. Hafen. *Powder River Campaigns and Sawyers Expedition of 1865*. Glendale, Calif.: Arthur H. Clark, 1961.

Hampton, H. D. "Powder River Indian Expedition of 1865." *Montana the Magazine of Western History* 14, no. 4 (1964): 2–15.

Hanson, Joseph M. *The Conquest of the Missouri: Being the Story of the Life and Exploits of Captain Grant Marsh*. New York: Murray Hill, 1946.

Hardorff, Richard G. "Packs, Packers, and Pack Details: Logistics and Custer's Pack Train." In *Custer and His Times: Bk. 3*, edited by Gregory J. W. Urwin and Roberta E. Fagan, 225–248. Conway: University of Central Arkansas Press, 1987.

Hedren, Paul L. *After Custer: Loss and Transformation in the Sioux Country*. Norman: University of Oklahoma, 2011.

Herskovitz, Robert M. *Fort Bowie Material Culture*. Anthropology Papers of the University of Arizona 31. Tucson: University of Arizona Press, 1978.

Heski, Thomas M. "Camp Powell: The Powder River Supply Depot." *Research and Review: The Journal of the Little Big Horn Associates* 17, no. 1 (2003): 13–24.

Hill, Michael D., and Ben Innis. "The Fort Buford Diary of Private Sanford, 1876–1877." *North Dakota History: Journal of the Northern Plains* 52, no. 3 (1985): 2–39.

Homans, John. *What's a Dog For? The Surprising History, Science, Philosophy and Politics of Man's Best Friend*. New York: Penguin Press, 2012.

Houston, James A. *The Sinews of War: Army Logistics 1775–1953*. Army Historic Series. Office of the Chief of Military History, U.S. Army. Washington, D.C.: Government Printing Office, 1966.

Hughes, David. *"A Bottle of Guinness Please": The Colourful History of Guinness*. Wokingham, England: Phimboy, 2006.

Hunt, William J., Jr. "Fort Union Trading Post National Historic Site (32WI17) Material Culture Reports, part V: Buttons as Closures, Buttons as Decoration: A Nineteenth Century Example from Fort Union." Lincoln: National Park Service, Midwest Archaeological Center, 1986.

Hutchins, James S. "The Cavalry Campaign Outfit at the Little Big Horn." In *The Custer Reader*, edited by Paul A. Hutton, 319–335. Lincoln: University of Nebraska Press, 1992.

Hutton, Paul A. *Phil Sheridan and His Army*. Lincoln: University of Nebraska Press, 1985.

Innis, Ben. "Bottoms Up! The Smith and Leighton Yellowstone Store Ledger of 1876." *North Dakota History: Journal of the Northern Plains* 51, no. 3 (1984): 24–38.
Keenan, Jerry. *The Life of Yellowstone Kelly*. Albuquerque: University of New Mexico Press, 2006.
Kilburn, C. L. *Notes on Preparing Stores for the United States Army*. Cincinnati: Bradley and Webb, Steam Printers and Stationers, 1863.
King, Charles. *Campaigning with Crook*. Norman: University of Oklahoma Press, 1964.
King, James T. *War Eagle: A Life of General Eugene A. Carr*. Lincoln: University of Nebraska Press, 1964.
Knight, Oliver. *Life and Manners in the Frontier Army*. Norman: University of Oklahoma Press, 1978.
Koch, Peter. "Historical Sketch: Bozeman, Gallatin Valley and Bozeman Pass." *Contributions to the Historical Society of Montana* 2 (1896): 126–139.
Larocque, Francois-Antoine. "Francoise-Antoine Larocque's 'Yellowstone Journal.'" In *Early Fur Trade on the Northern Plains: Canadian Traders among the Mandan and Hidatsa Indians, 1738–1818*, edited by W. Raymond Wood and Thomas D. Thiessen, 156–220. Norman: University of Oklahoma Press, 1985.
Larson, Robert W. *Gall: Lakota War Chief*. Norman: University of Oklahoma Press, 2007.
Lee, Ruth W. *Early American Pressed Glass*. Wellesley Hills, Mass.: Lee Publications, 1960.
Leeson, Michael, ed. *History of Montana*. Chicago: Warner, Beers and Company, 1885.
Lewis, Meriwether. *The Lewis and Clark Expedition*, 3 vols. The 1814 edition. Edited by Archibald Hanna and William H. Goetzmann. Keystone Western American Series. Philadelphia: J. B. Lippincott, 1961.
Libby, O. G., ed. *The Arikara Narrative of the Campaign against the Hostile Dakota June 1876*. North Dakota Historical Collections 6. Reprint. New York: Sol Lewis, 1973. First published 1920 in Bismarck.
Liddic, Bruce R., ed. *I Buried Custer: The Diary of Pvt. Thomas W. Coleman, 7th U.S. Cavalry*. College Station: Creative Publishing Co., 1979.
Lockhart, Bill. "The Origins and Life of the Export Beer Bottle." *Bottles and Extras: The Official Publication of the Federation of Historical Bottle Collectors* 18, no. 3 (2007): 49–58.
Lubetkin, M. John. "The Forgotten Yellowstone Surveying Expeditions of 1871: W. Milnor Roberts and the Northern Pacific Railroad in Montana." *Montana the Magazine of Western History* 52, no. 4 (2002): 32–47.
———. "'No Fighting Is to Be Apprehended': Major Eugene M. Baker, Sitting Bull, and the Northern Pacific Railroad's 1872 Western Yellowstone Surveying Expedition." *Montana the Magazine of Western History* 56, no. 2 (2006): 28–41.

Luhn, Gerhard L. "The Big Horn and Yellowstone Expedition of 1876 as Seen through the Letters of Captain Gerhard Luke Luhn." *Annals of Wyoming*, Spring 1973: 27–46.

Luscomb, Sally C. *The Collector's Encyclopedia of Buttons*. Atglen, Pa.: Schiffer Publishing, 2006.

MacDonald, John G. "History of Navigation on the Yellowstone River." M.A. thesis, Montana State University, 1950.

Madsen, Brigham D. *Glory Hunter: A Biography of Patrick Edward Connor*. Salt Lake City: University of Utah Press, 1990.

Malone, Michael P., and Richard B. Roeder. *Montana: A History of Two Centuries*. Seattle: University of Washington Press, 1976.

Marquis, Thomas B. *Wooden Leg: A Warrior Who Fought Custer*. Bison Book reprint. Lincoln: University of Nebraska Press, n.d. First published 1931 by Midwest Company.

McChristian, Douglas C. *The U.S. Army in the West, 1870–1880: Uniforms, Weapons and Equipment*. Norman: University of Oklahoma Press, 2006.

McClernand, Edward J. *With the Indian and the Buffalo in Montana 1870–1878*. Glendale, Calif.: Arthur Clark, 1969.

McHugh, Tom. *The Time of the Buffalo*. New York: Alfred Knopf, 1972.

McKearin, George L., and Helen McKearin. *American Glass*. New York: Crown Publication, 1948.

Meddaugh, Samuel L. Diary of S. L. Meddaugh, 6th U.S. Infantry, Covering the Indian Campaign along the Yellowstone River, from May to September, 1876. Newberry Library, Chicago.

Merrington, Marguerite. *The Custer Story: The Life and Intimate Letters of General George A. Custer and His Wife Elizabeth*. Bison Book reprint. Lincoln: University of Nebraska Press, 1987. First published 1950 by Devin-Adair Company.

Michno, Gregory F. *Lakota Noon: The Indian Narrative of Custer's Defeat*. Missoula: Mountain Press, 1977.

Miles, George M. George M. Miles Papers 1876–1878. Small Collection 318, Montana Historical Society Archives, Helena.

Millard, S. T. *Goblets*. Topeka: Central Press, 1938.

Morris, Roy, Jr. *Sheridan: The Life and Wars of General Phil Sheridan*. New York: Crown Publishers, 1992.

Murray, Robert A. *The Army Moves West: Supplying the Western Indian Wars Campaigns*. Fort Collins: Old Army Press, 1981.

———. "Wagons on the Plains." *By Valor and Arms: The Journal of American Military History* 2, no. 4 (1976): 37–40.

National Integrated Pest Management Network. "Public-Health Pesticide Applicator Training Manual, Chapter 6: Flies." Accessed January 14, 2013, http://entomology.ifas.ufl.edu/fasulo/vector/chap06.pdf.

National Park Service. "These Relics of Barbarism: A History of Furniture in Barracks and Guardhouses of the United States Army, 1800–1880." Report

prepared for Harpers Ferry Center by David A. Clary and Associates, Harpers Ferry, W.V., n.d.
Olson, Stanley J. "Post-cranial Skeletal Characteristics of *Bison* and *Bos*." *Papers of the Peabody Museum of Archaeology and Ethnology* 35, no. 4 (1960).
Paulding, Holmes O. "Dr. Paulding and His Remarkable Diary." Notes and introduction by Barry C. Johnson. In *Sidelights of the Sioux Wars*, edited by Francis B. Taunton, 47–69. Special Publication 2. London: English Westerners' Society, 1967.
Petsche, Jerome E. *The Steamboat* Bertrand*: History, Excavation and Architecture*. Washington, D.C.: National Park Service, 1974.
Pfaller, Louis. *Father De Smet in Dakota*. Richardson, N.D.: Assumption Abby Press, 1962.
Physician and Pharmaceutist 2, no. 7 (1870): 17.
Potter, James E. "The Great Source of Amusement: Hunting in the Frontier Army." *Montana the Magazine of Western History* 55, no. 3 (2005): 34–47.
Priess, Peter. "Wire Nails in North America." *Bulletin of the Association for Preservation Technology* 5, no. 4 (1973): 87–92.
Quivey, Addison. "The Yellowstone Expedition of 1874." *Contributions to the Historical Society of Montana* 1 (1876): 268–284.
Rafferty, Sean M., and Rob Mann, eds. *Smoking and Culture: The Archaeology of Tobacco Pipes in Eastern North America*. Knoxville: University of Tennessee Press, 2004.
Randall, Mark E. "Early Marbles." *Historical Archaeology* 5 (1971): 102–105.
Raynolds, W. F. *Report of the Exploration of the Yellowstone River*. Washington, D.C.: Government Printing Office, 1868.
Reedstrom, Ernest L. *Bugles, Banners and War Bonnets*. New York: Bonanza Books, 1986. First published 1977 by Caxton Publishers.
Reynolds, John D. "Archaeological Investigation at Old Fort Scott, 14BO302, Fort Scott, Kansas 1968 to 1972." Report submitted to the National Park Service, Omaha, 1983.
Rickey, Don, Jr. *Forty Miles a Day on Beans and Hay*. Norman: University of Oklahoma Press, 1963.
Risch, Erna. *Quartermaster Support of the Army: A History of the Corps 1775–1939*. Washington, D.C.: Center of Military History, U.S. Army, 1989.
Robertson, Francis B. "We Are Going to Have a Big Sioux War: Colonel David S. Stanley's Yellowstone Expedition, 1872." *Montana the Magazine of Western History* 34, no. 4 (1984): 2–15.
Rockwell, Ronald V. *The U.S. Army in Frontier Montana*. Helena: Sweetgrass Books, 2009.
Roe, Charles F. Letter from 2nd Lt. Charles Francis Roe to his wife dated August 18th, 1876 at Powder River, M.T. Marshall University Library, Huntington.
———. Letter from 2nd Lt. Charles Francis Roe to his wife dated August 21, 1876 at Powder River, M.T. Marshall University Library, Huntington.

Ronnenberg, Herman. *Beer and Brewing in the Inland Northwest 1850–1950*. Moscow: University of Idaho Press, 1993.
Rzeczkowski, Frank. "The Crow Indians and the Bozeman Trail." *Montana the Magazine of Western History* 49, no. 4 (1999): 30–47.
Sanders, Helen F. *A History of Montana*. Chicago: Lewis Publishing Company, 1913.
Schneider, George A., ed. *The Freeman Journal: The Infantry Campaign of 1876*. San Rafael: Presidio Press, 1977.
Scott, Douglas D. "Euro-American Archaeology." In *Archaeology on the Great Plains*, edited by W. Raymond Wood, 481–501. Lawrence: University Press of Kansas, 1998.
———. "An Officer's Latrine at Fort Larned and Inferences on Status." *Plains Anthropologist* 34, no. 123 (1989): 23–34.
———, ed. *Papers on Little Bighorn Battlefield Archeology: The Equipment Dump, Marker 7, and the Reno Crossing*. Reprints in Anthropology 42. Lincoln: J&L Reprint Co., 1991.
Scott, Douglas D., Richard A. Fox Jr., Melissa A. Connor, and Dick Harmon. *Archaeological Perspectives on the Battle of the Little Bighorn*. Norman: University of Oklahoma Press, 1989.
Scott, Henry L. *Military Dictionary: Comprising Technical Definitions; Information on Raising and Keeping Troops; Actual Service, Including Makeshifts and Improved Matériel; and Law, Government, Regulation, and Administration Relating to Land Forces*. New York: D. Van Nostrand, 1861.
Scott, Kim A. *Splendid on a Large Scale—The Writings of Hans Peter Gyllembourg Koch Montana Territory 1869–1874*. Helena: Bedrock Editions and Drumlummon Institute, 2010.
Smith, Victor G. *The Champion Buffalo Hunter: The Frontier Memoirs of Yellowstone Vic Smith*. Edited by Jeanette Prodgers. Guilford, Conn.: Globe Pequot Press, 1997.
"The Smith and Leighton Yellowstone Store Ledger of 1876." Ben Innis Collection. Fort Union Trading Post National Historic Site, Williston, N.D.
South, Stanley. *Method and Theory in Historical Archeology*. New York: Academic Press, 1977.
Spence, Clark C. *Montana: A Bicentennial History*. New York: W. W. Norton and Company, 1978.
Springer, Charles H. *Soldiering in Sioux Country: 1865*. Edited by Benjamin F. Cooling III. San Diego: Frontier Heritage Press, 1971.
Stanley, David S. *Report of the Yellowstone Expedition of 1873*. Washington, D.C.: Government Printing Office, 1874.
Stewart, Edgar I. *Penny-an-Acre Empire in the West*. Norman: University of Oklahoma Press, 1968.
Sudbury, J. Byron. "White Clay Pipes from the Old Connellsville Dump, 36 Fa 140." *Historic Clay Tobacco Pipe Studies* 1 (1980): 23–46.
Switzer, Ronald R. *The* Bertrand *Bottles: A Study of 19th Century Glass and Ceramic Containers*. Washington, D.C.: National Park Service, 1974.

"The Tarrant Explosion. A Million Dollars Damage." *American Druggist and Pharmaceutical Record: A Semi-monthly Illustrated Journal of Pharmacy* 37 (1900): 289–290.

Thuro, Catherine M. *Oil Lamps, the Kerosene Era in North America*. Des Moines: Wallace-Homestead Book Company, 1976.

Topping, E. S. *The Chronicles of the Yellowstone*. Reprint. Introduction, notes, and bibliography by Robert A. Murray. Minneapolis: Ross and Haines, 1968.

Toulouse, Julian H. *Fruit Jars*. Camden: Thomas Nelson, 1969.

U.S. Treasury Department. "Bottles—Capacity of Brandy, Ale, Beer, Porter, Treasury Department, February 21, 1884." In *Hand Book of the United States Tariff*. New York: F. B. Vandergrift and Co., 1897.

U.S. War Department. *Chronological List of Actions, &c., with Indians from January 15, 1837 to January, 1891*. Compiled and edited with introduction by Dale E. Floyd. Fort Collins: Old Army Press, 1979.

———. *Manual for Army Cooks*. Washington, D.C.: Government Printing Office, 1896. http://www.grandarmyofthefrontier.org/articles/manual_for_army_cooks-1896.pdf.

———. *Ordnance Memoranda No. 29, Horse Equipments and Cavalry Accoutrements*. Reprint. Introduction by James S. Hutchins. Tucson: Westernlore Press, 1984. First published 1891 by Government Printing Office, Washington, D.C.

———. Quartermaster Report of Persons and Articles Hired, August 1876. Record Group 92, National Archives and Records Administration, Washington, D.C.

———. Records of the Office of the Commissary General of Subsistence, Provision Books. Entry 36, Record Group 192, National Archives, Washington, D.C.

———. *Report of the Medical Department, Big Horn and Yellowstone Expedition, Montana, 1876*. Dr. B. A. Clements, Surgeon, U.S.A., Medical Directory. Record Group 94, National Archives and Records Administration, Washington, D.C.

———. *Report of the Secretary of War 1876*. Washington, D.C.: Government Printing Office, 1876.

———. *Report of the Secretary of War 1877*. Washington, D.C.: Government Printing Office, 1877.

———. *Report of the Secretary of War 1880*. Washington, D.C.: Government Printing Office, 1880.

———. *Returns from the Regular Army Infantry Regiments, June 1821–December 1916*. Record Group 94, National Archives and Records Service, Washington, D.C.

———. *Returns from U.S. Military Posts, 1800–1916*. Record Group 94, National Archives and Records Service, Washington, D.C.

U.S. War Department, Adjutant General's Office. *Official Army Register for January, 1876*.

U.S. War Department, Army Corps of Engineers. *Report upon United States Geographical Surveys West of the One Hundredth Meridian*. Washington, D.C.: Government Printing Office, 1889.

U.S. War Department, Quartermaster's Department. *U.S. Army Wagon Harness (Horse and Mule)*. Washington, D.C.: Government Printing Office, 1877.

Utley, Robert M. "The Bozeman Trail before John Bozeman: A Busy Land." *Montana the Magazine of Western History* 53, no. 2 (2003): 20–31.

———. *Cavalier in Buckskin: George Armstrong Custer and the Western Military Frontier*. Norman: University of Oklahoma Press, 1988.

———. *Frontier Regulars: The United States Army and the Indian, 1866–1891*. Bloomington: Indiana University Press, 1977. First published 1973.

———. *Frontiersmen in Blue: The United States Army and the Indian, 1848–1865*. Lincoln: University of Nebraska Press, 1967.

———. *Sitting Bull: The Life and Times of an American Patriot*. New York: Henry Holt and Company, 1993.

Vaughn, J. W. *The Reynolds Campaign on Powder River*. Norman: University of Oklahoma Press, 1961.

Vihlene, Shannon M. "Custer's Last Drag: An Examination of Tobacco Use among the Seventh Cavalry during the Nineteenth Century." M.A. thesis, University of Montana, 2008.

Wagner, David E. *Patrick Connor's War: The 1865 Powder River Indian Expedition*. Norman: Arthur H. Clark Company, 2010.

———. *Powder River Odyssey, Nelson Cole's Western Campaign of 1865: The Journals of Lyman G. Bennett and Other Eyewitness Accounts*. Norman: Arthur H. Clark Company, 2009.

Wagner, Fredrick C., III. *Participants in the Battle of the Little Big Horn: A Biographical Dictionary of Sioux, Cheyenne and United States Military Personnel*. Jefferson, N.C.: McFarland and Company, 2011.

Wagner, Glendolin D. *Old Neutriment*. Bison Book edition. Reprint. Introduction by Brian W. Dippie. Lincoln: University of Nebraska Press, 1989. First published 1934 by Ruth Hill Publisher, Boston.

Walker, Danny N. "Canid Remains from the Powder River Supply Depot, Prairie County, Montana, 24PE231." *Archaeology in Montana* 36, no. 2 (1995): 63–82.

Weibert, Don L. *The 1874 Invasion of Montana: A Prelude to the Custer Disaster*. Billings: self-published, Benchmark Printers, 1993.

West, Elliott. *The Saloon on the Rocky Mountain Mining Frontier*. Lincoln: University of Nebraska Press, 1979.

Willert, James. *After Little Big Horn: 1876 Campaign Rosters*. La Mirada: James Willert Publisher, 1985.

———. *Little Big Horn Diary: Chronicle of the 1876 Indian War*. La Mirada: James Willert Publisher, 1982.

Wilson, Rex L. *Bottles on the Western Frontier*. Tucson: University of Arizona Press, 1981.

Wylie, Lennon. "Belfast/Ulster Street Directory, 1880." Accessed April 22, 2012, http://www.lennonwylie.co.uk/BSD1880adverts.htm.

Index

Adams, Mary, 38, 76
African-Americans, 194n24. *See also* Adams, Mary
agate, 36, 103–4, 181
agriculture, in Yellowstone-Powder River region, 70
alcoholic beverages, 31, 54–55, 71, 73, 75–76, 88–89, 90, 96–99, 117–18, 136–47, 219n30. *See also* beer; bottles; goblets; tumblers; wine
Allison Commission, 45–46, 48
American Fur Company, 23, 193n6
Anheuser-Busch Co., 107
animals. *See* bones; buffalo; dogs; horses; hunting; mules; oxen
appendixes, as reference for future research, 4
Arapaho, 28, 194n23
archaeology: and Bureau of Land Management, 1–2; and definition of feature, 191n2; and investigations of battlefield of Battle of Little Bighorn, 1, 3–4, 226n60, 226n64–65; and investigations of Civil War campsites, 227n80; and investigations of precontact Native American sites in Yellowstone-Powder River region, 19. *See also* artifacts; dating; excavation; historical archaeology; Powder River Depot site
Arikara tribe, 56, 57, 71, 213n44. *See also* Red Cloud
Armells Creek, 42
Army, and management of supply and transportation, 13–18, 109–15, 199n66
Army and Navy Journal, 203n12
artifacts, from Powder River depot site: and alcoholic beverages, 96–99, 117–18, 136–47; and clothing, 105, 123–24, 174–75; and firearms, 105, 172–73; and food, 101–2, 148–59; and medicines, 99–100, 160–61; miscellaneous categories of, 176–81; and tobacco use, 162–64; and transportation, 165–72. *See also* bones; cultural materials
Ashton, Dr. Isaiah, 76, 211n12
Avant Courier (newspaper), 44, 198n56

Baliran, Augustus, 200n76
Bass ale, 96–98, 117, 127, 138, 142, 217–18n13–15, 218n17, 218n20
Beaver Creek, 38
beer, 96–99, 107–8, 118, 136–42, 218n27, 219n28. *See also* alcoholic beverages; Bass ale
Belknap, William, 205n39
Bennett, Lyman, 195n26
Benson's Landing, 54
Benteen, Capt. Frederick, 62
Bertrand (steamboat), 171, 216n1, 226n67, 229n10, 230n2, 231n5
Big Hadatsa Village (Crow), 22
Billings Curation Center, 148
Black Elk (Oglala), 85, 214n56, 214n58
Blackfoot tribe, 213n44
Black Hills, Custer's reconnaissance of in 1874, 45
Black Whetstone (Lakota), 195n31
bones: and artifacts at Powder River depot site, 101–2, 125, 157, *158–59*, 166, 182, 230n8; and cultural materials from Little Bighorn Battlefield, 122–23, 125. *See also* buffalo; dogs; horses
Bostwick, Henry, 205n33
bottles, 136–45, 154–56, 160–61, 228n2, 228–29n7, 229n9–10, 230n6
Bourke, Lt. John Gregory, 88, 102, 103–104
Boyer, Mitch, 55, 60, 193n7, 198n58, 208n62

245

Bozeman (town), 45, 47–48, 69, 116, 219n28
Bozeman Trail, 26, 28, 30, 34, 193n11, 197n50
Bradley, Lt. James, 55, 102, 202n97
Bridger, Jim, 22, 23, 29, 55, 193n11, 198n58
Brisbin, Maj. James S., 54, 116
Brockmeyer, Wesley, 80, 81, 83, 84, 213n38, 213n44, 213–14n50
Bronson, Nelson, 74
Brown, Lisle G., 233n9
buffalo: and bones from Powder River depot site, 101–2, 157, *158–59*; extirpation of in aftermath of Sioux War, 68–69, 106–7; and railroad surveys of 1871–1873, 35; and Raynolds expedition, 24
Bureau of Land Management, 1, 126
Burke, E&J, 96, 97, 98, 140, 218n17, 218n19
Burkman, John, 125, 126, 227n74
Burlington Northern Railroad, 8, 191n3–4. *See also* Northern Pacific Railroad
Burnett, Finn, 31
buttons, 105, 123–24, 174–75
Byrne, Lt. Bernard, 186, 187, 234n9

Calypso (railroad station), 70
Campbell, Dave, 80, 81, 83, 84
Campbell, Lt. William J., 187
candles, 104
cans and canned foods, 73, 87, 100, 101, 125, 148–53, 226–27n71, 230n2–3
Cantrell & Cochrane (C&C Group), 143, 144, 145, 219n34
Capron, Lt. Thaddeus, 103
Carr, Lt. Col. Eugene, 88, 102
Carroll (steamboat), 64, 66, 77, 79, 115
Carroll, Matt, 88, 98, 99, 120
cartridges. *See* firearms
cattle. *See* bones; oxen
Causby, Sgt. Thomas, 98
Chance, Lt. Josiah, 233n9
Chestnut, James, 54
Cheyenne: and conflicts in Yellowstone-Powder River region prior to Sioux War, 194n23, 197n50; and Powder River expedition of 1865, 28, 29; and Sioux War of 1876, 51, 59–60, 62, 85, 195n31; and Yellowstone-Powder River region at time of contact, 20, 193n10; and Yellowstone Wagon Road and Prospecting Expedition, 43, 44. *See also* Dull Knife; Little Wolf; Old Bear; Roman Nose; Wooden Leg
children, artifacts associated with at Powder River depot site, 105, 119–20, 221n77. *See also* dolls; marbles
"circular ridge," at Powder River depot site, 95
civilians: role of in Army supply system, 16–18; as scouts for Army, 57
Civil War: and archaeological investigations of campsites, 227n80; and field baking ovens, 121, 228n5; and organization of Army, 199n66; and Powder River expedition of 1865, 26, 30
Clark, Dr. Elbert, 211n12
Clark, William, 22, 23
Clark, William Andrews, 116–17, 223n28
Clark, Lt. William P., 86, 95, 214n63
Clarke, Capt. Francis, 77, 79
clay pipes, 103, 117, 119, 130, *132*, 162–64, 220–21n60–61, 224n30
Clifford, Capt. Walter, 84, 98
climate: and Sioux War of 1876, 49, 51, 65, 90–91; of Yellowstone-Powder River region, 23–24, 203n12
closures, for bottles, 136, 155–56
clothing, artifacts related to, 105, 123–24, 174–75
coal, 103. *See also* lignite
Cody, Buffalo Bill, 65, 67
Cole, Col. Nelson, 26–34, 194n24, 195n27, 195n28, 195n31, 196n42, 197n47
Coleman, James, 211n14
Coleman, Pvt. Thomas, 223n20, 226n66
Collins, M. H., 176
Colt firearms, 105, 123, 172, 173
Commissary Department (Army), 15, 73, 100, 113, 183–89, 210n5–6
Conner, Gen. Patrick, 26–34, 49, 194–95n25, 195n28, 195n32, 197n47, 197n49
Craft, Lt. David, 186
crates, and artifacts, 124, 168–69, 226n67, 231n5
Crazy Horse (Lakota), 30, 37, 59, 63, 68
Crazy Woman Creek, 193n11
Crook, Brig. Gen. George, 48, 50–53, 59–60, 63, 64–67, 68, 86–92, 112, 206n47, 222n8
Crow tribe, 20, 22, 43, 45, 55, 59, 60,

INDEX

193n10, 194n23, 197n50, 197n53, 201n87, 201n91
cultural materials: from Feature D at Powder River depot site, 96–106; and indicators of social and economic status, 118–19; from Powder River depot site compared to Little Bighorn Battlefield, 3–4, 122–26; preservation of after deposition, 130. *See also* artifacts
cultural norms, and alcohol consumption, 90
Custer, Lt. Col. George A.: and Battle of Little Bighorn, 61–64, 114, 127, 208n62; and dogs, 102, 125, 199n70, 227n74; and post traders, 205n39; and railroad surveys of 1871–1873, 37–38, 39, 41, 199n67, 203n12; rest and recreation at Powder River depot, 119; and Sioux War of 1876, 49, 55–56, 58–59, 60–64; and supply issues, 73, 200n81, 207n52, 222n8; and Yellowstone Wagon Road and Prospecting Expedition, 45
Custer Creek, 6, 38, 92

Dakota tribe, 56
Daniels, Zed, 205n33
dating: of Feature D at Powder River depot site, 106–108; and recovery of goods from steamboat *Bertrand*, 216n1
Deaver, Ken, 230n8
DeLacey, Sergeant, 89
Department of Fish, Wildlife, and Parks (FWP, Montana), 5–8, 191n1
Department of the Platte (Army), 14
DeSmet, Pierre Jean, 20, 34, 70
DeWolf, Dr. James, 115, 223n21
Dickson, Ephraim, 233n2
disciplinary problems, at Powder River depot, 76
disease. *See* dysentery; medicines; scurvy; typhoid fever
Division of Dakota (Army), 14
Division of the Missouri (Army), 13–18
dogs: bones of at Powder River depot site, 102, 117, 133, 157, 182; and Custer, 102, 125, 199n70, 227n74; and Little Bighorn Battlefield site, 125–26; and Sioux War of 1876, 75, 117; and Yellowstone Wagon Road and Prospecting Expedition, 42

dolls (toy), 105, 120, 178–79, 221n77, 225n48
Donahoe, Pvt. John, 80
DuBarry, Maj. Beekman, 113–14, 222n13
Dull Knife (Cheyenne), 30
dysentery, 100

eggs and eggshells, 101, 157
E. H. Durfee (steamboat), 80
Elk River (Yellowstone River), 20
English, Lt. William, 205n30
excavation: and analysis of Powder River depot site, 8–11; details of and formation of Features D and F at Powder River depot site, 129–35; of Little Bighorn Battlefield, 226n60
Export Bottlers Ltd., London, 218n19

Far West (steamboat), 57, 58, 60, 63, 64, 65, 66, 67, 71, 74, 80, 85–86, 91, 92, 94–95, 217n6
Fike, Richard E., 228n1–2
firearms: and cartridges from Little Bighorn Battlefield site, 123; and cartridges from Powder River depot site, 105, 172–73; and Yellowstone Wagon Road and Prospecting Expedition, 201n93
fish and fishing, 54, 157, 204n28
fly pupae, and preservation of artifacts, 130, 132–33, 157, 228n3
foil wrappers, and bottles, 136, 139–41, 142–43
foods: Commissary Department and supply of basic, 15, 16; and cultural materials from Powder River depot site, 100–102, 148–59; and post gardens and bakeries, 73, 211n17; and supplies at Powder River depot, 73, 87. *See also* bones; cans and canned foods; fish and fishing; hunting
Forsyth, Mjr. George, 199n68
Forsyth, Lt. Col. James W., 202n1
"Fort Beans," 64, 65
Fort Buford (North Dakota), 69–70, 193n6, 197n52
Fort Connor (Colorado), 30
Fort Ellis (Montana), 36, 54, 204n28
Fort Keogh (Montana), 69–70, 92
Fort Laramie (Wyoming), 31

Fort Laramie Treaty of 1868, 34–35, 37, 193n10, 202n101
Fort Larned (Kansas), 118
Fort Lincoln (North Dakota), 57
Fort Pease (Montana), 48, 54, 203n5
Fort Rice (North Dakota), 29
Fort Sarpy (Montana), 23
Fort Stambaugh (Wyoming Territory), 153
Foster and Sons, M. B., 96, 97, 141, 142, 143, 218n18–19, 229n7
Fourth of July celebration, 76
Fox, Richard A., Jr., 207n57
French, and early history of Yellowstone-Powder River region, 20, 22
Frozen Charlotte. *See* dolls
fur trade, 22–23, 193n6

Gall (Lakota), 30, 34, 36, 37, 39, 63, 194n16, 197n52
Gallatin valley, 41, 44–45, 202n98
Garlington, Lt. Ernest, 89
Garretry, Lt. Frank, 81, 84
"Garry Owen" (song), 74, 127
Gayle, Sgt. William G., 121, 217n9
geography, of Yellowstone-Powder River region, 19–20
George, Pvt. William, 7, 76, 84, 212n25
Gibbon, Col. John, 53–55, 63, 111–12
ginger ale, 99, 143–45
Glacier Park Company, 191n3
Glendive Creek, 38, 68, 183, 186, 187, 205n38
goblets, 146–47
Godfrey, Lt. Edward, 88, 90, 208n71, 215n75, 220n45
gold, Yellowstone Wagon Road and Prospecting Expedition and reports of, 41–46
Goose Creek, 59
Gore, Sir George, 22, 198n58
Grant, Lt. Col. F. D., 202n1
Grant, Ulysses S., 45, 48
gravestone, of Pvt. William George, 7
Great Sioux Reservation, 34–35, 45
greyhounds, 102
Guiness stout, 97, 98, 218n17

Hardoff, Richard G., 210–11n10
Hare, Lt. Luther, 62
harness fragments, 166–68, 231n4

Hazen, Col. William, 203n12
Heart River, 36, 38, 57
Hedren, Paul L., 222n81
Herendeen, George, 57–58, 60, 205n33, 208n62
Hero Glass Works (Philadelphia), 155
Heski, Thomas M., 217n12
Hibbert, E&G, 96, 97, 141, 218n19
Hill, Rick, 229n1
historical archaeology, 12–13
history: of American west and status of Battle of Little Bighorn, 1; connecting archaeology with at Powder River depot site, 93–96, 117–22; and context for understanding of events at Powder River depot site, 12–13; and documentary evidence for Powder River depot, 2, 3, 93–94; and record on Army management of transportation and supply in 1876, 109–15
Holmes, Booth and Haydens (Connecticut), 176
Hooten, Capt. Mott, 79
horses: artifacts and bones at Powder River depot site, 157, 165–68; and Little Bighorn Battlefield site, 122–23; and Powder River expedition of 1865, 28, 29, 31, 32, 33; and railroad surveys, 38, 40; and Sioux War of 1876, 51, 52, 87, 195n32, 207n53; and Yellowstone Wagon Road and Prospecting Expedition, 42, 201–2n93–94. *See also* harness fragments; horseshoes and horseshoe nails; transportation
horseshoes and horseshoe nails, 122, 165–66
Howard, James, 77, 79
Hunkpapa (Sioux), 29, 30, 34, 39, 43, 67, 194n16, 198n64. *See also* Sioux
hunting: Fort Laramie Treaty of 1868 and unceded grounds for, 34, 53, 197n53; and Sioux War of 1876, 54, 101, 196n42. *See also* buffalo
Hutchins, James S., 223–24n29
Hutton, Paul A., 199n69

Jackson, Bob, 213n44
Jens, Lester, 191n5
Jesuits, 20
Jordan, Walter, 115–16

INDEX

Josephine (steamboat), 38, 40, 56, 63, 67, 75, 77, 80, 202n1

Keogh, Capt. Myles, 68
kerosene lamps, 104, 176
Key West (steamboat), 199n68
Kidd, Col. James H., 28, 196n39
Killdeer Mountain, 194n17
Koch, Peter, 45, 202n96, 202n98, 204n28

labels, on bottles, 136
Lakota. *See* Sioux
Laroque, Francois-Antoine, 22, 193n9
Lea and Perrins Co., 155
leather. *See* harness fragments
Lee, Ruth W., 229n12
Leighton, Alvin C., 31, 57, 98, 196n34, 196n36, 206n40
Leighton, Joseph, 115–16
Lewis, Meriwether, 22, 23
lignite, 103, 133, 181. *See also* coal
line officers, 14–16, 17–18
Little Bighorn, Battle of: archaeological investigations of, 1, 3–4, 226n60, 226n64–65; company strength figures for, 192n11; cultural materials from compared to Powder River depot site, 3–4, 122–26; Custer and Sioux War of 1876, 61–64, 127; number of Native Americans at, 207n56; status of in history of American west, 1; and supply or transportation issues, 111, 114
Little Missouri River, 28, 38
Little Wolf (Cheyenne), 30
Livingston (town), 54
Lodge Grass Creek, battle on, 43
Long Dog (Hunkpapa), 67
Lovett, Maurice, 217–18n15
Ludwig, Capt. William, 200n75
Luhn, Capt. Gerhard L., 215n70

Mackenzie, Col. Ranald, 68
Macklin, Lt. James E., 77, 79
Manual for Army Cooks, 121
marbles (toy), 105, 119–20, 177–78, 221n77, 225n47
Marquis, Thomas B., 207–8n59
Marsh, Grant, 63, 80, 84, 94–95, 202n1, 208n63, 213n50
Maynadier, Lt. Henry, 23–24

McClure, Capt. Charles, 112, 114
McCormick, Paul, 54, 116, 203n5, 204–205n30
McDougall, Capt. Thomas M., 62
McDougall and Co. (Scotland), 103, 163, 221n61
McGowan, Pvt. Martin, 74
McKearin, George L. & Helen, 229n12
Meddaugh, Cpl. Samuel, 76, 77, 81, 84–85
Medical Department, 15, 16
Medicine Line, 68–69
medicines, and artifacts from Powder River depot site, 99–100, 160–61, 230n3
metal strapping/banding, 170–71
Miles, George, 80, 91, 116, 212n35
Miles, Col. Nelson, 65, 66, 80, 85, 92, 209n77
Miles City, 68, 69, 106, 116, 223n25
Millard, S. T., 147
Milwaukee Railroad, 68, 70
minerals. *See* agate; coal; lignite
mining. *See* coal; gold
Montana, Bureau of Land Management and archaeology in, 1–2. *See also* Department of Fish, Wildlife, and Parks
Moore, Maj. Orlando, 56, 63–64, 67, 77, 80–86, 91, 92, 94, 95, 186, 187, 212n30, 233n5, 233–34n9
Morgan, George, 80, 81, 84
Mounts, Matthias "Cy," 86, 214n60
mules: and harness fragments as artifacts, *167*, 168; and Powder River expedition of 1865, 29, 31, 32, 33; and railroad surveys, 38, 40; and Sioux War of 1876, 59, 74, 87, 196n45, 206n44, 206n51, 207n59, 212n30; and Yellowstone Wagon Road and Prospecting Expedition, 42. *See also* transportation
Murdock, Capt. Daniel H., 74

nails, as artifacts, 124, 169–70, 231n6. *See also* horseshoes and horseshoe nails
Native Americans: and abandonment of Powder River depot by army, 77–80; and Fort Laramie Treaty of 1868, 34–35, 37, 193n10, 201n101; and precontact groups in Yellowstone-Powder River region, 19, 193n10. *See also* Arapaho; Arikara; Blackfoot; Cheyenne; Crow; Dakota; Pawnee; Shoshone; Sioux

Newfoundlands (dogs), 42, 102
New York Herald, 84
Northern Pacific Railroad, 35–41, 69, 70, 106–108, 191n4, 199n69, 209n84. *See also* Burlington Northern Railroad
Northern (Texas) Trail, 69

O'Fallon Creek, 36, 67
Oglalas (Lakota), 30, 34, 51. *See also* Sioux
O'Kelly, James, 77, 79, 86, 104, 212n32
Old Bear (Cheyenne), 204n19
oral tradition, and precontact Native American groups in Yellowstone-Powder River region, 19
Ordnance Department (Army), 15
Oregon Trail, 193n11
Otis, Col. Elwell, 77, 79–80
oven, example of baking or field at Powder River depot site, 11, *12*, 95, 101, 120–22, 133–35, 225n57, 228n5
Overshine, Capt. Samuel, 86
oxen, and Yellowstone Wagon Road and Prospecting Expedition, 42

Palmer, Capt. Henry, 31
patronage scandals, and army supply system, 17
Paulding, Holmes O., 54–55
Pawnee tribe, 197n47
Pay Department (Army), 15
Peterson, Leslie Perry, 226n67, 230n2, 231n5
Pine Hills, 6
plains, and description of Yellowstone-Powder River region, 19
Platte River Road, 193n11
Pompey's Pillar, 39
Porter, Dr. Henry, 80, 81, 85
post traders, 17–18, 205n39. *See also* sutlers
Potts, Benjamin, 41, 47, 48, 116, 201n88
Powder River depot site: appearance of in 1876 contrasted to current, 69; chronology of events at, *72*; connecting archaeology and history of, 93–96, 117–22; cultural materials compared to Little Bighorn Battlefield, 3–4, 122–26; and cultural materials from Feature D, 96–106; and dating of Feature D, 106–8; discovery of, 2, 5–8; excavation and analysis of, 8–11; excavation details and formation of Features D and F, 129–35; and future fieldwork, 126; historic context for understanding of events at, 12–13; Native American activities at abandoned, 77–80; potential contribution of to future archaeological studies, 127; protection of grain stores at, 80–86; and provision books, 187, 189; rest and recreation during Sioux War at, 71–76, 119–20. *See also* artifacts
Powder River expedition (1865), 26–34, 197n49
Powell, Capt. James, 57
Prairie County Museum, 8
Press, Elizabeth, 217n13
provision books, and Commissary Department, 183–89, 233n2, 234n9

Quartermaster's Department (Army), 15, 16

railroads: construction of after Sioux War of 1876, 69; and surveys of 1871–1873, 35–41, 93, 198n64, 199n67. *See also* Burlington Northern Railroad; Northern Pacific Railroad
Raynolds, Captain William F., 23–25, 35, 49, 193n8–9
recreation, at Powder River depot, 76, 119–20
Red Cloud (Lakota), 30, 34
Red Star (Arikara), 71, 73, 99, 210n7
Redstone River (Powder River), 22
Reno, Maj. Marcus, 58–59, 62, 67
Reynolds, Col. Joseph J., 51, 53, 204n20
roads, construction of after Sioux War, 69–70. *See also* Yellowstone Wagon Road and Prospecting Expedition
Roberts, William, 37
"la Roche Jaune" (Yellowstone River), 19
Rock, James T., 229n1, 230n3
rodent burrowing, and preservation of archaeological features, 227–28n2
Roe, Lt. Charles, 98, 120, 215n68
Roe, Lt. Frances, 100
Roman Nose (Cheyenne), 30
Rosebud Creek, 42, 61, 183, 189
Royal Bottling Company (RBC), 96–98, 138, 139–40, 217–18n15

INDEX

Sanford, Pvt. Wilmot, 74, 75, 76, 81, 87, 88, 90–91, 94, 95–96, 99, 101, 103, 118, 119, 120, 121, 211n14, 214n58, 217n9, 220n44, 221n77
Sanger, Capt. Louis, 91, 92, 187, 189
sarsaparilla. *See* ginger ale
scalping, of Native Americans, 81, 83–84, 85
scientific corps, and railroad surveys, 38
Scott, Douglas D., 232n1
scouts, and Sioux War of 1876, 55, 56, 57, 58–59. *See also* Red Star
scurvy, 28, 100
shelters, at Powder River depot, 90, 211n15
Sheridan, Lt. Gen. Philip, 13–14, 17, 37, 47, 48, 49–50, 63, 66, 67, 68, 91, 109–10, 198–99n65, 203n12, 209n77
Sherman, Gen. William T., 35
Sheridan Butte, 6
Shoshone, 59, 63
Sioux: and conflicts in Yellowstone-Powder River region prior to Sioux War, 194n14, 194n23, 197n50; and Fort Laramie Treaty of 1868, 34–35; and Powder River expedition of 1865, 29; and railroad surveys of 1871–1873, 35, 36, 37, 39, 41, 198n64; and Sully campaign of 1864, 25–26; and Yellowstone-Powder River region at time of contact, 20, 193n10; and Yellowstone Wagon Road and Prospecting Expedition, 42–46, 201n91. *See also* Crazy Horse; Gall; Hunkpapa; Oglalas; Red Cloud; Sioux War of 1876; Sitting Bull; Spotted Eagle; Yellow Shirt
Sioux War of 1876: and Battle of Little Bighorn, 61–64; Bozeman residents as cause of, 45; and Commissary Department provision books, 183; Crook and beginning of, 50–53; and departure of Dakota column, 55–58; events after campaign, 68–70; historical association of Powder River depot with, 93–96; Lakota and Cheyenne attacks on Crook's forces, 59–60; and march of Montana column, 53–55; meeting of Crook's and Terry's forces, 64–66; Mjr. Reno and scouting, 58–59; preparations for, 47–50; rest and recreation at Powder river depot, 71–76; and resupply of Terry's and Crook's forces at Powder River depot, 86–92; separation of Crook's and Terry's forces, 66–67; and Terry's consolidation of forces, 60–61. *See also* Little Bighorn, Battle of
Sitting Bull (Lakota), 29, 34, 37, 39, 50, 53, 59, 63, 68, 194n16, 197n52, 198n64, 201n90
Slim Buttes, battle of, 67
Smith, Lt. Algernon, 123
Smith, John, 56–57, 61, 64, 65–66, 71, 73, 75, 87, 88, 89, 98, 99, 117, 118, 119, 206n40, 209–10n3, 211n14, 218n27, 219n30, 220n45, 223n23
Smith, Vic, 80, 81, 83–85, 211n18, 213n44–45, 213–14n48–50, 220n47
Smith and Wesson firearms, 105, 123, 172–73
socioeconomic status, cultural materials as indicators of, 118–19
soda water. *See* ginger ale
Spotted Eagle (Lakota), 198n64
Springer, Lt. Charles, 194n24, 196n36, 196n42
staff officers, 14–16, 17–18
staghounds, 102, 125
Stanley, Col. David, 36–41, 49, 102, 124, 186, 198n63, 199n70, 200n81
Stanley's Crossing, 56, 57, 183–87, 200n73, 233n5
steamboats: and railroad surveys, 37, 38, 209n84; and reconnaissance of Yellowstone River in 1875, 47; and Sioux War of 1876, 56, 110, 183; and Sully campaign, 25; and sutlers, 119. *See also Bertrand; Carroll; Far West; Josephine*
Stuart, James, 201n87
Subsistence Department (Army), 15, 16
Sully, Gen. Alfred, 25–26, 29, 194n17, 195n29
supply system: Army management of in 1876, 109–15; and organization of Army in 1876, 13–18; and Powder River expedition of 1865, 32–33. *See also* alcoholic beverages; foods; tobacco
sutlers: and army supply system, 17, 115–17; and foods available at Powder River depot, 73; and ledger records for sales at Powder River depot, 98, 100. *See also* Leighton, Alvin; Smith, John

Tarrant and Co., 100, 160, 219n41
Taylor, Muggins, 205n33
Taylor, Steven W., 218n15
tents. *See* shelters
Terry, Gen. Alfred: and Commissary Department, 113–15, 183, 186, 187, 189; and conduct of Sioux War, 53–58, 60–61, 64–67, 68, 74, 77, 80, 86–92, 208n65, 222n5, 222n13; and establishment of Powder River depot, 2; and Fort Laramie Treaty of 1868, 202n101; and preparations for Sioux War, 49, 50; and railroad surveys of 1871–1873, 37
Terry (town), 4, 70
Terry Badlands, 4, 22, 23
Texas (Northern) Trail, 69
Thibaut, Lt. Frederick, 75, 187, 189
Thompson, Lt. Richard E., 113, 187, 234n9
tobacco, 75, 88, 113, 123, 162–64, 215n74–75, 220n58. *See also* clay pipes
Tongue River, 31, 67, 68, 200n76
trade. *See* fur trade; post traders; sutlers; trading posts
trading posts, and fur trade in Yellowstone-Powder River region, 22–23. *See also* post traders
transportation: Army and management of in 1876, 109–15; and organization of Army in 1876, 13–18; and Powder River expedition of 1865, 32–33; and Yellowstone Wagon Road and Prospecting Expedition, 44. *See also* horses; mules; oxen; railroads; roads; steamboats
treaties. *See* Fort Laramie Treaty of 1868
tumblers, 145–46, 224n31, 224n38, 229n12
typhoid fever, 100

Utley, Robert M., 192n11, 192n13, 222–23n18

Virginia City (Nevada), 224n38, 225n47–48

Wagner, David E., 195n31
Walker, Danny N., 230n8

Walker, Lt. Col. Samuel, 26–34, 195n31
Warren, Lt. Gouverneur K., 22, 194–95n25
watches and watch keys, 105, 123, 176–77
Weibert, Don L., 201n93
Weir, Capt. Thomas, 89–90
Westminster Kennel Club Dog Show (New York), 125
Weston, Capt. John F., 187
Williamson, John, 57, 205n33
wine, 99, 117, 118, 141–43, 229n10. *See also* alcoholic beverages
Wolf Mountains, 42
Wolf Rapids, 66, 67, 77, 81, 91, 92, 94–95, 199n68
Wooden Leg (Cheyenne), 85, 123, 208n59, 214n56

Yellow Shirt (Lakota), 85
Yellowstone Depot M. T. provision book, 187–89
Yellowstone Depot-Stanley's Crossing provision book, 183–87
Yellowstone-Powder River region: first white visitors to, 20–23, 70; Fort Laramie Treaty of 1868 and continuing conflict in, 34–35; geography of, 19–20; map of, *21*; and Powder River expedition of 1865, 26–34; precontact Native Americans groups in, 19, 20, 193n10; and Raynalds expedition, 23–25; and Sully campaign of 1864, 25–26. *See also* Yellowstone River; Yellowstone valley
Yellowstone River: and agate, 181; and discovery of Powder River depot site, 5–8; map of river channel in 1878–1879, 95, 217n6; primary tributaries of, 20. *See also* steamboats; Wolf Rapids; Yellowstone-Powder River region; Yellowstone valley
Yellowstone valley, settlement of after Sioux War, 68–70
Yellowstone Wagon Road and Prospecting Expedition (1874), 41–46, 48, 200–1n86, 201–202n93–98